Education for All

There are two key questions at the heart of the ongoing debate about education and training for all young people, irrespective of background, ability or attainment:

- What counts as an educated 19 year old today?
- Are the models of education we have inherited from the past sufficient to meet the needs of all young people as well as the social and economic needs of the wider community?

Education for All addresses these questions in the light of evidence collected over five years by the Nuffield Review of 14–19 Education and Training – the most thorough investigation of every aspect of this key educational phase for decades. Written by the co-directors of the Nuffield Review, *Education for All* provides a critical, comprehensive and thoroughly readable overview of 14–19 education and training and makes suggestions for the kind of education and training that should be provided over the coming decade and beyond.

The authors acknowledge that much has been achieved by the respective governments – massive investment in resources; closer collaboration between schools, colleges, training providers, voluntary agencies and employers; and recognition and promotion of a wider range of qualifications. They are also optimistic about the good things that are going on in many secondary classrooms – enormous amounts of creativity; courageous efforts to meet problems; and a deep concern and caring for many young people otherwise deprived of hope and opportunity. But they argue for a radical reshaping of the future in the light of a broader vision of education – a greater respect for more practical and active learning; a system of assessment which supports rather than impoverishes learning; respect for the professional expertise of the teacher; a more unified system of qualifications ensuring progression into higher education and employment; the creation of strongly collaborative and local learning systems; and a more reflective and participative approach to policy.

Education for All should be read by everyone working in – or with an interest in – secondary-level education in England and Wales and beyond.

Richard Pring is Lead Director of the Nuffield Review of 14–19 Education and Training. **Geoff Hayward** is Reader in Education and Associate Director of the ESRC Centre on Skills, Knowledge and Organisational Performance (SKOPE) at the University of Oxford, and co-director of the Nuffield 14–19 Review. **Ann Hodgson** is Professor of Education and Faculty Director of Research, Consultancy and Knowledge Transfer at the Institute of Education, University of London, and co-director of the Nuffield 14–19 Review. **Jill Johnson** is Director of Policy and Communications at the Universities and Colleges Admissions Service (UCAS), and co-director of the Nuffield 14–19 Review. **Ewart Keep** is Deputy Director of the ESRC SKOPE Research Centre and Professor at the Cardiff School of Social Sciences, Cardiff University, and was co-director of the Nuffield 14–19 Review until 2006. **Alis Oancea** is Research Fellow at the Department of Education, University of Oxford. **Gareth Rees** is Professor at Cardiff School of Social Sciences, Cardiff University, Associate Director of the ESRC SKOPE Research Centre at Cardiff, and co-director of the Nuffield 14–19 Review. **Ken Spours** is Professor of Education and Head of Department of Continuing and Professional Education at the Institute of Education, University of London, and co-director of the Nuffield 14–19 Review. **Stephanie Wilde** is Research Fellow at the Department of Education, University of Oxford.

Education for All

The future of education and training for
14–19 year olds

Richard Pring, Geoff Hayward,
Ann Hodgson, Jill Johnson, Ewart Keep,
Alis Oancea, Gareth Rees, Ken Spours
and Stephanie Wilde

Routledge
Taylor & Francis Group

LONDON AND NEW YORK

First published 2009
by Routledge
2 Park Square, Milton Park, Abingdon, Oxon OX14 4RN

Simultaneously published in the USA and Canada
by Routledge
270 Madison Avenue, New York, NY 10016

Routledge is an imprint of the Taylor & Francis Group, an informa business

© 2009 Richard Pring, Geoff Hayward, Ann Hodgson, Jill Johnson, Ewart Keep,
Alis Oancea, Gareth Rees, Ken Spours and Stephanie Wilde

Typeset in Garamond by
Taylor & Francis Books
Printed and bound in Great Britain by
TJ International Ltd, Padstow, Cornwall

British Library Cataloguing in Publication Data
A catalogue record for this book is available from the British Library

Library of Congress Cataloging in Publication Data
A catalog record for this book has been requested

ISBN 10: 0-415-54721-0 (hbk)
ISBN 10: 0-415-54722-9 (pbk)
ISBN 10: 0-203-87359-9 (ebk)

ISBN 13: 978-0-415-54721-5 (hbk)
ISBN 13: 978-0-415-54722-2 (pbk)
ISBN 13: 978-0-203-87359-5 (ebk)

Contents

Acknowledgements

The Directorate would like to thank in particular:

- *The Nuffield Foundation* for so generously funding the Review, in particular Catrin Roberts, who, for four years, provided wise guidance and advice, and subsequently, Josh Hillman, who ensured an efficient completion of the Report. Velda Hinds at the Foundation has provided excellent administrative support during the Review.
- *The Advisory Committee* for the constant, detailed but sympathetic advice, especially in the concluding months: Sir David Watson (Chair until 2005), David Raffe (Chair from 2005), Gary Brace, Nick Pearce (until 2007), Anne Sofer, Geoff Stanton, Cathy Stasz, Hilary Steedman and Lorna Unwin.
- *Research Officers:* Alis Oancea, Stephanie Wilde and Susannah Wright, whose industry and thinking contributed so much to the production of the Annual Reports, Issues Papers, website and Final Report.
- *Secretariat:* Joanne Hazell who for five years managed every aspect of the Review so effectively and smoothly, and then, for brief periods, Helen Marson-Smith, and Phil Richards, who prepared the manuscript for publication.
- *The Core Group* (named in Appendix 2) who have supported the Review and given their expertise throughout.
- *Contributors* (named in Appendix 2) to Nuffield Review events and publications.
- *Partnerships* visited in Bradford, Kent, Kingswood, Oxfordshire, Stevenage and Wolverhampton.
- *Rathbone*, for its wealth of experience, enthusiasm and commitment to the Engaging Youth Enquiry.
- The following people, for all their efforts at different stages of the Review in terms of research, technical support, professional advice or organisation: Maria Coyle, Dan Hayward, James Butterworth, Sarah Margetts, Stephanie Sturdy, James Hall, Gerald Haigh, Alaster Douglas, Natalie Lundsteen, Niamh Moriarty, Christine Boyle and staff at Pall Mall Consult.

Foreword

Policy on 14 to 19 education in England and Wales is littered with an alphabet soup of acronyms, most of which can barely be recalled even by those who have had to teach in this kaleidoscopic qualifications landscape. Targets, priorities, curricula, assessment styles and qualifications have come and gone as often as secretaries of state, with few lessons being learned from past trials and errors.

The search for a more coherent, unified 14 to 19 qualifications structure, within which a high quality relevant curriculum and an appropriate assessment regime are available to every learner, goes on. Policy in England and Wales is now heading in different directions, but with some positive progress being made in each country.

If we are to avoid the mistakes of the past, a stronger collective policy memory is vitally important. If future generations of young people are to have a good educational experience between 14 and 19 and a valued qualification at the end, it is essential that policy makers are clear about values, structures, progression, learning and assessment and the potential for collateral damage if they get things wrong.

This review provides historical awareness, strong values and a clear way forward. Its analysis is thorough and its recommendations deserve to be read and acted upon. The debate continues about the right educational landscape for 14 to 19 year olds. This review is a very important contribution to that debate.

John Dunford
General Secretary, Association of School and College Leaders

1 Introduction

Why a review?

Why should there be a review of 14–19 education and training?

The main reason lies in a general perception, in England and in Wales, that there are problems in the education and training of young people, which need to be addressed both by policy decisions and in educational practice.

The controversies are familiar enough. Higher education worries about the readiness of new entrants for university-level studies; employers complain about the skills of new recruits; teachers resent the pressure from a testing regime they do not value; and too many young people leave education and training as soon as they can.

The visible result lies, first, in the large number of discussion papers by government and professional organisations and in the frequent interventions by government and its agencies; second, in the number of initiatives in curriculum, qualifications and structure of provision; but, third, in the controversies which such pronouncements and initiatives have provoked.

However those interventions and initiatives, especially in England, are too piecemeal – as though, for example, the interconnections between qualification reform and more learner-centred approaches, or between student progression and differentiated (and selective) provision, or between academic and vocational aims, have not been properly thought through. After all, Ofsted itself (2008b:14) says that '[although] 14–19 is treated as a single phase in education and training ... in practice, for many young people, and particularly those on vocational programmes, there is still a discontinuity at age 16'.

Moreover, many of the reforms are advocated without much sense of history. In many ways we have been here before. Today's problems are often repeated from a not so distant past, with lessons unlearnt. There has been a long-standing debate, for example, on the appropriate provision for the 'non-academic stream' (significantly referred to 40 years ago by the Newsom Report, 1963, as 'half our future') going back to the Crowther Report (1959) which argued for a new technical 'alternative system' alongside the traditional academic courses.

But a second question might well be asked. Why 14–19? What is so distinctive about this age range that a review should focus on those young people?

Reform of policy and practice is seen to be necessary because of the changes which are taking place both in young people and in the world in which they will soon be making their way. In one sense there are no clear breaks in the gradual transition from child to adult, although, historically, claims have been made for such breaks. For instance, the Hadow Report (1926:xix), aptly entitled *The Education of the Adolescent*, argued for the distinction between primary and secondary at the age of 11, because of the 'tide which begins to rise in the veins of youth at the age of 11 or 12. It is called by the name of adolescence'. However, despite the Hadow Report's claim, the division of education into distinct phases is inevitably arbitrary. The 'tide of adolescence' is in full flood in some 14 year olds, whilst only on the turn in others.

Nonetheless, for purposes of policy and administration, distinctions do have to be made, and both the Department for Children, Schools and Families in England and the Department for Children, Education, Lifelong Learning and Skills (DCELLS) in Wales have settled on age 14 as a transitional point because of a number of changes which do then take place in schools. These changes include an increase in the choices which young learners have to make about courses and subjects to be selected in the lead up to GCSEs and other qualifications, the introduction of work-related learning with a view to preparation for employment, and the English government's decision to extend the period of education and training to 17 by 2010 and to 18 by 2013. By contrast, in Wales, it will be left to young people themselves to decide whether they wish to take up opportunities for education and training up to 19 or not.

Furthermore, these changes to policy and practice are seen to correspond to changes in the young learners themselves, for example, the growing interest they have in the future career they would like to pursue and the further training and education they need. Many see themselves already as adults, finding the constraints of the traditional classroom irksome. Not very long ago they might well have been earning their living at 15, married at 16 and fighting for their country at 17.

Addressing the problem

In addressing the problems as perceived, governments in both England and Wales have been vigorous in the last few years, and much has not only changed but also been achieved. In pursuit of higher standards of a more inclusive system and of economic prosperity, both governments have given statutory entitlement to a broader curriculum, encouraged wider participation through 'applied' and 'vocational' routes, reformed qualifications (in Wales, through the introduction of a new Baccalaureate qualification), promoted 'personalisation' of learning, expanded opportunities for higher education, promoted collaboration between schools, colleges, higher education and employers, and created an integration of social, health and educational services.

In England, this is to be achieved through the quite radical proposals in *Every Child Matters* (DfES, 2003b), which advocated bringing together locally the range of social and educational services under one person so as to ensure the best possible cooperation between these services for the benefit of each child. In Wales, it is reflected in the *Extending Entitlements* approach to children and young people (NAWPU, 2000; Haines *et al.*, 2004), and in the recent *School Effectiveness Framework* in which pupils' well-being is placed alongside 'raised standards' as the purpose of education. The extensive *Building Schools for the Future* initiative is the largest schools' building programme ever in England and aims to revolutionise the design of school buildings in order to meet new styles of learning, especially 14–19. There has been a praiseworthy attempt to motivate young people from poorer backgrounds to remain in post-compulsory education through the introduction of a means-tested Education Maintenance Allowance.

All this heralds radical changes in the system of education and training. It challenges assumptions about the values and aims, about what should be taught, about the relation of the formal system of learning to the wider community, and about the appropriateness of the way in which learning is assessed and recognised in the qualifications offered.

And yet, despite what has been achieved (and that is quite considerable), problems stubbornly remain. There is continuing low achievement for many, lack of social mobility, constant complaints from employers and others about the standards of those leaving education, absence of good training opportunities and, in some instances, insufficient high-quality jobs that carry prospects of real fulfilment and progress.

A bit of history

Tri-partite mentalities

It is useful to remember that only 40 years ago, the salient features of the school system was its assumption that young people were 'academic', 'technical' or 'non-academic'. It was a persistent notion, the legacy of which is still detectable, and which has had its effect on every significant reform up to the present day.

The 80% of young people who were not in grammar schools took no public examinations, leaving school at 15 with no qualifications, although a sizeable number then moved into apprenticeships with day release to study at a Technical College. The vast majority of young people were thought not to be able to benefit from any further general education, although sterling efforts were made to include more general education within the part-time courses for apprentices and other trainees (Bailey and Unwin, 2008). The Crowther Report (1959) did argue for an extended school life for all, with an alternative technical education for those who would benefit from it.

Only following the recommendations of the Beloe Report (1960) was the Certificate of Secondary Education (CSE) launched, intending to provide this more general education for the next 40% who were thought not able to study for the Ordinary (O) Level examinations taken by the 'top' 20%. There remained a further 40% who, it was thought, should not take any nationally recognised leaving examinations.

'Tri-partitism', embodied in the threefold division of schools into grammar, technical and secondary modern, following the recommendations of the Norwood Report (1943), seemed deeply ingrained in the English and Welsh psyche.

However, that division between the academic few and the rest was difficult to sustain, as when, in 1972, the school-leaving age was raised to 16 and as the majority of secondary schools became comprehensive. There was the belief that all young people are capable of responding to a general education up to the age of 16.

Innovative reforms to the teaching of the humanities, science and mathematics, supported by the Schools Council (created in 1964) and financed equally by the Ministry of Education and the local authorities, showed how such an inclusive approach to general education could be achieved. It supported the professional role of the teachers in shaping curriculum and pedagogy. Assessment embraced what would now be called 'wider key skills'; teachers were deeply involved through the countrywide network of 'teachers centres' in adapting the curriculum to the needs of the young learners; and their judgements, carefully moderated, were a significant part of the assessment. There are still huts with the acronym ROSLA (Raising of the School Leaving Age) bearing witness to the vigorous attempts to provide a general, though more practical, education and a relevant preparation for the future for those who were remaining in school for a further year.

Coming of the GCSE

It was only a matter of time before the two examination systems – CSEs and O-Levels – would be brought together in the new General Certificate of Secondary Education (GCSE) in 1986. But there are features of this merger which demand attention because they continue to shape our perceptions of the present system and which affect what might be aspired to in the future.

First, within GCSE, there was less room for the more practical and relevant learning which had been a feature of the CSE; the pursuit of respectability seldom values the practical. Second, there was less room for teacher judgement in the assessment of the learners' work. Third, the importance of oral skills, much valued in the 1975 Bullock Report *Language for Life*, gave way almost completely to the more easily assessable writing skills. Fourth, although the new GCSE claimed to be criterion referenced rather than norm referenced, the top three grades were defined as equivalent to the pass grades at O-Level; Grade C in fact, if not in theory, came to be perceived as the 'pass mark', with the proportion of pupils gaining five A*–C grades becoming a major school performance indicator for the 1990s (A* was introduced in 1994). This legacy is to be seen in the significance attached to 'good GCSEs' and the proportion of these required for avoiding the label 'failing student' or 'failing school'.

Meanwhile, the development of an inclusive system, which would meet the educational needs of all, received a challenge in the late 1970s when the downturn in the economy left many school leavers without the prospect of employment or vocational training. They neither wanted to repeat the increasingly academic courses, which many had failed, nor had in mind a specific vocational route they wanted to pursue. What kind of education and training would better prepare them for adult life and the world of work?

The further education perspective

The Further Education Unit's (FEU, 1979) pioneering *A Basis for Choice* (ABC), and its subsequent publication *Vocational Preparation*, established the principles of a *pre-vocational* education which would develop general understanding based on occupational interests, equip young learners with key skills, and guide them in choosing a satisfying career path and the further training which such a career required. In many respects, one could see the present Diplomas as the inheritors of this pre-vocational tradition as it was continually transformed through a series of short-lived qualifications – City and Guilds (CGLI) 365 courses, Certificate of Pre-Vocational Education, the Diploma of Vocational Education and General National Vocational Qualifications (GNVQ). Simultaneously the Technical and Vocational Education Initiative (TVEI), under the aegis of the Manpower Services Commission, provided the framework for imaginative attempts to integrate theoretical and practical learning, academic and vocational studies, in a general education for all.

However, a major difference between the development of the new Diplomas (which the government has introduced from 2008 and which are described in Chapter 8) and that of the earlier pre-vocational tradition is that they focus primarily upon qualification reform rather than upon the curriculum development principles embodied in ABC, Vocational Preparation and TVEI (Stanton, 2008:23–27, gives a clear account of the differences). It is perhaps instructive that Diplomas have not been adopted in Wales, although pre-vocational provision remains a contentious issue.

In the 1970s and 1980s, there were initiatives for those who were not in full-time education, vocational training (as in the apprenticeships) or employment, arising in the main from concerns about the collapse of the youth labour market following the oil crisis – a context which has many parallels with today. The Youth Opportunity Programme provided 'pre-vocational preparation'. The later Youth Training Scheme (YTS), on the other hand, had two pathways: Mode A placing young people in jobs with employment contracts; Mode B for those deemed not ready for work or with learning difficulties. When YTS was expanded to a two-year programme in 1986, a qualification was attached as a mandatory outcome at National Vocational Qualification (NVQ) Level 2. Hence, from about 1990 onwards, qualification attainment began to dominate. There were initiatives, too, for those who were in employment but without any further training, such as the Unified Vocational Preparation. What we see today has its roots in these earlier initiatives as is reflected in accounts of 'young people's perspectives' (Unwin and Wellington, 2001).

Apprenticeships

There is a similar story to be told about apprenticeships, which have long been a coveted route into employment, particularly strong in certain sectors such as manufacturing, engineering, catering and construction. But problems, which still prevail, were tackled, though not very successfully, as long ago as 1964 through the Industrial Training Act – namely, the encouragement of employers to make a fair contribution to apprenticeship training through the imposition of training levies and the redistribution of money so received. Problems, however, continued as the traditional apprenticeship, with a contractual relationship between apprentice and employer, gave way to various government-sponsored training schemes (Ryan and Unwin, 2001; NR, 2008a). Subsequently there has been a series of 'reforms' with Modern Apprenticeships introduced in 1994 and then again reformed following the recommendations of the Cassells Report (2001).

The persistent A-Level itch, and Tomlinson

It often looks as though the problems involved in educating 14–19 year olds were confined to the areas of vocational preparation and training. All is well, we might conclude, with the education of those pursuing the academic routes. That is far from the truth, as shown in the almost universal welcome given to the recommendations of the Tomlinson Report (2004) for a unified system of qualifications with an entitlement to a broader education *for all*. Indeed, ever since the arrival of A-Levels in 1951, the degree of specialisation post-16 has been a constant source of concern, reflected in the continual, but failed, attempts at reform – for example, the recommendations of the Higginson Committee, 'Advancing A-levels', in1988, the problems arising in England from Curriculum 2000, the support for a Baccalaureate from Prime Minister Blair (and its adoption in Wales, albeit in a more attenuated form than that of the International Baccalaureate), and the fleeting attempts to provide greater 'stretch', first, through the extended essay and now through the more 'stretching' questions for obtaining an A* grade.

Learning the lesson

It is important to be reminded of this history because the problems which the English and Welsh governments are tackling are not new. The present can be understood only as shaped by the past – and, in many respects, 'played out' in the past.

So what are the lessons from history that might help us to avoid making the same mistakes?

First, we identify five legacies that have to be addressed:

- Persistent 'tri-partite mentality' that constantly threatens to revert to seeing young people as 'academic', 'technical/vocational' and, to be brutal, all the rest.

- Continuing failure to obtain parity of esteem between 'academic' and 'vocational' qualifications except by distorting the very aims of the new courses.
- Ambivalence towards what is meant by 'vocational'.
- Inability to get the necessary recognition of new qualifications from employers and higher education.
- Transient nature of new qualifications.

Second, we identify from this history, three further points for action:

- The need for the local adaptation of central qualifications by those who understand the local scene.
- The training and recruitment of teachers with the relevant practical experience to teach the courses.
- Assurance of progression from qualifications obtained to further learning, training or employment.

This history and the lessons it contains might be summed up in the words of one teacher who contributed to the review and who has taught through all these changes:

> With ROSLA 1972 the school leaving age came to overlap the age of marriage; new legislation has simply been bolted onto old; curriculum reform has played with deckchairs. 19th century schools were *sanctuaries*; after ROSLA they became *containers*, and since 1988 the curriculum in the containers has become closed in and two-dimensional. What the writer calls 'academicism' distorts education and our ideals of 'success'. To turn *containers* into *bases for dispersal*, we must broaden the recruitment of teachers, turn the curriculum outwards towards community providers and facilities, and restore a third dimension to education which admits genuine respect for the 'practical'
>
> (Fox, 2004)

It is necessary to ask why the present reforms should succeed when so many of the ones in the recent past have failed, as reflected in the need to review those changes so soon after they have been made – the national curriculum in England by Dearing in 1994, the NVQs by Beaumont in 1995, the GNVQ by Capey in 1995, 16–19 Qualifications by Dearing in 1996, Modern Apprenticeships by Cassells in 2001, and Curriculum 2000 in England by Tomlinson in 2004.

Parity of esteem: Holy Grail or red herring?

Perhaps the search for parity of esteem which lay behind so many of these and other changes is not so much a false as a meaningless aim. There are different kinds of learning experience, different kinds of courses. This book argues that, rather than pursue parity of esteem in a highly divided system (with all the fabricated equivalences which that entails), the basic structure of the qualifications system has to be addressed. We argue for a more unified approach in which different pathways can be pursued, each pathway justified in terms of the quality of learning it offers and opportunities for further learning and employment opened up. The book explores the idea of a common baccalaureate structure for England (it already exists in Wales, although in an attenuated form) with both a common core of education and the chance to specialise. This could be the way forward.

The Nuffield Review – what it has tried to do

The book is based on a review of 14–19 education and training in England and Wales funded by the Nuffield Foundation. It has been shaped by the question:

What counts as an educated 19 year old in this day and age?

Whilst recognising what has been achieved, the Review looked ahead to what can and should be done to overcome the problems encountered. It put forward, in the light of the evidence explored, its own vision for the future. That vision is outlined in detail in the following chapters. It aims to be comprehensive in its considerations, examining: educational aims; quality of learning; appropriateness of assessment; qualifications framework; progression into higher education, further training and employment; institutional provision; and government control and responsibility.

The Review pointed to changes which are already taking place within the system but which are rarely acknowledged and failing to enter the mainstream. They could wither on the vine unless they receive more widespread support. There is an enormous amount of creativity amongst schools, colleges, independent training providers and voluntary (third sector) organisations, courageous efforts to meet the problems the Review identified, a deep concern and caring for young people otherwise deprived of hope and opportunity. Indeed, in reviewing evidence, members of the Review team visited schools and colleges; they have examined evidence put to it by teachers and by those working in the youth service, higher education and the voluntary bodies. They have spoken to young people with different degrees of engagement within the education and training system. They came away from those visits inspired by what they heard and saw. This surely bodes well for the future.

The Review was commissioned by the Nuffield Foundation in 2003 to review the whole of 14–19 education for England and Wales. It is a comprehensive and independent review, which has been led by a directorate of six people from the University of Oxford Department of Education, the Institute of Education in London, UCAS, the University of Warwick Business School and the Cardiff School of Social Sciences, supported by three researchers and working with a 'core group' of about 60 people drawn from schools, colleges, universities, unions, professional bodies, independent training providers, employers, examination boards and government agencies, engaged in widespread reviewing of evidence and experience. It addressed over 100 conferences during the five years of the project, visited schools, colleges and partnerships, and met with government and shadow government ministers as well as their civil servants.

The Review conducted a thorough review of evidence with a view to an informed debate about the way ahead for 14–19 education and training. It also conducted research in two areas. The first concerned the views of over 200 admissions tutors from 22 universities about the preparation of young people for university work, which is drawn upon in Chapter 10. The second was the extensive work with the charitable body, Rathbone, on the engagement in learning of those who are disaffected with the system. That is drawn upon in Chapters 4 and 5.

The Review's three Annual Reports and subsequent Issues Papers have pulled together evidence which has contributed to this book. Much of the evidence presented to the Review has been published on the Review's website (www.nuffield14-19review.org.uk) for all to see and to add critical comments.

Wales

The Review covered England and Wales. The brief historical account given above is, for the most part, common to both countries. Nevertheless, there have been long-standing differences in the organisation of the education and training systems of the two countries. In particular, since 1999, education and training in Wales has been the responsibility of the National Assembly for Wales, with a distinctive programme of policies developed by the DCELLS, as it is now termed, of the Welsh Assembly Government (WAG). Although so many of the issues dealt with in this book are common to both countries, important differences have increasingly emerged which contribute significantly to the analysis presented here.

This will be dealt with in detail, chapter by chapter. But it is worth pointing out here that there have always been significant differences in the contexts of the two countries, shaped by their respective economic situations, political allegiances and cultural traditions. The Welsh education system has a long-standing commitment to maintain and develop a distinctively Welsh culture, expressed not only through the promotion of Welsh-medium and bilingual schools and through the teaching of the Welsh language in all schools, but also through the general curriculum (e.g. in the Curriculum Cymreig). Since parliamentary devolution, however, the distinctiveness of the Welsh education and training system has increased significantly. Wales has preserved a fully comprehensive and community-based school system that has not been diluted, as in England, by a large independent sector or by the variety of differently funded Specialist Schools and Academies. It has also moved away from 'league tables' and a regime of assessment in schools based on repeated testing, preferring to trust the professional judgements of teachers on pupils' progress (with appropriate moderation).

Wales has also adopted, as we shall see, what is arguably a broader view of general education, reflected in the development of its 'Learning Pathways 14–19' (WAG, 2002a). The development of the Welsh Baccalaureate (Bac) also reflects this broader vision. Both the Learning Pathways and the Welsh Bac illustrate the need to offer genuine choice of 'academic' and 'vocational' routes to all 14–19 year olds and a commitment to cultural breadth and community engagement.

This divergence from the English system provides a valuable contrast from which both countries can learn as they look to the future.

Major themes

It is widely recognised that respective governments have attempted to raise levels of attainment, to promote a 'skills revolution' and to make education more inclusive.

The intention of the Fisher Act of 1918 and of the Butler Act of 1944, namely, that education and training should be engaged in by all young people up to 18, seems finally to be in our grasp. Nevertheless, problems, identified long ago stubbornly persist: continued low levels of post-16 participation in comparison with other advanced industrial countries; despite rising exam results, the lack of agreement as to whether 'standards' have indeed risen; the related concern about the currency and complexity of qualifications for 14–19 year olds; and over-assessment and its negative effect on the quality of learning.

We argue for:

Broader aims

The aims of education – namely, the initiation into a worthwhile form of life which is distinctively human – should embrace a wider set of achievements and understanding of personal and social development than those which are covered in the targets, performance indicators and assessments that dominate policy and practice.

Values not targets

Neither the aims and values, nor their embodiment in educationally worthwhile programmes of learning, can be captured in the target culture of modern 'performance management'.

More active and practical learning

Attention should be given to more active and practical modes of learning as part of the general education for everyone, whether in school-, college- or work-based learning.

Teacher as curriculum developer

The central importance of the teacher as creator rather than deliverer of the curriculum needs to be recognised, affecting the control and organisation of professional development.

Increased collaboration

Attainment of the educational aims and of improved standards requires a vigorous development of the collaborative arrangements between providers of education and training – formal and informal. Few providers can go it alone.

A move from controlling to enabling

The relatively recent appropriation by the state of control over the details of education and training has brought its own problems. The relationship between central control and local responsibility needs close examination. There should be a shift from a controlling state to an enabling one. England might learn from the more consultative processes in Wales.

Acceptance that schools cannot do it all

As Basil Bernstein (1970) once argued, 'education cannot compensate for society'. Too much is expected of schools and colleges. Their apparent inefficacy is in part due, not to their own inadequate efforts, but to wider and often pernicious social influences outside the formal educational and training system.

In looking to the future, therefore, the Review argues for a more devolved system of education and training, based on a new balance between national, regional and local levels of governance. This would emphasise partnerships between providers, on the one hand, and, on the other, those who have a stake in the system – the parents, local employers, voluntary bodies, youth services, higher education, the communities and, not least, the learners themselves. It argues for a wider vision of learning, less beholden to an impoverishing regime of assessment. It argues for a different role for central government in determining the shape of education and training – a role which is more responsive to the needs identified by local communities, educational professionals, parents, learners and employers.

2 Aims and values

The central question

The central question posed by the Review, which should constantly be asked by those planning and implementing 14–19 education and training, is:

What counts as an educated 19 year old in this day and age?

Is he or she the one who has succeeded in 'academic studies'? Or the one who is well adjusted to the demands of the entrepreneurial society in which success goes to the enterprising? Or the one who demonstrates practical capability in everyday matters? Or are there specific personal moral qualities which an educated person should have?

Even if the question is not systematically asked, answers are implicit in the very content of the curriculum, in the way in which young people are expected to learn, in the relationships between teacher and taught, and in the organisational arrangements for education and training. If you separate children at the age of 11 to give them different sorts of learning experience, then you are subscribing to different aims for different children – which is one sort of answer to the general question. If you make some subjects part of a core curriculum and not others (e.g. the arts and the humanities), then you are in fact saying that those subjects have more value than the others – and that is another kind of answer.

Therefore, ideals and values, and definitions of what we mean by 'educated', though rarely articulated, are embodied in the practices of people and institutions. It is important to make these aims and values explicit and to see whether they withstand closer scrutiny.

Therefore, let us take that first question and expand it.

What are the understandings, knowledge, skills, attitudes, dispositions and capacities which, in different degrees, an educated 19 year old should have developed in this day and age?

Immediately we need to clarify three key phrases.

'understandings, knowledge, skills, attitudes ... '

Distinctions have to be made between understanding, knowledge, skills and other attributes because an overemphasis on knowledge, say, or upon skills would not do justice to the range of qualities which are part of being a fully rounded person. A knowledgeable person might be practically useless. A skilled person might be disposed to use those skills for bad ends. In reviewing the aims of the 14–19 education and training, we need to address questions about what it means to be a person and to be one more fully.

'in different degrees'

Different learners have different capacities, motivations and opportunities for learning. Many learners are the victims of the social and economic disadvantages described in the next chapter. It would be mistaken, therefore, to set exactly the same criteria of being educated for all young people irrespective of their different capacities, opportunities or motivations. But that is compatible with insisting that education requires a basic grasp of the concepts and principles needed for the intelligent management of life and for participation in the wider community. There are different degrees of understanding.

'this day and age'

Reference to 'this day and age' is also important. 'Intelligent management of life' is different in the twenty-first century from what it would have been in the twentieth. We know, for instance, more about how to be healthy; the economic context in which young people need to carve out a career has changed massively; technology has transformed access to information; there are problems of environmental change which have to be addressed. Our understanding of an 'educated person' needs constantly to be updated.

The core purpose remains

These changing contexts and these different capacities should not distract us from the more constant concerns of education, namely, that of introducing young people to a form of life which is distinctively human, which enables them to be and to feel fulfilled, which equips them to live independent economic lives, and which enables them to participate positively within the wider community. The need remains for broad educational aims which can survive contextual changes. At the level of policy, governments in England and Wales have made it clear that the aim for education is 'to raise standards' (i.e. to put it more correctly, to improve performance in relation to standards as they have been defined), to prepare young people more effectively for the world of work, and to create a more equal and fair society. 'Standards' (bearing in mind that the definition of 'standards' is constantly changing), 'employment skills' and 'social justice' are the watchwords. More recently the DfES (2003b) widened its vision – one which takes seriously the more general welfare and happiness of the young person. In England,

Every Child Matters: Change for Children emphasises the 'well-being' of all young people – a notion which extends beyond knowledge and understanding to the sense of personal fulfilment and to healthy and safe lifestyles, a more holistic approach. In Wales, the Welsh Assembly Government has spelled out the *entitlements* that children and young people should have by virtue of their citizenship, through, for example, the *Extending Entitlements* and *Children First* programmes. These include considerations of education and employment, but also relate to their safety, health and access to wider services, as well as their rights to express their views in developing policies which affect them.

Furthermore, a spin-off from the policy of greater collaboration between providers has been the more intensive debates about the aims of learning and about the best ways of improving the learning experiences of everyone.

Clarity about the different and often competing aims of education and about the values which they embody was important for the Review. They affect, often without acknowledgement, what should be taught, how the teachers should teach, and above all how the schools and local authorities and the system as a whole should be judged. For example, choice of 'performance indicators' should relate to the acknowledged aims of education. A narrow understanding of aims leads to a narrow set of performance indicators. Or, put the other way round, a narrow range of performance indicators (e.g. five GCSEs graded A*–C) reflects a narrow understanding of educational aims. Too often during the course of the Review, we visited schools and colleges, and met teachers, where the aims and values embedded in their practice received little recognition in official 'performance indicators' – for example, facing racism and its causes in the communities from which they came or undoing the damage created through the experience of constant failure.

This chapter, therefore, as it moves on, divides into four further sections:

- It raises difficulties over clarifying the aims of education.
- It examines one particular difficulty, namely, the increasingly impoverished language in which policy and practice of education are spoken and deliberated about.
- It spells out what we believe these aims should be, recognising that there will not be universal agreement.
- It questions the predominant role of the state in determining what the aims of education should be. There are many voices that have the right to be heard in that debate. The government is but one of them.

Clarifying the aims

There is a strong tendency, especially on the part of government, to emphasise one kind of educational aim. Many official papers and pronouncements, especially in England, give priority to the development of the skills and attitudes, which will ensure a more prosperous future, and to the distinctive role which business people might and should play in making schools more 'effective' (Hatcher, 2008 reviews the influence of business and 'economic success' on the aims and provision of education). There would seem to be good reasons for this. As Prime Minister Blair said in a speech at Sedgefield in 2005, 'Education is our best economic policy ... The country will succeed or fall on the basis of how it changes itself and gears up to this new economy, based on knowledge. Education is now the centre of economic policy making for the future' (www.number10. gov.uk/page8547). And, therefore, for example, business partners are sought to sponsor and help run the new academies, and to be role models in the educational process.

The government, then, set out a set of aims for education that are dominated by the need to develop skills for the economy (e.g. DfES, 2003c; 2005a). Indeed, a more prosperous economic future for both the community and the individual should be an aim of education. And there is no necessary reason why such an emphasis should exclude the wider vision of education. In practice, though, there is a danger of other aims being crowded out by such a dominant form of discourse.

Then there are differences that appear when broad general aims are interpreted at school level. Every school can sign up to equality and justice, or to promoting autonomy. But the meaning of a statement of aims lies in the practical consequences of espousing it. What sort of behaviour, according to that general aim, is pursued or excluded? What practically happens in a school where respect for the learner is an aim? Is, for example, the learner's voice taken seriously in the planning of the curriculum?

Overlying all that is the *ethical* nature of establishing the aims of education – of establishing what is worth learning, what counts as a valuable and flourishing life to be pursued, and what sort of society ought we to be preparing the next generation for.

Ethical questions are notoriously difficult to get agreement on. In fact, we live in a society where there is inevitably disagreement on such questions.

That, of course, makes ethical deliberation about the aims of education (e.g. 'what counts as an educated 19 year old in this day and age?') central to any review of 14–19. It is a question which has been posed in the past – at the creation, for example, of the Schools Council in 1964. The Schools Council was established to provide a forum through which professional bodies, local education authorities, government and others might support curriculum development within a framework of deliberation about what was worth learning. Since there was lack of consensus over the aims of education at a time of rapid social change, it was felt necessary to find ways of living with diversity. The Schools Council was an attempt 'to democratise the process of problem solving as we try, as best we can, to develop an educational approach appropriate to a permanent condition of change' (Morrell, 1966).

How then can we, in the face of such difficulties, establish the aims of education – namely, what counts as an educated 19 year old in this day and age?

The language of education

The language of business and performance management

Language matters and so do the metaphors we employ. Language shapes our thinking. It embodies how we see and experience the world. It is very noticeable that pursuing the relevance of education to the economic world has given rise to the increasing use of a particular sort of 'management language', where the performance of schools and colleges is described and evaluated in terms usually used of business organisations. Where have these changes come from, and what lies behind them?

Much of the answer to that undoubtedly lies in the increased central control of education which brings with it the need for a management perspective and language of performance management – for example, *levers* and *drivers* of change, and *public service agreements* as a basis of funding. The *consumer* or *client* replaces the learner. The curriculum is *delivered*. *Stakeholders* shape the aims. Aims are spelt out in terms of *targets*. *Audits* (based on *performance indicators*) measure success defined in terms of hitting the targets. Cuts in resources are euphemistically called *efficiency gains*. Education, in its descriptive sense, becomes that package of activities (or *inputs*) which are largely determined by government. In other words, the ghost of 'rational curriculum planning' comes back to haunt (Chapter 7), assisted, in England, by a *delivery unit* at No. 10, whose *management models* for running education include that of *command and control* – a process well described in Seddon's (2008) paper on 'deliverology'. It is arguable that in Wales these developments have been somewhat more muted. However, even here, there has certainly been no *wholesale* escape from this style of management and regulation (Rees, 2007).

Changing metaphors

As the language of performance and management has advanced, so we have proportionately lost a language of education which recognises the intrinsic value of pursuing certain sorts of question, of trying *to make sense of* reality (physical, social, economic and moral), of seeking understanding, of exploring through literature and the arts what it means to be human or what Plato, in the Symposium, referred to as the 'desire and pursuit of the whole'. In that respect the distinctive features of 'school' are being obscured.

How different the provision of education and training might be if we employed different metaphors, for the words we use embody the way in which we conceive the world, other people, the relationships between them and the way in which they should be treated. Oakeshott (1972; 1975) referred to education as an *initiation into the world of ideas*, a world of ideas which had arisen from *the conversation between the generations of mankind*, in which the young person is introduced to the different voices in that conversation – the voices of poetry, of science, of history, of philosophy. There is an *engagement* between learners and teachers who are able to relate that conversation to the interests and needs of the learner.

Yet other metaphors enable one to conceive of education differently still. The American philosopher, John Dewey (1916), seeing the danger of the 'false dualism' of 'academic' (the transmission of knowledge) and 'vocational' (the narrowly conceived training to hit a target) emphasised the integration of practice with the world of ideas ('the accumulated wisdom of the race') as the young person adapted to new situations, faced problems that need to be solved, endeavoured to make sense of experience and learned to extend and benefit from relations within the wider community. Education as growth and adaptation was the metaphor. But this blurring of the distinction between academic and vocational, and between subject- and activity-based curriculum has been vilified as 'the cause of all the problems in our schools' (Pring, 2007:3) and undermining standards (O'Hear, 1991:28). Arguments about educational aims can get exciting.

These and other different understandings of education and its aims, each with its own distinctive metaphors, compete for allegiance – one which sees teaching as *delivering* knowledge and skills in order to meet targets, another as an *engagement* between teacher and learners in order to help them to enter into a *conversation* and to appreciate the world of ideas, yet further as a continuing and intelligent adaptation to reality as problems arise and are solved, though drawing upon the knowledge and experience of previous investigations.

The danger is that, in seeking wholesale 'reform' of 14–19, we shall depend upon a particular language and a particular set of metaphors – a language which lends itself to more effective control and management, rather than to an engagement between minds.

False dualisms

Academic and vocational

Language continues to bewitch policy and practice in other ways too, for example, in the questionable distinction between academic and vocational. Vocational usually refers to those studies which are relevant to employment both because of the skills and knowledge which they cover and because of the motivation for undertaking them. Academic, on the other hand, refers to those studies, aimed at theory rather than practice, which are deemed to be intrinsically worthwhile and thus 'studied for their own sake' rather than for their relevance to employment.

However, we can easily get into trouble here. First, this dichotomy excludes important activities, especially in the arts which have been 'disapplied' from the national curriculum post-14. Are these academic or vocational? They can become 'academic' (theorising about drama or studying the history of art), but then they lose their distinctively practical and aesthetic character. Second, many 'academic subjects' are indeed vocational in that they are chosen with a view to a specific career (e.g. English so as to become a journalist or biology with medicine in mind). Third, much so-called 'academic', at its best, has a lot of practical (often confused with vocational), 'hands on' experience, as in science, and much that is called 'vocational' requires not a little theory, as in plumbing. Fourth, 'vocational' is used so 'elastically' as to stretch from very narrow skills training to intellectually demanding apprenticeships in engineering, through which young people can move into higher education.

In fact, the distinction between 'academic' and 'vocational', assumed to be self-evident in almost every document, becomes highly complex upon further examination. The Review found it necessary, when examining the quality of learning and the qualifications framework for the future, to question this simplistic distinction.

Ends and means

Equally seductive is to treat the ends to be achieved (critical thinking, appreciation of poetry, thinking scientifically, moral commitment) as quite distinct from the means of getting there, as though 'effectiveness' in teaching is a scientific matter of finding empirically the best way of attaining these measurable outcomes. The means/end model of educational improvement is reflected in the language of effectiveness, and of management and control. Improvement requires the setting of targets; having accepted those targets from others, the school or teacher needs to know the most effective means for attaining them, based on rigorous research. According to Reynolds (1998) speaking of 'teacher effectiveness: better teachers, better schools, teaching is or ought to be a science'.

However, the ends are not necessarily separate from the means. An educational practice embodies the aims and values; it is not something distinct from them. There may well be spin-offs from the teaching of Macbeth (the meeting of externally imposed targets and the passing of exams), but the educational value lies in the engagement with a valuable text. The end or purpose should be shown and captured in the very act of teaching. Teaching is a transaction between the teacher and the learner, not the delivery of something to the learner. The humanities is the place where the teacher shares his or her humanity with the learner.

After these cautionary notes we shall address the question which is central to the book as it looks to the future. What counts as an educated 19 year old in this day and age?

An educated person ...

Bruner (1966) posed three questions which should shape our thinking about the curriculum. What is it that makes us human? How did we become so? How can we become more so?

In sorting out the aims of education and training for 14–19 year olds, we need to look at the development of the person as a whole – those qualities and attainments which make him and her distinctively human and the ways in which those qualities might be enhanced. There is a danger otherwise of having too narrow a view of the aims. The following sets out what the Review sees to be the different characteristics of being a person and, through education, of being one more fully.

Intellectual development

There is a common association between 'education' and the initiation into the different forms of knowledge which constitute what it means to think intelligently – the acquisition and application of key concepts, principles and modes of enquiry to be found in the physical and the social sciences, in the study of literature and history, in mathematics, in language and the arts. It is concerned with the development of the intellect, and thus with the capacity to understand, to think critically about the physical, social, economic and moral worlds we inhabit, and to act intelligently within them. It is, as Stenhouse (1983:i) argued, to 'value the emancipation of pupils through knowledge'. It is to enter into the world of ideas. But such entry can be achieved at different levels – no one need be excluded.

For some, therefore, 'intellectual excellence' is what constitutes an educated person. The following words of Newman (1852:121) have been echoed many times: 'Liberal education, viewed in itself, is simply the cultivation of the intellect, as such, and its object is nothing more or less than intellectual excellence'.

But care is needed, for often excellence is achieved on a narrow front (the cult of the specialist) and sits alongside ignorance of other matters which those deemed less well educated would be familiar with. Intellectual excellence is but part of the whole person. There is more to development and fulfilment as a person.

Practical capability

Indeed, as the Royal Society of the Arts pointed out in its 1986 Manifesto *Education for Capability*, the pursuit of 'intellectual excellence' can create an imbalance towards what is often referred to as academic content and modes of learning.

> The idea of the educated person is that of a scholarly individual who is able to understand but not act. ... Education should ... also include the exercise of creative skills, the competence to undertake and complete tasks and the ability to cope with everyday life ... Educators should spend more time preparing people for a life outside the education system.
>
> (RSA, 1986)

The Royal Society of the Arts (RSA) represents a broader view of excellence where theory and practice are integrated in intelligent doing and making, and in giving recognition to 'competence, coping, creativity and co-operation with others'. Practical *know how* is not reducible to *knowing that* – practical intelligence to theoretical knowledge. There is a need to recognise and respect practical capability, that capacity to face and to solve practical problems, including working intelligently with one's hands – the abilities reflected in the achievements of great engineers such as Morris (later Lord Nuffield) and Brunel. This is developed at length in Chapter 5, and the 'skills agenda' (functional skills and skills for employment), elevated in successive government pronouncements, needs to be seen within that broader education and training tradition.

Community participation

The economic and social historian, R.H. Tawney, argued that 'men possess in their common humanity a quality which is worth cultivating ... a community is most likely to make the most of that quality if it ... establishes on firm foundations institutions which meet common needs and are a source of common enlightenment and common enjoyment' (1931:15).

That sense of community – acknowledging common needs, recognising the importance to personal growth of common enlightenment and pursuing common enjoyment – lies at the centre of education for citizenship. The community shapes the lives of each of us, but is itself shaped by the thinking and activity of its members. Hence, the importance of education for democracy and the embodiment of democratic principles in the life of school and college. Part of that would be the acquisition of the knowledge and skills whereby each was able to contribute fruitfully to the community.

Moral seriousness

Part of what is distinctive to being a person is the capacity to shape one's life according to what one believes to be right – to take responsibility for the direction of one's life. The young learners can, and should be helped to, reflect on how they should live their lives, commit themselves to notions of justice, care about the environment and other social and moral issues. It is a matter of *seriousness* in asking what kind of life is worth living, what is worth pursuing in leisure or career, what obligations are to be considered sacred. It is to have certain moral virtues (e.g. concern for those in trouble) and intellectual virtues (e.g. openness to evidence, argument and criticism).

One important aspect of that moral seriousness must be a concern about the 'the big issues' which affect the wider society into which the young person is entering – those concerning the conflicts which so easily arise, the capacity of a multicultural society to live in harmony, the steps which need to be taken to confront ecological and climate change. It is not enough to have knowledge; one needs also the dispositions to apply that knowledge in the creation of a better world.

Pursuit of excellence

Schools have often seen part of their educational mission to be that of inspiring young people with ideals which enable them to aim high, to pursue excellence in its different forms – the ideals of selflessness as manifest in the lives of people, of holiness as in the lives of the saints, of artistic accomplishment as in the lives of musicians, of courage as in the lives of sports men and women. This need not be something remote. Many are those for whom the field trip (e.g. to Snowdonia or Lake District) has opened up possibilities of fulfilment and pleasure previously not dreamed of.

Self-awareness

'Know thyself' instructed Socrates. Knowledge of oneself, of one's strengths and weaknesses, of what one might aspire to, of the contribution one might make to the wider community and of what one would find fulfilling, must be at the heart of education. Such self-knowledge and exploration is achieved in many ways – through the arts, drama and literature, through group activities and individual pursuits. Confidence in oneself, though tempered by realistic appraisal, and resilience in the face of failure are part of the educational ideal for all young people irrespective of background or ability. But developing that 'realistic appraisal' requires a range of expertise, including a highly professional Information Advice and Guidance service working in close collaboration with the schools and colleges, knowing the young persons but also the social and economic context in which they live – a point developed further in Chapter 5.

That then is the educated 19 year old: one who has a sufficient grasp of those ideas and principles to enable him or her to manage life intelligently, who has the competence and skills to tackle practical tasks including those required for employment, who has a sense of community and the disposition to make a contribution to it, who is morally serious in the sense that he or she cares about fairness and responsibility to others, who is inspired by what has been done by others and might be done by oneself, and who has a sense and knowledge of self – confident and resilient in the face of difficulty. Such an educational aim is open to everyone, irrespective of ability or background. Such an aim should shape the education for the future.

Social justice

Much of what has been said would seem to focus simply on the educated individual, although such a person would, as it was said, develop the kind of knowledge and dispositions to contribute to the wider community – to become a good and active citizen. But that does not quite do justice to the aim of producing a fairer society, created in part through a more inclusive system of education. The system of education should be equally concerned about the distribution of these educational opportunities, if it is to be an education for all, irrespective of background.

One useful definition of equity derived from Gutierrez (2002) is the 'erasure of the ability to predict ... achievement and participation based solely on characteristics such as race, class, ethnicity, sex, belief and creeds, and proficiency in the dominant language'. Perhaps a total erasure will never be possible, but there are considerable differences between countries over the predictability, in terms of background factors, of success in measured outcomes. 'Erasure of the ability to predict ... ' should remain an ideal to be aimed at, even if it is never totally attained. And the assessment of system performance would need to show how, over a period of time, such an ideal is at least being embodied successfully in practice.

But 'social justice' must extend beyond this useful, if narrow, definition. To what extent do diverse cultural backgrounds, so important for the learners' self-respect and identity, have a place in the curriculum? And how far is the creation of social cohesion amidst such diversity promoted not only for the well-being of the community but also for the subsequent creation of a more just society?

Implications 14–19

Such aims and values affect the appraisal of what is happening and how one might see what the future should be. For example:

Performance indicators

The indicators, whereby teachers, schools, colleges, local authorities and the educational and training system as a whole are assessed and evaluated, should reflect the broader educational aims. Many schools working in difficult social and economic contexts, have, in England, been publicly charged with failing, when, set against these broader educational aims, they might well be regarded as highly successful (see Chapter 4).

Content of the curriculum

The content of learning should be more locally determined by those who know the special circumstances of the learners and their needs, albeit within a centrally agreed curriculum framework which ensures initiation into those forms of experience through which we understand the physical, social, economic and moral worlds we live in. In drawing upon this cultural inheritance, the curriculum should address themes or topics of importance to the learners and to the society into which they are entering. Furthermore, the curriculum needs to emphasise the importance of practical learning and of the integration of theory and practice (Chapters 5 and 7).

Pedagogy

Curriculum reform has too often focused on targets which are 'hit' through the coverage of content, and not on the most appropriate pedagogy. But 'practical capability' and, for many, self-esteem require a more active and practical engagement of the learner both in determining what is to be learnt and in the learning itself. The learner's voice should be built into the learning experience (Chapter 5).

Qualifications

The needs of the learners and the quality of their learning come first, and the qualifications should reflect those needs and that quality, not the other way around. Therefore, there should be a framework of qualifications which does justice to the range of learning experiences and achievements, and which motivates the learner to continue with his or her education and training (Chapter 8).

Sense of community

Traditional emphasis upon individual autonomy must be balanced by a sense of community – cooperative learning, community involvement, commitment to wider social well-being (Chapter 5).

Provision of education

Aims and values are embodied in the very institutional provision of education and training. Therefore, in implementing the above aims, there is a need for a close look at that provision: the selection still of young people into 'different types' at 11 and 16, the choice of different courses for 'different types' at 14, the competition between providers for young people especially at 16 and the exclusion of others, and the effect that the sheer size and organisation of the school or college has upon the relationship between teacher and learner (Chapter 11).

Relation of education to the labour market

Clearly the education and training of all young people must prepare them to be economically autonomous and to make a contribution to the well-being of the wider community – vocational in this wide sense. But economic relevance and skills for the world of work should not be allowed to crowd out the wider understanding of personal well-being and fulfilment (Chapter 9).

Who decides upon the aims?

'Quis custodiet ipsos custodes?' Who are the 'moral experts' for deciding on the aims of education? Educating the next generation is one of the most important obligations of society. But the aims of education, especially when translated into practical detail, do not gain universal assent.

The respective educational policy-makers must take on a major responsibility in this regard. But it is as well to be reminded of the fact that it was not always thus. When Marjorie Reeves was invited to be a member of the Central Advisory Committee for England in 1947, she was told by the Permanent Secretary, Redcliffe-Maud, that her main duty was to be prepared to die at the first ditch as soon as politicians get their hands on education (conversation with Richard Pring, 2004). When Mr Callaghan became the first Prime Minister to make a major speech on education at Ruskin College in 1976, he was reprimanded through his political adviser for having spoken without the prior approval of the Chief Inspector of Schools.

Few, we suspect, would want to return to such a position. The government is mandated democratically to ensure that all young people have access to the range of knowledge, understanding, practical capabilities and skills which enable them to live fulfilling and economically valuable lives. But as the brief history in Chapter 1 indicates, there is a constant tension between central control and local autonomy. The state, given its mandate and its responsibilities, must be in a position to identify and implement certain educational aims, and ensure an enriching curriculum framework for all. On the other hand, it is but one voice amongst many. It is important, in the shaping of policy and in the enforcement of education and training, to ensure a place for those different voices – 'the social partnerships' as developed in the final chapter. The state might be exercising more control than it can wisely manage.

Who are those voices that need to be heard?

Teachers and academics

The culture, which we have inherited and through which we have come to understand the world, is itself both protected and enhanced through academic and professional bodies, not least of which are the teachers in our schools and colleges, and academics within universities. One important aspect of education must be the safeguarding and development of what Matthew Arnold referred to as 'the best that has been thought and said'.

Wider community

The relevance to the wider community of what is taught is clearly a matter of deep concern to those who live within those communities and to their representatives on the local councils and other bodies.

Local business

The welfare of those communities depends upon economic well-being and the success of local businesses and enterprises. Those who manage and work in such businesses have a rightful voice, too, in determining the relevance of what should be taught and on the attitudes and skills which are to be nurtured.

Parents

In both England and Wales, arrangements have long been in place for parents to express their own distinctive educational aims through the maintenance, within the state system, of voluntary-aided and voluntary-controlled schools. The voice of parents in a pluralist society must be respected. They have the ultimate responsibility for their children.

The learners

By no means least in importance are the learners themselves. Respect for their voices must be part of the respect for them – part of the educational task of giving them a sense of dignity as well as ensuring their engagement in the learning process. The context in which young people grow up affects profoundly their learning needs as they aspire to adult status.

Therefore, there are many voices in the deliberations about the aims of education and about the implementation of those aims in practice. Reconciliation of differences or the accommodation of differences within the system as a whole or within the school or college is, as with all moral discourse, a matter of constant deliberation. But it requires the right sort of forum, both nationally and locally, for such deliberations to take place. No one voice, not even the government's, should be allowed to drown out the others. Chapter 11 argues for 'strongly collaborative learning systems' to meet the needs and entitlements of all young people – the obvious place for such constant deliberation about aims and values to be pursued.

Recommendations

1. The aims and values outlined above should be a constant focus of deliberation at every level of education.
2. The impoverished language of 'performance management' needs to be challenged as we help young people to find value in what is worthwhile, lead fulfilling lives, gain self-esteem, make sense of experience and become responsible members of the community.

---

3 Context

The context in which learning takes place matters. Aims and values need to be hammered out by the people most affected by them, in the light of dominant social and economic forces. This chapter highlights some of the principal features of this context in the light of our earlier consideration of the aims and values which should shape education in the future.

In looking to the future, the Gilbert Review (2007) attempted a brief summary of what they referred to as the 'drivers of change', namely, young people being less passive, biddable and deferential; technological advances transforming access to knowledge; economic changes affecting work-based skills and knowledge; environmental changes making urgent demands on our way of life; social changes affected by greater ethnic diversity and by shifts in typical family structures. That review and others (e.g. Green *et al.*, 2005) have referred, too, to the increased emotional and mental problems which young people suffer from, which affect their educational progress and are doubtless exacerbated by some of these changes. All have implications for the aims of education, the work of teachers, the nature of educational provision and the relationship of schools and colleges to the wider public services.

Adolescence

Before we look at the social and economic context in detail, there is a need to reflect on the transitional period in all young people's lives – their so-called 'adolescence' – since the progress through that transition is likely to be affected by the social, economic and cultural forces impinging upon it.

Educational discourse is replete with what philosophers have called 'contestable concepts', and of this 'adolescence' must win first prize. By 'contestable' is meant that, although there is agreement in meaning at a level of everyday usage, such agreement conceals controversial differences on how reality, especially social reality, should be described. Is adolescence not a good example of what sociologists (e.g. Mills and Frost, 2007) refer to as a 'social construction', where reality could have been 'constructed' in a different way – and is so by different people?

Therefore, adolescence is the period of transition between the *perceived* dependency of childhood and the *perceived* independence and autonomy of adulthood, heavy in the possibility of conflict and misunderstanding. The word 'perceived' is used because there are different perceptions both of this dependency and of the adult's independence. And these different perceptions affect considerably our understanding of this transition and of the relationship between adolescent and teacher. Young persons, perceiving themselves as adults, might resent the use of authority in circumstances where the adult perceives them as children. To parent or teacher it is the 'use', to the young person it is the 'misuse', of authority.

In such a transition, adjustments have to be made. Young persons have to learn to stand on their own feet, to accept responsibility, to face choices about the future which are a cause of anxiety. Their parents or carers have gradually to concede this responsibility. Coleman and Hagell (2007) refer to the 'risk' and 'resilience' of young people in that transition – 'risk', because, unless parents and teachers are careful, things can go wrong, 'resilience', because normally young people find the strength to cope perfectly well with these adjustments (although the UNICEF Report (2007) revealed that our young people are the least happy in the Organisation for Economic Co-operation and Development countries).

There are different indicators of this transition having been made, for instance, earning one's living, being held responsible for one's actions, and settling down in a long-term sexual relationship. However, in that sense, adolescence has become prolonged and not a little confused as a result of material and social changes. Puberty comes earlier; economic independence comes much later. On the one hand, within 15 years, there has been a reduction from 60% of 17 year olds in full-time employment to about 30% today. On the other hand, as economic independence decreased, there has been a radical increase in the independence of young people to form sexual relationships, once associated with adulthood. Whereas in 1964, 14% of males and 5% of females reported having had sexual relations before the age of 16, by 2002 the figures had risen to 38% and 33%, respectively (Coleman and Schofield, 2007:56).

Therefore, the young person has to deal with confusing messages. What we are telling our young people is that they cannot have a sexual relationship before 16, though many do and though it is legally acceptable for young people to have such relationships at 15 in the rest of Europe. They cannot buy alcohol before the age of 18, even though drinking alcohol before that date is extensive; according to the NHS Report (2006), 45% of 15 year olds and over 30% of 14 year olds reported having drunk alcohol within a given week in 2005. Teenagers can marry at 16, yet cannot vote until 18 – signalling to them both maturity for making lifelong commitments and immaturity for influencing policies which affect their lives.

What does this mean for schools and colleges?

Unsurprisingly, there is confusion over the role (and indeed the capacity) of schools to provide the appropriate help and guidance. There is little clarity, as once there was, in what society thinks (and therefore amongst teachers, parents and young people) about the age at which young people are to be considered 'grown up', and able to have an equal voice and to make independent decisions about behaviour or the learning programmes to pursue. Different perceptions over status lead to confrontation and disengagement. When, and to what extent, should the 'adolescent' be treated like an adult in terms of participation in important decisions affecting their future and in the kinds of programmes affecting their present?

Certainly, many young people show their disillusion with, or dislike of, schooling through indiscipline, leading to exclusion and truanting. Although permanent exclusions of pupils from state primary, secondary and special schools have been declining since the late 1990s, it remains the case that in both England and Wales around 1% of the school population is excluded annually. In England, this amounts to some 9000 individuals and in Wales some 450. Schools themselves might be a cause of this disaffection.

Clearly, there are problems in how to manage this transition into adulthood as the period of dependence is prolonged and yet as independence in other respects is increased. This inevitably affects relationships between many adolescents and their teachers, as they demand a different sort of relationship from what so long has prevailed. It also affects the appropriateness of the institutional arrangements for education and training – the rules and regulations, the freedom of action and the choice of learning pathways, the responsibility for one's own learning and the degree of compulsion over the continuation of learning to 19.

One consequence would be, in attempting to raise attainment and levels of happiness in schools, to take seriously the growing movement towards more 'human scale' educational provision, which gives priority to supportive relationships between teacher and learner (see Fielding *et al.* (2006), and Tasker (2003), for research on the importance of 'human scale' organisation of schools). An answer to a parliamentary question (*Independent*, 10 April 2007) points to permanent exclusions from the largest secondary schools with 1500 or more pupils having risen by 28% since 1997. And temporary exclusions are now 10% of pupils in schools with more than 1000 children, compared with 3% in schools with 1000 or fewer pupils. Where personal relations are less easy to maintain, schools themselves might be a cause of disaffection.

Demographic changes

In looking to the future arrangements for education and training, two demographic factors are important because they will increasingly make themselves felt over time.

First, the number of 14–19 year olds is set to decrease. According to Social Trends (2006), there is a decline over time of those in the 14–19 age range. This is likely to lead to greater competition between schools and colleges for the declining numbers, and also between these providers and employers in the latter's demand for labour. This will need to be handled with care if the policy of collaboration (see Chapter 11) is not to be compromised by increased competition.

Second, the ethnic mix of our population is changing. The proportion from minority groups in Britain in 2001 was 4.5 million out of a total population of 57 million (Social Trends, 2004). This proportion will grow because, in some minority ethnic groups, young people below the age of 18 constitute a larger proportion of the total ethnic group than is the case with the majority white group (General Household Survey, 2004). For example, whereas the proportion of 'white British' aged 0–15 is 15%, the corresponding figures for those of Pakistani and Bangladeshi origin are 36% and 41% – and these are groups which come disproportionately from economically poorer households. As is shown below, there is a strong correlation between poverty and educational outcomes.

The implications of this for the future of education are several and important. Unless issues of ethnic diversity become a central focus both in the provision of education and in the learning programmes of our schools, then the warnings of the Ousley Report (2001) – namely, of a socially segregated Britain and of a growing minority feeling alienated from mainstream society – will be fulfilled. Indeed, as is pointed out below, a disproportionate amount of the very poor (with all the implications of that for educational outcomes) comes from these ethnic minority groups.

A broken society?

Politicians have spoken of the 'broken society', the sort of society in which the adolescents, just referred to, have to steer their course through the 'crags and torrents of the distant scene'. They point to the decline of stable marriages, lone parents, increasing crime amongst young people, increased drug and alcohol abuse, and the criminalisation of more young people. However, one needs to be careful with such apocalyptic analyses.

A more accurate picture would be that, despite significant behavioural changes, and despite this being a period of experimentation, the vast majority of young people turn out to be mature and responsible grown-ups, have caring adults to help them, get jobs and do not commit crimes. As Coleman and Schofield (2007:xi) argue, there has been 'too much emphasis on anti-social behaviour, and a too ready willingness to attribute blame either to parents or to young people themselves'. They then tell the 'good news' stories over the last decade which contradict the assumptions of the 'broken society' sirens.

Nevertheless, a significant minority is affected by social and economic changes, especially in relationship to changing family structures and to the concentration of poverty and social immobility, which affects the 'resilience' that Coleman and Hagell speak of.

Families and educational engagement

Family disadvantage seems to be one obstacle to engagement in education. Family support, generally speaking, is important for achievement at school or college. But parenting is in many respects much more challenging today. For example, recent research shows that conflicts between parents adversely affect children's academic attainment, especially where children blame themselves for parental difficulties (Harold *et al.*, 2007).

There are several aspects of changing patterns of family life which are relevant. In a recent speech as General Secretary of the Association of Schools and College Leaders, John Dunford speaks of the 'lost art of conversation because many young people rarely experience the family meal' (*Guardian*, 10 March 2008). Indeed, 'for all children, schools have had to take the place of the institutions that used to set the boundaries of acceptable behaviour – that was, fundamentally, the family and the church'. Research on shared family meals, therefore, is relevant. Though the source is American, the following may well reflect a similar trend in Britain. The family meal time, we are told, is a vital institution for socialisation and development, but going the way of the dinosaur. Not only do 30% of those aged 12–18 not share a family meal within the week, even of those who did share a meal, 70% did so with the television on (Larson *et al.*, 2006).

Changing family patterns might well affect the educational prospects of our core group. For example, 25% of young people are growing up in households with one parent – a shift from 8% in 1971 (General Household Survey, 2004). In addition, the proportion of young people up to the age of 17 living in 'workless households' is 16.5% in the UK (compared with 10% in the European Union as a whole and 4% in Portugal), according to the Eurostat Yearbook (2006).

Lone parents are much more likely to suffer from poverty. In 2004, 60% of lone parents with dependent children had a weekly income of less than £300 per week, whereas only 11% of married couples with dependent children had less than £300 (General Household Survey, 2004). They are much less likely to be able to spend time with their growing children. Perhaps basic resources and time from sympathetic adults (indeed, having meals together) are significant factors in the smooth transition into adulthood.

Furthermore, as Coleman and Hagell (2007) report, summarising the evidence, parents living in poverty are likely to have a higher rate of depression and other mental disorders, as well as being less effective in their parenting behaviour.

One clear implication is the importance of support for parents if the educational achievements of many young people are to be raised, and such support, as the Gilbert Review (2007:23) acknowledged, may for many require steps towards the development of positive parenting styles (see Chapter 5).

Poverty and educational opportunities

The Chief Inspector pointed to the link between poverty and poor performance in her Annual Report for 2006/2007. Particularly insidious in its effects is child poverty (by definition, where the household has less than 60% of the median income), which, in the UK, remains worse than in most European countries. A child in the UK still has nearly twice as much chance of living in a household with relatively low income than a generation ago. Whilst the numbers of children living in poverty fell during the early years of the present century, more recently they have begun to increase again (Hirsch, 2006). A recent Joseph Rowntree report (Berthoud, 2007) notes that, although there has been rising employment, much of it has been in families already with an income. Hence, that rise coincides paradoxically with a rise also in 'work-poor families', where there is no income from employment. The proportion of all children who had no resident working parent increased from 8% in 1974 to nearly 20% in 1993 then fell to 12% in 2003 – still a very substantial number. According to a report by the Institute for Public Policy Research (Cooke and Lawton, 2008), 1½ million children were living in poverty despite having a working parent – moving into work has not necessarily meant moving out of poverty. Women without a partner but with dependent children rose from 7% in 1974 to 23% in 2003 – with a high risk of family unemployment (Coleman and Schofield, 2007:6). Hence, there is increased polarisation between 'two-earner families' and 'no-earner' families – between work-rich and work-poor.

What is relevant to the argument of this book is not simply the number of poor or of workless families, but the changing distribution of poverty and wealth and the growing polarisation between the extremely wealthy and the very poor. Indeed, a recent report (Spencer and Hirsch, 2008) speaks of 'an epidemic of poverty' in Britain and its impact on a range of social service outcomes, and the failure to close the inequality gap between rich and poor. This is confirmed by a further report (Paxton and Dixon, 2004) which shows that wealth distribution became more unequal during the 1990s. The wealthiest 10% of the population increased their wealth holdings from 47% to 50% of total wealth.

Further research by the Joseph Rowntree Foundation (Dorling *et al.*, 2007) distinguishes between 'core poor', 'breadline poor', 'not poor, not wealthy', 'asset wealthy' and 'exclusive wealthy'. Since 2000, there has been an increase in both the 'exclusive wealthy' and the 'core poor', and no narrowing of the education access gap between the categories. Furthermore, the 'asset wealthy' group is increasing most within 50–100 miles of London, and falling in the cities of the north of England. Areas that are wealthy are disproportionately wealthy. The main significance of this is that the connection between family income and educational outcomes is exacerbated by increasingly segregated neighbourhoods. Increasingly there is no interrelationship between the 'exclusive wealthy' and those in the poorest neighbourhoods, where young adults aged 16–24 are 20 times more likely to be in the 'not in education, employment or training' (NEET) group than those in the top economic class (Thomas and Dorling, 2007).

None of these factors by themselves are a necessary cause of personal difficulties at school or elsewhere. Indeed, such difficult circumstances create in many cases levels of responsibility which are beyond what would be normally expected of young people and often are not recognised in school or college.

An estimated 175,000 young people start the day by washing and feeding sick parents (Children's Services Network *TES*, 5 May 2006). But such circumstances create the conditions in which the difficulties encountered are less easy to cope with. Much greater resilience would be required.

Social class, mobility and reform

More generally, sociologists have established over many years that how well children do in school and college is strongly influenced by social class background. More specifically, the more disadvantaged the social class background, the lower the level of educational attainment that is likely to be achieved. Moreover, young people from less advantaged class backgrounds are less likely to take up the opportunities available to them to progress through the educational system, even where they are sufficiently qualified to make the progression (Heath, 2000). In other words, the achievement of full academic potential is far from being realised, despite the manifold educational reforms of recent decades. Where class inequalities in educational attainment have been reduced, this has been attributable to much wider programmes of social reform, as for instance in the Scandinavian countries. Alternatively, where, for any given level of attainment, educational provision is organised to enable nearly all of the most advantaged class to reach that level, then the next most advantaged class can catch up, and so on (Paterson and Iannelli, 2007).

There is also extremely robust evidence on the relationships between educational attainment and young people's subsequent life chances. Hence, we know that the increases in upward social mobility that were characteristic of large parts of the second half of the twentieth century have more recently contracted; and that there has been an increase in downward mobility during this more recent period (Goldthorpe and Mills, 2004). But the role of educational attainment in these changing patterns of mobility is limited. Achieving high-level qualifications remains important in attaining professional, managerial and scientific jobs, which bring with them not only higher incomes, but also higher status and improved life chances generally.

However, it is changes in the occupational structure which provide the principal explanation of shifts in mobility patterns. It is the expansion of non-manual jobs, the decline of manufacturing and general up-skilling during much of the second half of the twentieth century which accounts most substantially for increased upward mobility during this period. Similarly, more recently, as the expansion of 'middle-class' jobs has slowed, so upward social mobility has decreased and downward mobility grown. Moreover, this is a pattern shared by many other countries. In short whilst people have clearly experienced changing patterns of social mobility, there has been relatively little change in the inequalities of opportunity experienced by people born into different social classes. Again, changes in the structure of educational provision have had very little impact (Paterson and Iannelli, 2007).

This latter point cannot be emphasised enough. Lack of social mobility amongst the poorest in our society, where – as we have seen – the contrast between rich and poor is rapidly and dramatically increasing, is often seen to be an educational problem. There has been a fashionable emphasis on education as a mechanism for ensuring a more 'meritocratic' society. Thus, those schools, struggling within areas where there is an increasing concentration of the 'core poor', are disproportionately within the 'list of failing schools', under threat of closure, from which they can escape only by hitting narrowly defined targets of educational success.

There have been various initiatives to meet the problems outlined above: Excellence in Cities, 1996–2006, which aimed at raising the attainment of disadvantaged pupils in our most deprived cities, towns and rural areas and which worked through more than 1300 secondary schools nationwide; the Connexions Service, which focused particularly on young people at risk providing more personal guidance with regard particularly to progression to further education and training and to employment; Education Maintenance Allowances, to enable those over 16 to continue with their education and training; Full Service Extended Schools, leading eventually to the multiservice approach created by *Every Child Matters* and the *Children's Plan*. Evaluations of these initiatives have been generally favourable. They have had a positive impact on individuals and schools (Middleton *et al.*, 2005; Cummings *et al.*, 2006).

However, as the studies of educational attainment and social mobility would indicate, both in England and Wales, the role which education plays in shaping life chances is very limited. As a recent Rowntree Foundation report argues, 'all the evidence over many decades and from many countries seems to show that family background continues to be a major determinant of educational outcomes ... far from offering a route out of poverty, education simply seems to confirm existing social hierarchies' (Raffo *et al.*, 2007).

As Bernstein (1970) argued, 'education cannot compensate for society' – at least not completely.

Nonetheless, given the limitations in the school and college attempts to compensate for society, if they are expected to do so, then there should be, as the New Vision Group argued in its letter to the Prime Minister (10 July 2007), extra resources and recognition in the league tables for taking on a disproportionate number of disadvantaged young people – a recommendation promoted also by a recent report of Policy Exchange, namely, 'pay schools extra for taking children from poorer homes' (Freedman and Horner, 2008). At the moment, despite their best efforts, such schools appear disproportionately in the list of 'challenging schools'.

Vulnerable young people

Increase in mental ill-health in adolescence is the subject of another Nuffield project, directed by Ann Hagell, from which the Review has benefited. A recent study by Green *et al.* (2005) of mental health amongst young people in England and Wales estimates that 10% have a 'psychological disorder'. The largest ever study of self-harm amongst 15–16 year olds says that one in ten teenagers self-harm, arising from depression, seeking relief from a terrible state of mind, bullying anxiety, impulsiveness and low self-esteem (Hawton *et al.*, 2007).

Some of these emotional or mental health problems arise from a range of factors such as the abuse which the young people have suffered, children taken into care, homelessness and so on. Seventy-five per cent of teachers say they have taught children they believe to have been sexually or physically abused (TES' Big 5 Series – investigation into the impact of *Every Child Matters*, *TES*, 7 March 2008). Twenty-eight thousand children are on child protection plans. Sixty thousand young people and children in England are in care (11,000 aged 16 or over), 4400 in Wales. A recent report from the charity Barnardo's points to these young people as having been 'failed by the system', eight out of ten leaving education without any qualification (Barnardo's, 2006). It is estimated that homelessness amongst young people aged 16 and above is over 32,000 and 'runaways' (by definition under 16) many more each year (Ghosh, 2006). Furthermore, there is a strong correlation between mental health problems and poverty within their families. Those in the most economically disadvantaged homes are three times more likely to suffer from mental health disorders than those from well-off families (*End Child Poverty* Report, *Observer*, 24 August 2008).

There are clearly many young vulnerable people.

But schools, colleges and the teachers within them are not well equipped to handle the difficulties and needs which are no doubt partly created by the wider social culture. In England, for that reason, the government is requiring every school, by 2009, to be 'certified' as a 'healthy school', following government policy to encourage schools to widen their responsibilities under *The Children's Plan* and to gain 'healthy school status' which emphasises emotional well-being. In Wales, too, *Extending Entitlements* and the recent *School Effectiveness Framework* place all young people's well-being at the centre, requiring multi-agency involvement in their welfare.

Changed behaviour: drugs and crime

We have already pointed out that the nightmare vision of young people out of control is exaggerated. But we have also acknowledged that problems exist and have a disproportionate impact on those who are affected or who have to deal with them. There are considerable changes in the behaviour of young people which affect the public's perception of adolescence and of their vulnerability, and which are relevant to the achievement of educational aims.

First, the UK Drugs Policy Commission (Reuter and Stevens, 2007) reports the popularity of illegal substances amongst young people, especially the use of cocaine and cannabis. 'It now seems that what might be called "recreational" drug use has become firmly established as an experience that many young people will go through' because the consumption is so prevalent in the age group. According to British Crime Survey (2005), 40% of 16–19 year olds have used drugs at some time – much greater than our European neighbours. However, the figures for later years show a decrease in the use of any illicit drugs amongst 16–24 year olds (British Crime Figures, 2007/2008). Overall 21.3% of people in this age group said they had used illicit drugs in the last year reflecting falls in the use of cannabis, as well as ecstasy, hallucinogens and amphetamines since 2006/2007 – indeed, its lowest ever level since 1995. Cocaine use has, however, increased since 1995, reflecting large increases in the prevalence of cocaine powder use between 1995 and 1999.

Second, there has been recent reporting of violent crime amongst young people, particularly within certain inner city areas, with much news coverage of knife crime. The significance of these figures can be exaggerated; most young people live in safety and few schools are affected by such violence. Nonetheless, despite this cautionary note, approximately 216,000 children and young persons (10–17) are criminalised each year, a rise of nearly 26% in the period 2002–2006. The figure includes formal pre-court warnings and on the spot fines (which count as convictions and are citable), and indeed the increase might partly reflect changed approaches to the administration of justice (Morgan, 2008). Even so, the figures are both startling and worrying, and reflect a considerable number of vulnerable and emotionally deprived young people, often concentrated in relatively few schools. There are 3000 in penal custody. Britain locks up 23 children per 100,000 compared with six in France, two in Spain, 0.2 in Finland, a larger proportion absolutely and proportionally than in any other jurisdiction in Western Europe (YJB, 2006).

Most schools and colleges are not affected by such levels of criminality, but particular areas are, making demands on the schools and colleges which serve them. In certain neighbourhoods, fear is such that young people feel unable to travel to nearby areas to benefit from opportunities such as local youth services (Hayward *et al.*, 2008). In many schools and colleges serving those areas, one sees inspiring efforts, not simply to ensure security, but also to turn anti-social behaviour into an opportunity to educate those young people who are most vulnerable. The increasing links between schools, colleges, parents and the community police seek to protect young people from the criminal world, which the most vulnerable so easily get caught in. Through such programmes as 'restorative justice', pioneered by the Thames Valley Police, they can be enabled to live more effective lives.

But schools and colleges cannot solve such crises in the wider society which impinge so emphatically upon their educational and training mission. Education and training have to be seen within the broader context of social change and reform.

Economic context

The transition to adult status in the past for many young people was symbolised by employment, earning a living and economic independence. But, as has been pointed out, this significant indicator of maturity (seen as such both by the young person and by others in society) has largely disappeared. By the beginning of the present century, only about 9% of 16 year old school-leavers went into a full-time job, down from 22% some 15 years previously. Even at age 18, only about 30% were in full-time employment, compared with over 60% 15 years earlier (Croxford *et al.*, 2006).

The collapse of manufacturing industry from the 1970s and the consequent decline in the availability of manual jobs led to a sharp fall in the demand for 16 year olds leaving school, often with minimal qualifications. In place of such employment, there was a dramatic growth in government-sponsored youth training schemes, designed to combat rising youth unemployment. However, for many participants, these did not provide a viable route into employment; nor did they bring the same sense of status and independence as employment. Some contemporary apprenticeships do not bring with them any contract with an employer. There is inevitably, with such a collapse of an established youth labour market, a feeling of insecurity and possibly uncertainty about status. There is a continuation of dependency. One isn't quite an adult.

Moreover, that dependency could well be in a family context where there is not much income to depend on. As Catan (2003) argued,

> the withdrawal of State support to youth transitions has impacted most severely on young people whose families cannot make up the deficit experienced in the areas of earned income, income support and housing and who lack the resources to support their near-adult children through a lengthy period of further education or training.

It is important, however, to see the impact of economic changes upon educational aspirations and outcomes more widely. Over the last few decades, there has been a growth in the proportion of the work-force in 'white-collar' jobs, as a result of the growth of the services sector and the tendency toward the up-skilling of occupations in all sectors (Gallie, 2000). Government pronouncements have emphasised the necessity for the education system to respond to the needs of the 'knowledge-based economy' by raising levels of educational participation and attainment, as well as to develop the sorts of 'key skills' and personal qualities that are now deemed necessary to function effectively in an economic environment characterised by 'enterprise' and 'entrepreneurialism'. Schools and colleges are increasingly required to equip young people to benefit from the new economic opportunities (Ball, 2008).

At least partly in response to these changes, there have been dramatic increases in the proportion of young people opting to continue in education and training beyond the minimum school-leaving age. For example, Croxford *et al.* reveal that the proportion of 16 year olds in full-time education rose from 42% to 72% during the period from the mid-1980s to the beginning of the present century (with a further 9% being in government-supported training). Even for 18 year olds, 41% remained in full-time education (with a further 8% in government-sponsored training). Likewise, there have been significant increases in young people's levels of educational attainment, as reflected in the qualifications that they gain, and in the proportion of the age cohort entering higher education (Croxford *et al.*, 2006; Chapter 4 discusses these patterns at greater length).

It remains a moot point, however, how far this growth in participation and educational attainment has been matched by the growth in jobs that require the higher levels of skills that educational expansion is supposed to produce – see Chapter 9. Certainly, there is strong evidence for a general increase in the levels of skills required over the last two decades. However, it can equally be argued that this increase in demand for skills has been out-stripped by the growth in the supply of highly qualified individuals from the education and training system, resulting in young people being 'over-qualified' for the jobs that are actually available. Certainly, there has been no eradication of jobs that require only very limited skills (Felstead *et al.*, 2007). It seems likely that any disjuncture between, on the one hand, an official rhetoric of economic growth and upward social mobility through education and, on the other, a reality of limited employment opportunities will ensure that many individuals see themselves as educational failures and feel dissatisfied with their transition to adulthood. There must be more to the 'educated 19 year old' than that.

Community and political engagement

In many respects young people form their own communities through their shared interests, and such communities might often be 'on-line'. Moreover, in some areas, these youth communities find their identities in opposition to other 'gangs' living in different neighbourhoods. Indeed, visits to certain inner city schools and youth clubs by members of the Nuffield Review revealed young people's deep reluctance to move from one school to another despite collaborative arrangements or partnership, or to a youth centre which was in a nearby but different area (Hayward *et al.*, 2008).

But these very same young people are growing up in a world where, in some important respects, there is a decline in community – where, according to the evidence (Thomas and Dorling, 2007), clear divisions are growing between rich and poor neighbourhoods, with little or no interaction between them and where the emphasis on choice has led to many schools serving only the most disadvantaged – those unable to exercise choice. This decline in community is reflected in what Marquand (2004) refers to as the 'decline of the public' – that tradition of public service, nurtured through strong local government and the central role of voluntary bodies in public affairs. The significance of this is recognised in the efforts by the National Assembly for Wales to engage young people in the political process through its 'Funky Dragon' and its schools' councils.

It would seem that increasingly, in place of this 'sense of serving the community', there is an emphasis upon individual choice, pursuit of personal interest and growth of inequality which militates against a shared form of life and shared values. The importance of this and the concern for the values which should be pursued in the public tradition (which Marquand sees to be in decline, thereby affecting the lives of young people) were succinctly expressed by Tawney in his influential book, *Equality*.

> In spite of their varying characters and capacities, it is the fact that men possess in their common humanity a quality which is worth cultivating, and that a community is most likely to make the most of that quality if it takes it into account in planning its economic organisation and social institutions – if it stresses lightly differences of wealth and birth and social position, and establishes on firm foundations institutions which meet common needs and are a source of common enlightenment and common enjoyment.
>
> (Tawney, 1931:15)

In place of this more community-based governance and responsibility, which would otherwise be an educative force amongst young people, is the stronger but more distant central government exercising control through arm's length agencies and steering mechanisms, such as targets and performance tables that are the hallmarks of New Public Management. It is understandable why many young people do not feel part of a civic tradition in which they are being asked to contribute.

Such considerations were at the heart of the arguments for the renewal of citizenship studies (significantly referred to as 'community understanding' in Wales) in schools – with particular reference, according to those conducting the National Foundation for Educational Research Citizenship Education Longitudinal Study, to the 'literature which discusses the contemporary breakdown of "traditional" forms of community life and indicates why traditional neighbourhood and community loyalties and networks may now be peripheral to the lives of young people in modern society' (Cleaver *et al.*, 2006). That civic tradition, which in the past shaped the attitudes and dispositions of so many, may have less formative influence upon young people as they enter into adulthood, and are expected to participate in the political process and contribute to the community not simply through self-interest (Kimberlee, 2002).

The renewal of citizenship studies and related activities in the community is an admirable response to the changing social scene, but once again it is necessary to be reminded that 'education cannot compensate for society', and there is only a limited impact which such curriculum developments can be expected to have.

Conclusion

Transition from dependent childhood to independent adulthood requires adjustments on the parts of the young persons themselves, of the adults responsible for them and of the institutional provision of education and training. In making those adjustments, the young person needs support, advice and sympathy when the occasion arises. Because this is generally available from caring adults, whether at home or in school, the transition into higher education, further training or employment is not so bumpy after all.

But for a sizeable minority of young people the transition is bumpy indeed. Their consequent vulnerability might be due to many factors and exacerbated by significant changes in family patterns and extended financial dependence. It is inevitably acute amongst those who suffer most from poverty in an increasingly polarised society. And it is reflected in the range of behaviours, including criminal, which have been outlined above.

Most young people will have the resilience and the support to go through this period of transition smoothly enough. But even they are affected in three ways.

First, the substantial number of vulnerable young people, unless excluded from school, is distributed across schools, although with more significant concentration in areas of greater disadvantage. And, as indicated above, within such areas, the 'core poor' are themselves more and more isolated from other social groups. They need help and support within the system. Very often, however, neither resources available to schools and colleges nor the expertise of the teachers are able to provide that support. It is in recognition of this that the governments respectively in England, through *Every Child Matters* and the *Children's Plan*, and in Wales, through *Extending Entitlements* and the *School Effectiveness Framework*, have adopted a much more holistic approach to the development of young people. The school is the centre not only of teaching, but of the coordinated application of a wider range of social and health services, including community police who have instigated such valuable contributions as 'restorative justice' procedures (Marshall, 1999).

Second, even the majority of young people, who might not be deemed vulnerable, can so easily become disillusioned with the apparent contradictions between the dependent status of learner and growing social independence – between continuing economic dependence and their burgeoning sense of adulthood. There is inevitably a tension between the growing sense of adult status and the constraints of the system through which they are to enter the next stage of their lives. There is a greater awareness of the right to challenge authority – the recognition of rights vis-à-vis the teacher, and the power (e.g. through internet and texting) to question the teacher's knowledge or even character (see the nasty emails on 'MySpace'). Are they adults or aren't they? All this calls for a re-appraisal of the institutional framework in which the extended period of education and training is to take place. How far should adolescents be treated as adults?

Third, however, it is important to keep in mind the wider social context, in particular, the growing inequality and separateness between rich and poor, and the limited impact which schools and colleges can have in a society which increasingly militates against the aims and values that these organisations are pursuing.

Schools and colleges, therefore, need to adjust to the changing social and cultural context, in particular: the ambiguity in the relation between young learners and the 'authorities' in learning; the greater sense of personal *independence* coinciding with greater sense of economic *dependence*; the increasing emotional stress amongst a growing number of young people; the expectation of 'greater voice' in shaping the social and learning experience; but also the decline in family security, support and socialisation.

Certain questions need to be asked:

- How can the curriculum be dovetailed more closely with this world of the adolescent?
- How can schools, colleges and workplaces manage the confused and questioned relationship between adult and learner?
- Are schools and colleges, as presently constituted, the right kind of institution, in terms of rules and relationships, to enable the aims of education to be pursued?

On the other hand, the context just outlined, which inflames the problems for some and reduces the resilience for others (e.g. poverty, lack of caring adults, pressure for examination success, anxiety in choices to be made for the future), is beyond the power and responsibility of school and college, a matter ignored in so much criticism of educational performance and even in the frequent 'visions' of education for the future. The Gilbert Review (2007:5) asserts that 'schools, local and national governments need to work towards a society in which a child's chances of success are not related to his or her socio-economic background ... [There is a need to] design a new school experience'.

That may be. But the evidence would indicate that, if schools and colleges are to improve educational outcomes, there is a need for a much broader approach to social and economic change. 'Education cannot compensate for society', and should not be held to account for wider social ills.

Recommendations

3. The systems should recognise and respond to the very different economic and social conditions which affect learning – education cannot compensate for society.

4 Measuring system performance

The Welsh and English governments' agendas (*Learning Pathways* in Wales and *Every Child Matters* in England) require the education systems to provide all 14–19 year olds with the best possible opportunities. The systems should seek out and develop talents and abilities, consciously addressing class, gender and ethnic barriers. To that end we have seen a prolific growth of institutions, courses and qualifications, assuming that there is something, somewhere, for every one.

But are they, collectively, doing their jobs? And if there are gaps, through which young people can fall, what can be done to fill them?

Levels of system performance

Chapter 2 sets out the aims of the education and training systems, and the values that they embody. It noted a tension between policy aims, operationalised through targets and performance measures, and the aims and values embedded in pedagogy and institutional ethos. This tension is reflected in different conceptions of how the systems are to be monitored – whether through measurable targets to support management or through ethical deliberations about what is worth learning. The current chapter has the task of negotiating between these as it addresses the question 'How well are the systems currently working?'

A first step in thinking about system performance is to conceptualise the 14–19 education and training system. A three-level model based on that of Raffe *et al.* (2001), comprising national, local and individual levels, is used to match the values and outcomes suggested in Chapter 2. Within such a model the *national* level can be construed as setting the administrative and governance arrangements for organisations operating at the *local* level, which in turn will produce outcomes of importance to *individuals* through provision of teaching and learning opportunities.

The relationships between and within these three levels are complex. At best, the national systems as a whole can be described as loose confederations of organisations with variable funding and governance arrangements, trying to meet the needs of a diverse population of learners. Any assessment of system performance, in order to capture the systems' contribution to achieving educational, as well as social and economic aims, needs to reflect the properties of each of the three levels. The exclusive focus on the national level or on aggregate measures that do not discriminate between the three levels is likely to produce evidence of limited use.

At national and local levels, a number of properties emerge from the connections between the various components of the system that are different from the properties of individual agents. For example, the degrees of inclusiveness or coherence are properties of the system, not of the individual. Because each system as a whole, despite its enormous internal heterogeneity, has such properties, we can consider how to reach judgements about how well the system is working that go beyond the aggregate activities (e.g. participation) and achievements (e.g. General Certificate of Secondary Education [GCSE] attainment) of individuals within it. For example, we need to judge the extent to which the system qua system is coherent, provides fair treatment for all, and allows for different voices to influence democratic decision-making. Such judgements may use evidence from, but cannot be based exclusively on, aggregate data on enrolments or examination results.

Judging the performance of the system at the three levels is not therefore just a technical problem, such as that of accumulating more detailed information in ever increasing databases. There *is* collective knowledge and experience in the system, but no single body or agent can hold it comprehensively. Thus, judging how well the system is performing against the criteria developed in Chapter 2 will require 'layered' judgements, that is, made by more than one agent (such as the inspectorate) and adopting more than one standpoint. Such differing perspectives can then be brought together to form some overall qualitative judgement about system performance.

However, the extent to which we are able to do this is hampered by the availability of information. This is to be expected because of the way the current system is measured. The data that are collected to enable measurement do not necessarily map onto the aims and values outlined in Chapter 2. Consequently, we also recommend in the final section of this chapter how data collection systems need to be developed to make possible more holistic judgements about system performance.

The national level

The English machinery of government for education consists of the two education departments (Department for Children, Schools & Families [DCSF] and Department for Innovation, Universities and Skills [DIUS]), local authorities, and non-governmental agencies that advise, finance and monitor the system. These include the Qualifications and Curriculum Development Agency (QCDA – formerly the QCA); Ofqual; the Learning and Skills Council (LSC); the UK Commission for Employment and Skills; Sector Skills Councils (SSCs); the Office for Standards in Education, Children's Services and Skills (Ofsted); and the Specialist Schools and Academies Trust. These organisations have overlapping responsibilities for 14–19 education and training. In addition to the two education departments, Her Majesty's Treasury and the Departments for Work and Pensions and Business, Enterprise and Regulatory Reform also have an active interest in education and training.

The relationship between these various bodies and their roles and responsibilities is extremely complex. Coffield *et al.* (2008), in attempting to represent the relationships in just one part of the machinery of government for 14–19 in England, produced a picture that looks like a complex electrical wiring diagram. That diagram, presented in early 2008, was already redundant when this book was being written in the autumn of 2008 because of changes to the 'machinery of government'. For example, the LSC's role in funding 16–19 education and training is being transferred to local authorities and the new National Apprenticeship Service by 2010. It is important to have this constant state of flux in the machinery of government clearly in mind when attempting to assess overall system performance.

In Wales, developments since parliamentary devolution in 1999 have produced a somewhat less complex institutional structure. Responsibility for 14–19 provision rests with a single department of the Welsh Assembly Government (WAG), namely, the Department for Children, Education, Lifelong Learning and Skills (DCELLS). Moreover, in April 2006, a number of 'quangos' were absorbed into WAG itself, including Education and Learning Wales (ELWa) – the Welsh equivalent of the LSC – and the Qualifications, Curriculum and Assessment Authority for Wales (ACCAC). However, there remain some organisations which are independent of central government, with Estyn – Her Majesty's Inspectorate for Education and Training in Wales – playing a key role. There is also the further complication that, in some instances, Wales is represented in UK-wide organisations, such as the UK Commission for Employment and Skills (through the chair of its own Wales Employment and Skills Board) and the Sector Skills Councils.

Awarding Bodies, as the providers of qualifications (albeit subjected to the specifications of QCDA in England and WAG), are another set of key players that have to be considered when assessing system performance. Are the qualifications on offer and the mode of assessment employed appropriate for producing an educated 19 year old as described in Chapter 2, including the more practical learning to be argued for in Chapter 5, and responsive to the changing social and economic contexts outlined in Chapter 3?

This collection of national institutions is supposed to support, monitor and govern an education and training system in meeting nationally agreed outcomes, which constitute one aspect of system performance. In terms of current policy in England, for example, this is carried out through the Public Service Agreement (PSA) targets and an emerging set of performance indicators around the *Every Child Matters* agenda. These are typically targets and indicators based on aggregates of data about individuals, for example, 90% of 19 year olds to achieve a Level 2 qualification by 2015 or reducing the inequalities in educational attainment between different socioeconomic groups. In Wales too, there is a wide range of such targets, although they are applied in

a much less formalised way. Attaining such targets does matter but constitutes a limited judgement of system performance which fails to capture
aspects of the system that lie beyond the 'sum of the parts'.

Participation

High rates of participation, retention and progression are taken to be indicative of a well-performing education and training system in most countries.
Given the available data, this is the area where we have the greatest understanding of how well the English and Welsh systems are performing (see NR
Annual Reports, 2003–6).

Figure 4.1 shows the historical trends in participation rates (full-time and
part-time) for 16, 17 and 18 year olds in England. A significant increase in
participation rates up to the mid-1990s has been followed by a more stagnant
phase. It is only recently that a possible further increase in participation can
be detected. In Wales, although the broad patterns of change parallel those in
England, levels of participation are appreciably lower. The outcome is that,
compared to other Organisation of Economic Co-operation and Development
(OECD) and European Union countries, England and Wales can be characterised as having only low participation rates 14–19. In 2005, the OECD
average participation rate for 15–19 year olds was 81% and the EU19 average
was 84%. By comparison the UK's participation rate for this age group was just

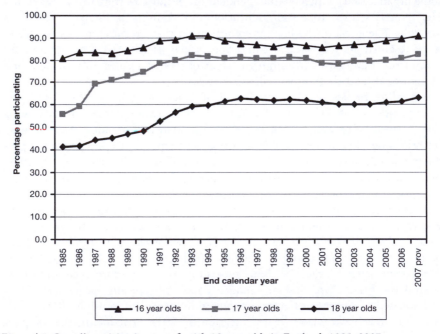

Figure 4.1 Overall participation rates for 16–18 year olds in England, 1985–2007
Source of data: DCSF (2008g)

79%. This placed the UK 24th out of 30 countries (OECD, 2008). Furthermore, countries such as Greece, which historically had poor participation rates, have witnessed major increases, from 62% in 1995 to 97% in 2005.

Both England and Wales are therefore performing poorly on this indicator. One reason may be a major shift in the mode of participation. In the 1970s, both countries could be described as having a mixed model of participation, with a sizeable proportion of young people participating through a work-based learning route such as apprenticeship. However, through the 1990s, participation via work-based learning declined rapidly, from 30% of 16 year olds in 1985 to less than 10% today. This means that the sharp increase in participation rate occurring in the late 1980s and early 1990s (see Figure 4.1) was driven by a rapid expansion of post-compulsory full-time education. Young people became increasingly likely to remain in school sixth-forms or enrol in college courses once they had reached the end of compulsory education.

However, too many young people judge such provision to be unsuitable for them, or they are judged to be unsuitable for the provision on offer.

The Not in Education, Employment or Training (NEET) problem

The corollary of comparatively low participation rates by international standards is that the proportion of young people who are NEET in England and Wales is unacceptably high. At the end of 2007, 9.4% of 16–18 year olds in England (189,000) were NEET. While there was a welcome decrease from the figure of 10.4% in 2006, this is still unacceptably high. In Wales, the proportion of 16–18 year olds classified as NEET has remained between 10% and 12% for over a decade. WAG has set out a new strategy for tackling the problem (DCELLS, 2008b).

Young people enter the NEET population in different ways. Some start the process of disengaging from school early in their secondary school. This is reflected in continuing high levels of permanent exclusion and persistent absence (truanting). Such disengagement seems to have more to do with an inability to cope with the necessary authority structures of schooling than with an inadequate curriculum. Ofsted (2008b) and Estyn (2008a) reports have suggested that being provided with more practical learning opportunities helps young people at risk of disengagement, but, if true, these positive messages are not reflected in the participation statistics.

Young people who disengage from school before the age of 16 are typically from socially disadvantaged backgrounds, especially where parents too are not in work – a problem highlighted in Chapter 3. They are far more likely to become long-term NEET and their future prospects are bleak. Others may enter the NEET group because they have caring responsibilities. This is indicative of inadequate welfare provision rather than a poorly performing education and training system. Yet others become NEET for a short period of time after completing secondary school, and can be relatively easily helped by appropriate information, advice and guidance (IAG) into employment or further education and training (Hayward *et al.*, 2008).

The proportion of young people who are NEET is much higher in the old industrial and coal mining areas in northern England and in South Wales, where unemployment and economic inactivity amongst the adult population are also high. The NEET rate in the northeast region was twice as high as that in the southeast of England. Rates in Blaenau Gwent in Wales remain some of the highest in the whole of the UK. This is due to long-term restructuring of the economy rather than an inadequate education and training system.

Retention

Figure 4.1 reveals another characteristic feature of the 16–19 system in England and Wales: a steady decline with age in the proportion of young people participating. Part of the reason is that young people start a programme but find they have chosen the wrong course, and they leave within the academic year. Such behaviour could be seen as a natural process of experimentation but it is also indicative of inadequate and less than impartial IAG (Foskett *et al.*, 2008). Dropping out in this way is a particular problem for those taking vocational programmes. A learner taking four General Certificate of Education (GCE) AS Levels in Year 12 (the first year of the sixth-form) can easily drop one AS-Level and still have a viable learning programme. By contrast, a learner taking a vocational course, such as a Business & Technology Education Council (BTEC) National Diploma, can only drop the whole programme not an element of it. Given that the students who participate in vocational programmes post-16 have, on average, lower rates of attainment and come from poorer backgrounds than those taking GCE A-Levels, this seems inequitable. Here the structure of qualifications acts against the interests of some learners compared to others.

Progression

Attrition also occurs at the end of an academic year. For example, young people who enrol on Level 1 and 2 qualifications at the beginning of Year 12 typically embark on a one-year learning programme. When they reach the end of that year and complete their qualification, they would then have to embark on a qualification at a higher level in order to carry on participating.

Analysis by Watson (2008) of a sample of 100 Year 12 students who started courses below Level 3 in further education (FE) colleges in 2004 revealed that two-thirds of them carried on with their learning in Year 13. That means one-third of the original sample left, entering employment or the NEET group. Those who started Level 2 qualifications in Year 12 and successfully completed those qualifications were the most likely to stay on into Year 13 to take a Level 3 course. However, a significant number of those who do continue into Year 13 do not make progress. They were already at least one year behind the majority of their peers, as they did not achieve five 'good' GCSEs. At the end of Year 12, only those who progressed to Level 3 (16% of the sample) were still one year behind. The others were two or more years behind. Of five learners selected at random from the sample of 100 for more detailed analysis, only two progressed to Level 3, and they both abandoned their courses with no achievement. After two years in post-compulsory education, none of these five had achieved Level 3, nor were any still on course to achieve Level 3 in the following year.

The implications are clear. For those who do not achieve five good GCSEs at 16 there are second-chance learning opportunities at Level 2, typically provided in FE colleges. Many who start subsequently do achieve a Level 2 qualification. However, the likelihood of progression to and successful completion of subsequent Level 3 courses, essential to access higher education and better paying jobs, seems small.

For those entering post-compulsory education on courses below Level 2, the opportunities for successful progression seem remote. Of course, there will be individual instances of success. In particular, where individual colleges offering Entry and Level 1 courses have forged good links with employers, there may be progression to employment for such learners. But at a system level the implications are clear: failure in the 14–16 phase of education with little, if any, GCSE attainment at 16 seems hard to remediate in further education colleges.

Attainment

A key indicator of system performance is the extent to which it enables young people to achieve qualifications that have an impact on their future lives, including economic well-being. The use of attainment as an indicator highlights the inequities that persist in the English and Welsh systems between different social groups. In particular, the OECD has noted the high association of social class with educational performance in the UK generally. The Programme of International Student Assessment (PISA) is the survey, conducted every three years by the OECD, of students towards the end of their compulsory education to see how far they have the knowledge and skills (in maths, science and reading) to equip them for participation in society. Though the UK does reasonably well on average compared with other OECD countries on the PISA tests, particularly science, good outcomes are not achieved by a significant number (OECD, 2007).

The Welsh results were below the OECD average, as well as lower than those of the other countries of the UK, in each of the three areas tested. Measured in these terms, therefore, the performance of the education system in Wales is especially poor. This fact could be interpreted as casting doubt on the efficacy of the distinctive policies which have been adopted in Wales since parliamentary devolution in 1999 (Reynolds, 2008). Moreover, the very unequal outcomes achieved by different social groups in the UK's education systems explain the higher dispersion of PISA scores in the UK compared with other OECD countries (OECD, 2007).

Attainment at the end of Key Stage 4

In England, five or more GCSEs at grades A*–C was the key performance measure of attainment used by the government in setting PSA targets. It seems a reasonable measure to use but there is some ambiguity which needs to be noted. The 2004 Comprehensive Spending Review set a target by 2008 of 60% of 16 year olds achieving the *equivalent* of five GCSEs at grades A*–C. This means that a range of other qualifications approved for study pre-16 other than GCSEs are included. For example, from 1997/1998 to 2002/2003 the figures included attainment in Intermediate General National Vocational Qualification (GNVQ) where a pass was deemed equivalent to four GCSEs at A*–C. Intermediate GNVQs are no longer available but qualifications such as BTEC First Diploma can now be offered in schools pre-16. A pass in this qualification is also deemed to be equivalent to four GCSEs at grades A*–C. The extent to which the achievement of these 'equivalent' qualifications has resulted in the ongoing increase in GCSE attainment cannot be estimated from the available aggregate data.

Nonetheless, the last 10 years appear to have been a phase of continuous increase in attainment. The proportion of English 15 year olds achieving five or more GCSEs at A*–C has increased from 45.1% in 1996/1997 to 64.2% by 2007/2008. The proportion achieving five or more A*–C grades, including English and maths, rose from 35.6% to 47.0% over the same time period (DCSF, 2008f). But a word of caution: the time series data reported here are based on the older methodology for deriving figures at the end of Key Stage 4 which did not accurately account for the number of pupils in pupil referral units and hospital schools.

This is a key performance indicator for the English and Welsh education systems. For many institutions the attainment of five GCSEs at grades A*–C is the minimum level of attainment needed to undertake GCE A-Level programmes and so access higher education. Providing this minimum level of attainment is reached by the end of Key Stage 4, the chance of accessing higher education by those from lower socioeconomic groups is the same as for higher socioeconomic groups (though access to elite universities remains more probable for those from better off backgrounds) (Marcenaro-Gutierrez *et al.*, 2007).

As Table 4.1 shows, the chances of reaching this level of attainment still remain predictable on the basis of characteristics such as social class, ethnicity and gender. Nonetheless, it is important to recognise that there have been significant improvements in the proportion attaining five A*–C GCSEs in certain minority ethnic groups. For example, the proportion of young people of Black ethnic origin attaining five good GCSEs rose from 34% to 50% between 2003 and 2006. In 1991 only 14% of young people of Bangladeshi ethnic origin achieved five GCSEs at A*–C compared with 57% in 2006, virtually the same as young people of White ethnic origin (58%).

Large differences in GCSE attainment across social classes have persisted over the last decade, although long-term comparisons are complicated by changes in reporting, especially that of social class. Young people whose parents are not classified as having an occupation have the lowest rates of academic attainment, but as Table 4.1 indicates the gap is closing.

Nonetheless, it remains the case that, at a system level, patterns of attainment remain inequitable and restrict social mobility. For example, young

Table 4.1 Percentage attainment of five or more GCSE grades A*–C in Year 11 by learner characteristics: 1997–2006

	1997[1]	1999[4]	2001	2003	2006
All	46	49	51	54	58
Sex					
Male	42	44	46	50	54
Female	51	54	56	59	63
Ethnic origin	47	50	52	55	58
White	29	38	36	34	50
Black	45	48	52	55	64
Asian	54	60	60	72	72
Indian	29	29	40	38	52
Pakistani	33	29	43	44	57
Bangladeshi	61	72	64	65	77
Other Asian	47	42	53	59	56
Other ethnic group					
Parental occupation (NS-SEC)[2]					
Higher professional	n/a	75	77	76	81
Lower professional	n/a	62	64	65	73
Intermediate	n/a	49	51	53	59
Lower supervisory	n/a	34	34	41	46
Routine	n/a	26	31	33	42
Other/not classified[3]	n/a	24	26	34	34

Source: DCSF/DIUS (2008c)

Notes
1. From 1997 includes equivalent GCSE qualifications achieved in Year 11
2. Data from 1999 onwards use the Family NS-SEC to describe overall economic status of the family
3. Includes many respondents for whom neither parent had an occupation
4. Data from 1999 onwards for England only

people eligible for free school meals (FSM) (a proxy indicator for poverty) remain the most likely to achieve no GCSEs at all (8% of those eligible compared with 3% who were not). Young people who are disabled are also far more likely to achieve no GCSE passes (18%) compared with those who are not disabled (4%). Finally, and unsurprisingly, only 13% of those who persistently truant achieved five GCSEs grades A*–C compared with 67% who never truanted. The extent to which current increases in GCSE attainment among previously poorer performing groups will lead to an increase in social mobility remains to be seen (Cabinet Office, 2008).

In Wales, in addition to these problems of the distribution of educational opportunities between different social groups, there has also been a crisis of low attainment in general. As in England, there have been rising levels of attainment, measured in terms of GCSE performance. However, the rate of increase in Wales has been significantly lower, resulting in a widening gap between the two countries and their education systems. Hence, in 1999, 47% of pupils in Wales achieved five GCSEs at A*–C, only two percentage points behind the English figure. By 2008, this gap had widened to some eight percentage points, with only 56% of pupils in Wales achieving this threshold of attainment. Moreover, when English and maths are included in the five GCSEs, the Welsh deficit again stands at some seven percentage points.

It could be argued that the lower attainment levels reflect Wales's relative economical and social disadvantage in UK terms. However, it is not clear that Wales has become more disadvantaged over the time period during which the attainment gap has been widening. Moreover, Welsh performance (in 2007) was not only below the English average, but also below the attainment levels of all the English regions, many of which are much closer to Wales in terms of economic and social conditions (WAG, 2008a). In addition, up until the end of primary schooling (Key Stage 2), Welsh attainment levels are higher than those in England. Clearly, much more sophisticated analysis would be required to provide definitive conclusions on this issue (Gorard, 2000). Nevertheless, it is not surprising that the quality of provision in Welsh secondary schools has come to be a particular focus of attention and policy development and is seen to be a key element in the wider development of 14–19 provision.

Attainment post-16

Examining attainment post-16 is far more difficult given the range of institutions young people attend and the wide range of qualification types and levels they attempt. The majority of learners are in FE and sixth-form colleges, not in school sixth-forms. For example in 2007, in England, of the 79.3% of 16 year olds participating in full-time education, 41.8% were in colleges, compared with 37.1% in schools. Across the 16–18 age range, and including those in full-time and part-time study, 52.4% were in colleges, compared with 34.6% in schools.

GCE A-Levels remain the most popular single qualification taken by 16 and 17 year olds, with nearly half of all 16–18 year olds in education and training taking this qualification in 2007. By comparison, only one-sixth of all 16–18 year old learners were taking Level 3 vocational qualifications. The proportion taking Level 2 and Level 1 qualifications post-16 is also small, compared with GCE A-Level provision: only just over one in five 16–18 year old learners were taking such programmes full-time in 2007. This is despite the fact that under 50% achieved five GCSEs at grades A*–C including English and maths by the end of Key Stage 4. In part, this low uptake of Levels 1 and 2 provision post-16 may reflect lack of coherent provision at a local level without an overall local planning process. It could also represent a lack of demand by learners for such programmes.

Attainment across different qualifications is collated in England by QCA into point scores for use in the Achievement and Attainment Tables. Qualifications covered include GCE A and AS-Levels, BTEC National Diplomas (deemed equivalent to three GCE A-Levels) and the International Baccalaureate Diploma (five GCE A-Levels). Using these points, overall achievement in GCE A-Levels and equivalent Level 3 qualifications increased from 721.5 per candidate in 2005/2006 to 733.5 in 2006/2007. On this measure, system performance is clearly improving. However, the proportion of candidates passing a Level 3 qualification (equivalent in size to at least two GCE A-Levels) has remained at about 95% over the last two years, while the proportion achieving three or more A grades at A-Level has also remained the same at 11.9%. In Wales, attainment at Level 3 has also been rising, although again there is an attainment deficit relative to England.

Attainment rates in Levels 1 and 2 qualifications post-16 overall are lower. However, it is not possible to provide figures across the whole of the 16–19 sector owing to the way that data are collated. Nonetheless, attainment at these levels of qualification is also improving. For example, success rates for young people taking LSC-funded full Level 2 qualifications was 70% in 2006/2007, a considerable rise over previous years. This compares favourably with success rates for learners taking LSC-funded full Level 3 qualifications in FE, which stood at 69% in 2006/2007. However this does not take account of the higher success rates on Level 3 programmes in school sixth-forms and sixth-form colleges.

Completion of apprenticeship frameworks has also improved steadily. In the case of Level 2, it went up from 41% in 2004/2005 to 62% in 2006/2007. Comparable figures for the Level 3 apprenticeship frameworks are 41% and 65%, respectively. Certain things are clearly improving across the system at a national level. Nonetheless, rates of attainment remain low compared with our European neighbours, as recognised in the Leitch Review (2005, 2006).

Conclusion

Poor rates of participation, high rates of attrition and low levels of attainment remain endemic features of the English and Welsh 14–19 systems compared with our European neighbours (OECD, 2008). This suggests that the system, as it is currently configured, is performing poorly by international standards. In addition, the system is highly inequitable in terms of participation and attainment; those from poorer backgrounds, certain ethnic groups, and boys perform less well than other young people at age 16. Many rounds of curriculum reform and other initiatives over the last 20 years seem to have had little impact on these indicators. This suggests that the problem does not lie wholly within the education and training system and is not resolvable by further rounds of curriculum and qualification reform, the favoured policy instruments in both countries. Thus we should not necessarily attribute the poor performance on these indicators exclusively to the functioning of the education and training systems. We have to take account of the wider, particularly economic, context. The 'problem' of low participation rates relative to European neighbours may be indicative of weak incentives to participate in education and training being signalled by the labour market, especially for those with low levels of attainment at the end of compulsory schooling (Chapter 9).

This argument does not mean that high participation rates are not desirable for delivering a range of non-economic benefits derived from schooling, which contribute to the production of educated 19 year olds, but it does call into question the economic imperative that drives so much education policy.

Young people do not seem to respond to messages that, to get ahead economically, they need to stay in education, unless on the 'royal route' to higher education. In particular they seem to avoid opportunities to take Levels 1 and 2 vocational programmes post-16. This may be, economically, a wise decision. The economic value of holding a particular qualification can be estimated by using the wages of people who hold that qualification. Results from such analyses indicate big returns (on average) to those holding degrees, and reasonable returns for those holding GCE A-Levels and some Level 3 Vocational qualifications such as BTEC Nationals. GCSEs on their own provide a limited return but most vocational qualifications at Level 2 and below provide little if any return for most groups. This indicates the low value placed on them by employers. This issue is explored further in Chapter 9.

These national outcomes arise from outcomes generated at the local level.

The local level

This level consists of the organisations and people that provide formal and non-formal learning opportunities. The most obvious of these are schools (including special schools) and further education and sixth-form colleges, but they also include independent training providers, employers, youth clubs, detached youth workers, Children's Trusts and a range of third-sector voluntary organisations such as Rathbone, Barnados and the Prince's Trust. Such third-sector organisations are particularly important for providing services to disadvantaged young people and those at risk of becoming NEET. Independent training providers are local, regional or national private companies established to offer a range of training at different levels. The JHP Group Ltd, for example, is one of the largest vocational training providers in the UK – over 2400 apprentices and over 1000 on other training programmes.

The exact configuration of these organisations at a local level varies considerably largely for historical reasons. Figure 4.2 provides a simple descriptive taxonomy based on the balance of school sixth-forms and colleges. An obvious, but until recently unanswered question is: 'To what extent do different local arrangements of providers produce more or less effective performance?'

Participation rates

Might different configurations of learning providers affect staying-on rates? Policy in England seems to suggest so with its presumption of establishing new school sixth-forms in areas where 11–16 schools dominate (the 'sixth-form presumption') and establishing new academies with sixth-forms. Analysis of the Youth Cohort Survey suggests that, taken on face value, this is a sound policy;

overall staying-on rates in areas with school sixth-forms are 80% compared with 78% in areas where sixth-forms are absent (Fletcher and Perry, 2008:19).

However, when social background is taken into account, this difference disappears. 11–16 schools are more common in working-class areas, 11–18 schools in middle-class areas. Socially determined staying-on rates affect the type of school structure, as local authorities seek to maximise the efficiency of post-16 provision in areas with low staying-on rates by pooling such work into viable units such as tertiary colleges. Furthermore, in areas with a significant proportion of post-16 students in school sixth-forms, this seems to decrease the probability of learners in that school remaining in post-16 education.

> Other things being equal [in a school with a sixth-form] the average child is between two and five percentage points less likely to stay in education at school or college than pupils from similar backgrounds in 11–16 schools. Lest anyone should think that this effect is minor we should remember that it is about the size of the improvement in staying on rates bought about by Education Maintenance Allowances at a cost of over £500 million per year.
>
> (Schagen *et al.*, 2006:19)

This depressing outcome is particularly pronounced for those of greatest concern to policy-makers: pupils with below average attainment at 16. Of learners who achieve five or more grades D–G in an 11–16 school, 59% stay on compared with 45% of pupils with a similar level of attainment and social background in an 11–18 school. The outcome is even starker for those with no GCSE attainment at the end of Key Stage 4: 38% stay on if they are in an 11–16 school compared with 27% in an 11–18 school.

There are two possible explanations for this negative school sixth-form effect. For those in 11–18 schools, progression into the sixth-form, which is overwhelmingly progression onto GCE A-Level provisions, is seen by pupils in the school only for the academically able. Second, when this is combined with the poorer and more biased quality of IAG available to pupils in 11–18 schools, it is not surprising that staying-on rates in areas dominated by school sixth-form

Figure 4.2 Patterns of post-16 provision

| | | Colleges | |
		FE and sixth-form colleges	Few or no sixth-form colleges
School Sixth-forms	*Many*	**Mixed provision** Worcestershire, London	**FE colleges and school sixth-forms** Kent
	Few	**Mainly FE and sixth-form colleges** Hampshire, Oldham, Solihull	**Tertiary college** Bridgwater, Selby, Truro

Source: Fletcher and Perry, 2008, p.12

provision are lower (Foskett *et al.*, 2008). Suggestions, therefore, that adding school sixth-forms to 11–16 schools will reduce the NEET problem, for example, fly in the face of such evidence. This is not to argue against the value of sixth-forms for schools in terms of their ethos or recruiting specialist teaching staff, but it does call into question a policy of adding school sixth-forms as a simplistic policy tool to increase participation rates at a local level.

In addition, providers operate with high levels of autonomy at a local level. While senior managers and governors value such autonomy, it may not result in coherent local provision. This may act against the interests of lower attaining learners, as illustrated in the Welsh experience of 14–19 Learning Pathways. The Pathways were designed to foster institutional collaboration at the local level precisely in order – *inter alia* – to improve the post-16 opportunities for learners with modest levels of attainment. As is shown in Chapter 11, however, there are difficulties in achieving this objective.

Attainment

There is considerable variation in post-16 attainment across different learning providers. For example, in England, on Level 3 qualifications such as GCE A-Level, candidates in comprehensive school sixth-forms achieved 723.1 points on average compared with 676.8 in FE colleges and 786.4 in sixth-form colleges. This compares with 962.1 per candidate in grammar schools and 885.6 in independent schools. At face value, school sixth-forms and sixth-form colleges outperform general FE colleges, at least when it comes to GCE A-Levels. Ofsted (2008a) concluded that sixth-form colleges were more effective providers of Level 3 qualifications than school sixth-forms and FE colleges.

However, in the previous section, it was demonstrated that local institutional arrangements affect staying-on rates in a counterintuitive way. Could the same be true of attainment rates? Could these differences in attainment reflect important underlying differences between learners attending different types of post-16 learning provider?

The Youth Cohort Survey and other data sources indicate that, when provision within an area is made through a differentiated set of learning providers, the characteristics of their intakes differ sharply:

> Put simply some institutions are more white, more middle class, are more likely to contain high achieving learners and those without disabilities than others. In England school sixth-forms and sixth-form colleges contain many more such learners than general FE colleges: evidence supplied to the Foster Report suggested that school sixth-forms were actually less socially inclusive than universities.
>
> (Fletcher and Perry, 2008:18)

Given that achievement at Level 3 is highly correlated with prior achievement at Level 2 and social background, it may be in the interests of providers to 'restrict' their intake and the evidence suggests this is what happens (ibid:21). This is not necessarily an attempt to 'game' the system but could reflect an underlying cultural commitment to Level 3 provision, particularly GCE A-Levels, in school sixth-forms and some sixth-form colleges, which in turn raises the popularity of these learning providers with middle-class parents.

There is considerable selection and sorting of learners occurring at age 16, which apparently causes no concern to policy-makers (unlike selection at 11), and into higher education at 18. The result is that general FE colleges become providers of last resort for many young people, especially those from poor and certain minority ethnic backgrounds, notably of Black ethnic origin. Many of these will be taking programmes below Level 3. This means that a sixth-form college or school specialising in providing GCE A-Level programmes, which have a higher success rate than other types of provision but with a more restricted range of learners, will automatically have higher performance, when that is based on raw examination results, than a college offering a wide range of provision to a diverse range of learners. This problem can be overcome through the use of 'curriculum-adjusted success rates', as developed by the LSC. These provide a more accurate comparison between two institutions, but this rarely makes the front page of the local paper (or the tables of the nationals) come results day. A system of performance assessment that focuses on crude scores in individual institutions tends to exacerbate these distinctions. The most effective institutions according to these measures are the ones best able to restrict their intake (ibid:22).

When a more balanced perspective is taken of post-16 attainment and outcomes, including the incorporation of young people on Entry, Level 1 and Level 2 programmes, who are overwhelmingly found in FE colleges, the performance of FE colleges emerges more strongly compared with school sixth-forms and sixth-form colleges.

Policy-makers are then faced with a dilemma: to support systems that increase participation, namely, those with smaller 11–16 schools and separate sixth-form provision in colleges (a tertiary system) or to support a system that affords high levels of Level 3 attainment by fostering selective school sixth-forms and sixth-form college provision. Such decisions, the Review has argued, are best made at local level through democratic processes which give all interested parties a voice. However, government policy in England, though delegating responsibility for 14–19 education and training back to local authorities, is not delegating the power to make such decisions at local level. Policy emphasises strongly autonomous providers, even when such arrangements may act against the interest of the least successful learners. In Wales, government policy favours local collaboration more strongly. However, implementation at the local level has proved uneven, reflecting the essentially voluntarist nature of the 14–19 Learning Pathways strategy.

Local autonomy in England is further strengthened by government policy on specialist schools and academies and the 'sixth-form presumption'. What is the impact of these policies on system performance?

Specialist schools and academies programme

Key government policies in England for raising educational attainment are the specialist schools and the academies programmes. The Conservative party is also wedded to promoting academies. Raw examination results indicate that many specialist schools and academies are performing better in terms of the proportion of pupils receiving five or more GCSEs A*–C, although these claims are disputed and questions have been raised about rates of exclusion from some and selection by others. Nonetheless, on the basis of raw examination data, it appears that the rate of improvement is greater in some, but by no means all, academies than in standard comprehensive schools. It is hoped by government that a wider roll-out of the programme to cover all schools would reduce differences in attainment between social groups while raising attainment overall.

The question that needs answering is: 'To what extent have specialist schools or academies achieved examination results in excess of what they would otherwise have achieved if they had not acquired specialist status?' (Taylor, 2007) – and also, one might continue, if they had not received such a large injection of funds (almost £30 million per academy). It is suggested that higher exam scores achieved on average by schools which take on specialist or academy status are due primarily to sample selection bias, exclusions and extra money, not to benefits accruing from adopting a particular status. The rate of exclusion is greater in academies than elsewhere, even though they were established initially to help young people in disadvantaged areas. One study concluded that 'the specialist schools programme. ... has been mildly successful, but only in four specialist areas [business and enterprise, technology, science and arts]' (Taylor, 2007:9).

The same study points to the distributional impact of specialist schools. Those schools with a high proportion on free school meals (FSM) have benefited from specialist status far more than those with a small proportion of pupils on FSM. Why this is the case is difficult to ascertain. For example, a change in a school's status to a specialist school may result in a change of pedagogy but it also brings extra funding. Is the improvement in performance, especially for those schools with a higher proportion of poorer young people, a result of better teaching, extra funding, a combination of both or a better match between pupils' interests and the curriculum on offer?

'Sixth-form presumption'

There is continuing emphasis in England on competition as the best way to improve quality of provision, despite the recent advocacy of collaboration around the implementation of Diplomas. Such emphasis on competition is evident in the desire to encourage new providers to operate within the 14–19 system. These could include independent training providers, third-sector voluntary bodies and new types of school. Such initiatives can however be wasteful, and not lead to desired outcomes.

For example, policy thinking about raising attainment at 18 focuses on school sixth-forms as providing a panacea, the so-called 'sixth-form presumption' (DfES, 2004). Such sixth-forms might be established by being bolted onto 11–16 schools or by the introduction of new types of school, such as academies. The likelihood in both cases is that such sixth-forms will, in the first instance, be small. Here evidence on standards is absolutely clear: small sixth-forms produce poorer results, less choice and use resources far less efficiently than large ones or college provision. The advice is consistent with that of the Audit Commission report (1996), namely, that sixth-forms need, on average, to have at least 150 pupils – preferably more than 200 – to produce good standards and use resources effectively.

Given the demographic decline over the next 10 years, further expansion of post-16 provision through the development of inevitably small sixth-forms will reduce choice, lower attainment and raise costs. It would be much better to develop local learning opportunities based on strongly collaborative models, as argued in Chapter 11, to raise both participation and attainment. However, collaboration is expensive, and costs and benefits have to be weighed against simpler options, such as local reorganisation. This is as much a matter of politics as rationally weighing the evidence. Sixth-forms are popular with middle-class parents whose children are most likely to use them. Moreover, as Welsh experience of attempting to achieve more strongly collaborative local systems of provision through the 14–19 Learning Pathways demonstrates, even where central government is strongly supportive, actually achieving such systems is in practice extremely difficult.

Does the system make efficient and equitable use of resources?

Overall level of public expenditure in education in the UK has risen over the past decade to be near the OECD average as a percentage of gross domestic product (GDP) (OECD, 2008). Current arrangements for funding 14–19 are informed by a wider public sector reform agenda. In particular, in England there is emphasis on a purchaser–provider split to prevent providers from using resources to further their own agenda rather than meet the needs of learners. The outcome is 14–19 funding arrangements that are judged to be 'broadly fit for purpose' (Fletcher and Perry, 2008).

There are nonetheless inequities in the current system. Learners on Level 3 programmes in schools in England are funded at a higher level than equivalent learners in FE colleges, despite the fact that such learners in colleges have lower levels of prior educational attainment and come from less privileged back-grounds. Also Levels 1 and 2 learners in FE colleges (i.e. those who have lower levels of prior educational attainment and a greater distance to travel educationally if they are to progress) are funded at a lower level and receive less teaching than their Level 3 counterparts. This seems to be an example of an inverse care law as reported in the Webb Review (2007) on further education in Wales.

Writing of health care over 30 years ago, Tudor Hart argued that an Inverse Care Law was in operation: those who were most in need received less care than the less needy. There is a distinct danger that this is also the case in education. Moreover, the total expenditure on disadvantaged groups is falling short of what is needed. Certainly the size of the groups remains stubbornly high. While these decisions are for politicians, the Inverse Care Law also raises questions about the proportionality of spend on these most needy people compared with that on such undifferentiated groups as university students and adult leisure learners.

The most needy learners of all, those in the NEET category, are the ones who receive the least. Voluntary sector organisations, who seek to help them, receive least money, typically in the form of short-term initiative-led funding. It is hardly surprising that helping such people to achieve is such an uphill struggle. In particular, there is inadequate resourcing of the work of detached youth workers, who are essential in reaching the most disengaged young people (Hayward *et al.*, 2008; NR, 2008i).

Increasing funding has led to an increase in the number of qualified teachers (9% FTE increase between 1997 and 2007 in England) and of adult/learner ratio. Chapter 6 explains this consequence of the new 'work-force agreement'. This has led to a decrease in class size, although not to the levels experienced in independent schools. Evidence from the Engaging Youth Enquiry (Hayward *et al.*, 2008) speaks to the importance of the pastoral role of teachers and spending enough time to support disadvantaged learners. Some evidence of improving performance comes from the Chief Inspector's Annual Report 2006/07, which notes that 'increasingly, schools are providing academic and pastoral mentors who guide and support pupils well' (Ofsted, 2007a:29). But there is no evidence to indicate that the potentially available additional adult time has been used in such a way as to produce a reduction in indicators of unequal access to learning, such as exclusion rates, persistent non-attendance or NEET rates. This would suggest that the increase in adult/learner ratio has had little impact on the educational chances of the most disadvantaged young people.

Such concerns lead us to the final level of the system: the individual learner.

Individual level

The data available may have enabled the production of the (incomplete) picture of system performance at national and local levels, presented above, but do not permit systematic connections between the functioning of the system and the educational aims described in Chapter 2. The nearest approximation of the individual level based on such data only gets as far as descriptors of institutional performance (e.g. how well institutions do in providing young people with opportunities to learn and develop meaningfully, enjoyably and safely). Such evidence is briefly outlined below. However, in order to get closer to the individual level, one would need more textured data from focused research, of a different nature from the aggregate performance measures currently available.

Educational benefit

It is the relationships and interactions between learners and teachers (broadly conceived), embedded in the practices of course and programme 'delivery', and the organisational values of the learning providers, that ultimately lead to the development of the educated 19 year old. The ongoing conversation between teachers and learners as they engage in the process of developing their understanding and practical know how gives rise to so many of the educational benefits.

But the available evidence is inadequate for making definitive judgements about the development of most of the important attributes. The best available evidence comes from Ofsted (2007a) and Estyn (2008b) reports. These provide a general impression of what is happening based on the detailed inspection of schools and colleges countrywide. For example, 'a focus on gaining purely factual knowledge leaves too little room for pupils to apply what they have learned, to carry out research and to develop as creative and independent learners' or 'the pupils' understanding of what they have learned, as opposed to their ability to recall the basic facts, is often superficial' (Ofsted, 2007a:34). Since these school inspections do look for the broader qualities described in Chapter 2, then we should be able to get some idea of how young people are doing in terms of general health and happiness as well as the other qualities. Ofsted's (2008b) recent evaluations of progress in implementing 14–19 reforms are, as yet, not too helpful in this respect, but this broader view of education is now reflected in the indicators used in school and college inspections.

Social and economic benefits

There is considerable evidence that young people who disengage from the system early face long-term social and economic disadvantage (Bynner, 2004; Parsons and Bynner, 2007). Not only will they find it more difficult to obtain sustainable employment, they are more likely to suffer from ill-health and less likely to engage politically. However, the government's vision of education and training as providing the key means for engendering social mobility and thereby redistribution of income remains, as demonstrated in Chapter 3, highly problematic. Those who benefit most are those who are on the 'royal route' to higher education, the GCSE to GCE A-Level pathway, where certain social groups are over-represented. If young people from poorer backgrounds, for instance, are enabled to attain the requisite level of GCE attainment, then they too can participate in this progression pathway with an equal likelihood of progressing to higher education. But for those progressing through vocational pathways the outcomes are far less certain (Chapter 10) and in some cases the outcomes can have little if any economic return (Chapter 9).

Well-being

The UNICEF Report (2007) revealed that our young people are the least happy in the OECD countries. Nonetheless, Ofsted inspection reports note that schools responded well to the *Every Child Matters* agenda and that 'a very large majority of schools provide well for pupils' enjoyment, safety, health and their contribution to the community' (Ofsted, 2007a:5). However, in a high proportion of secondary schools, behaviour is judged as only satisfactory, 29% (p. 29), and levels of bullying remain unacceptably high, especially bullying of those with special educational need and disabilities (DCSF, 2008d). Furthermore, bullying is known to have a negative effect on attainment.

System performance: the overall judgement

Does the system contribute to achieving the educational aims set out in Chapter 2? To be able to judge this, we would need to draw on evidence about the quality of the learning experience throughout the system, and on holistic assessments of understandings, skills, attitudes and capacities in relation to the different contexts of the learners' lives (rather than simply on atomistic proxies of attainment such as qualification levels achieved). In light of the discussion in Chapter 3, a further question would be:

To what extent does the system respond to social, environmental, and economic challenges? To answer this question, one would need detailed evidence about the effectiveness and limitations of the education system in relation to other systems in addressing, for example, inequality, exclusion, violence and abuse, or narrow horizons of individual and local aspirations and sense of responsibility, and concern for the wider national and global problems.

Both these questions are more fundamental than the question that has dominated recent policy discourse – namely, whether the system meets minimum thresholds of performance as set out in relation to top-down targets and performance measures. However the data available to answer them remain limited. Consequently we aim to address in this section two more overarching questions about system performance that we believe can be answered. Then finally we turn to how the mechanisms of system performance might be developed to enable us to provide a more holistic assessment.

What contribution does the system make to wider social cohesion and economic performance? Overall, the system, as it is currently configured for 14–19 year olds, serves well the interests of higher attaining pupils, typically from wealthier backgrounds. More often than not, such learners will be on the 'royal route' to higher education, from which will flow preferential access to better paid and more interesting work. Those who are left behind are ill-served. As discussed in Chapter 9, the qualifications they obtain at Levels 1 and 2 have little value in the labour market, routing them into low-paid work. This polarisation of the labour market proceeds apace and the education system seems to have little to offer to ameliorate this process. Indeed, it is not a problem that the education system can solve. High levels of income inequality, described in Chapter 3, are known to have a corrosive effect on social cohesion, political participation and community engagement (Gibbons *et al.*, 2006a; 2006b). Society is becoming more, not less, divided.

There have been attempts at the level of policy to embed education and training more firmly with other social agencies and institutions. For example, the idea of a more employer-led vocational component is intended to make the system more responsive to the needs of the labour market, as construed by policy-makers, while also drawing in employers to act as agents of change. It is too early to judge whether such initiatives will bear fruit and lead to a more responsive system, but history does not augur well (Chapter 9).

In addition, there have been many attempts to involve parents more closely either in the direct running of the system (e.g. as school governors), or indirectly, by exercising choice over where their children learn. However, the impact of choice on school standards and pupil outcomes remains equivocal (Gibbons *et al.*, 2006b).

Efforts to embed local developments of the education and training system within community development projects have borne some fruit. For example, Hillsborough in Sheffield has seen a rapid improvement in its participation rates as educational reform processes have sought to involve the whole of a very deprived community. This has led to action at a local level that has run counter to government policy, such as the establishment of an 11–16 academy within an overall tertiary system. This decision was reached democratically with a wide range of stakeholders participating.

Such local activism, while promising, runs counter to central government policy, in England, to maintain a clear line of sight between centrally devised educational initiatives and their outcomes. Thus, while responsibility for 14–19 provision is being devolved back to local authorities the power to reorganise local provision is apparently not.

This leads us back to the issue of how to ensure coherent local provision in 14–19, a key aspect of system performance that is virtually ignored by current national policy. Local collaborative models may help to overcome the lack of local planning but local reorganisation of provision, especially in the face of a demographic downturn, may produce a more efficient and equitable allocation of resources. Reorganisation would also provide the opportunity to develop smaller scale 11–16 schools, along lines suggested by Human Scale Education (Tasker, 2003), which may benefit lower attaining learners and those most at risk of disengagement, as resources could be targeted more accurately to meet their needs.

Is the system just and equitable? Judging whether all young people are treated fairly by the system is important, but highly problematic. Assessments of teaching tend to focus on outcomes, such as GCSE results. These are important but, as indicators, tell us little about whether teachers have attempted to provide the best service to all learners, in a way comparable to medical practitioners (in whose case quality of treatment is arguably a stronger criterion than outcome). Judgements made by Ofsted and Estyn about teaching quality do not provide a systematic enough evidence base to constitute useful information about such an indicator.

Despite recent improvements in attainment outcomes for those from lower socioeconomic groups and certain minority ethnic groups, there remains a substantial achievement gap. The system currently fails the test of equity referred to in Chapter 2: the 'erasure of the ability to predict students' … achievement and participation based solely on characteristics such as race, class, ethnicity, sex, belief and creeds, and proficiency in the dominant language' (Gutierrez, 2002:9).

Current policy direction in England, in particular the school 'sixth-form presumption' and the academies programme, will, according to available evidence (Fletcher and Perry, 2008), potentially reduce participation and attainment by the lowest achieving learners who are a clear policy concern. This development speaks to the continuing inability of the system to respond nationally to evidence about what works at the local level. Furthermore, political interference at the national level in England to promote, for example, school sixth-forms and academies at the local level at the expense of other existing and more equitable provision, is all too apparent.

Beyond aggregate performance measures

The evidence available allows us to judge some aspects, particularly at the system level (e.g. inclusiveness and attainment), but does not support judgements about the local and, in particular, individual level (except for attainment, which is however used as a proxy for too much). We lack evidence for other, often more important, indicators. Some of that evidence is provided by research, but not systematically across the aims we have outlined. There has been some progress in terms of government measures (e.g. PSA indicators and *Every Child Matters* outcomes), but the emphasis on targets driving the system has the side effect of converting crude measures into aims, to the detriment of the educational aims outlined in Chapter 2.

The data available are structured around measures that are currently used in the performance management system. This is problematic for several reasons.

First, they do not fully reflect the aims that education ought to have (nor, in fact, current policy objectives). It is conceivable that the system meets its participation, achievement and progression targets, first, without being equitable (e.g. the small percentage excluded is precisely that of young people who were most at risk from the start); second, without nurturing learning that is worthwhile (including stimulation of critical attitude); or, third, without generating outcomes through educationally valuable processes. In other words, good performance is not necessarily educational; and an 'output' of high achievers does not equal an 'output' of educated people.

Second, rounded judgements of system performance at all levels necessarily involve more than simply counting young people in schools and colleges, and registering the number of examinations they have passed. For example, simply counting the number of GCSEs passed at different grades fails to capture what was deemed important in terms of the pursuit of excellence and the development of self-awareness or moral seriousness. Even in terms of intellectual development, using GCSE or GCE A-Level attainment as a proxy measure requires faith in an assessment process that is not necessarily designed to capture holistically the wide range of understandings, intellectual virtues or practical capabilities. The use of aggregate qualification performance to represent individual development is even further called into question when the Chief Inspector in England expresses her concern about teaching to the test (HoC, 2008), or when higher education admissions staff agree that certain intellectual and practical capabilities – the ability to read critically, write fluently, and discuss and apply ideas – are consistently under-developed in their new entrants (Wilde and Wright, 2007). The narrowness of the English post-16 curriculum, in particular, and the almost total lack of general education in our vocational pathways compared with European systems (Chapter 9) should also concern us if we are simply relying on examination results to assess the extent to which the system is enabling young people to develop intellectually.

Towards better performance assessment and management

Four improvements are needed to how we think about and handle data and develop performance indicators intended to illuminate system performance.

Performance indicators should not themselves become the aims. Not all important attributes, particularly at local and individual levels, can be expressed as targets. Trying to do that risks damaging the transactions and collaborative relationships that make worthwhile learning work.

There needs to be a shift in accountability which encompasses both a 'tightening up' (at the system level) and 'letting go' (at the local level). At national level, 'tightening up' would mean holding people in government and its agencies accountable for producing learning communities capable of nurturing the development of the attributes described in Chapter 2. At the same time, at local level, 'letting go' means shifting accountability from individual providers to a broader area or context. A school embedded in local institutional arrangements that contain grammar schools, creaming off the top 25–30% of measured ability, should not be held accountable for meeting government targets in the same way as a comprehensive in a local authority with no grammar schools.

Assumptions behind public assessment should be challenged. Too much focus is on the technical detail of public assessments of system performance as these are measured against prescribed indicators. As argued in relation to research assessment (Oancea, 2007), there is a strong connection between the narrowing of the 'official' concept of *quality* to 'measurable performance', the narrowing of *practice* to 'production and delivery', and the narrowing of *assessment* to what can be quantified.

Data collected should enable judgements to be made about performance in relation to the qualities that the Review has identified. Much of the data available in fact simply provide information on whether top-down targets have been met.

Somewhat ironically, it may well be that the relative paucity of such data in Wales reflects the rather different approach to policy monitoring and target setting that has been adopted here. What is clear is that such quantitative measures cannot readily be turned into the information needed to make the judgements about system performance that the Review had identified as being of importance.

We need to consider how best to develop performance measurement systems for the future.

Conclusion

What are we able to say, then, about how well the system is working?

National level

Participation rates have stagnated since the mid-1990s up to very recently, and are lower than those of other OECD and EU countries. At the same time, the proportion of young people who are NEET is unacceptably high. The GCSE attainment of those who do participate is still predictable on the basis of social class, ethnicity or gender. While overall achievement in GCE A-Levels and Level 3 qualifications has improved, the students enrolled on vocational programmes at Levels 1 and 2 have on average lower rates of attainment. Completion of apprenticeships has improved steadily, although the rates of attainment are lower than in other European countries.

Local level

There is considerable selection of learners at 16, with the result that FE colleges offer much of the Level 2 provision, particularly for young people from poor and certain minority backgrounds, while schools and sixth-forms 'specialise' in GCE A-Level programmes. This selection is not reflected in the current assessments of performance of different types of institution on the basis of raw examination results. Some of the policy messages are confusing at local level; for example, there is evidence that adding small sixth-forms to 11–16 schools will reduce choice, lower attainment and raise costs, and that it would be much better to develop strongly collaborative models (Chapter 11).

While funding arrangements have led to improvements, such as more qualified teachers and smaller class sizes, the system remains inequitable, with provision and support for those most in need (NEET) being the most under-resourced.

Individual level

Existing data did not permit adequate judgements about the extent to which the system contributes to the attainment of the educational aims outlined in Chapter 2.

Overall

The system serves well the interests of higher attaining pupils typically from more advantaged backgrounds, but the groups that are most in need of support are ill-served. Part of the problem lies elsewhere, for example, with long-term structural unemployment or with the welfare system. However, improvements are possible and necessary in the education and training system, although they will not be likely to solve all the problems.

Inspection

A better inspection system would use a wider range of criteria to judge quality. Such inspection could be linked to greater use of self-report measures, as is currently being suggested for FE colleges, relying on teacher, institution, parent and learner-based judgements. Moderation of such judgements could be augmented by an approach pioneered in the 1970s by the Assessment of Performance Unit to assess the wider range of individual learner outcomes on the basis of stratified light sampling testing that went far beyond current approaches (see Chapter 5).

Improving performance indicators

Judgements of performance need to be driven by deliberation about system aims in a revised accountability environment. More textured research evidence is also needed of how well the system works in relation to its aims.

Recommendations

4. Performance indicators should be 'fit for purpose' – reflecting the broader aims of education and different kinds of learning.
5. These indicators should measure the achievements of learning partnerships as a whole, not solely those of individual providers.
6. The essential contribution of the FE sector should be recognised, through equal funding for equal work, and through performance indicators which reflect FE's distinctive aims.
7. Performance indicators at every level should encourage the attainment of greater equality between genders, ethnic groups and social classes.
8. The variation between school and college providers in funding and governance should be reduced.
9. Predictable and long-term funding should be provided to the voluntary, community agencies and youth service, which are essential partners in the 'education of all'.

---

5   Learning

Introduction

It is clear from Chapter 3 that, in the field of learning, 'no one size fits all'. There are different barriers to learning to be overcome, different experiences to be taken into account. For many, learning is a slow struggle to make sense of the experience and to find interest and inspiration in what schools and colleges have to offer. But, as Chapter 4 argued, the 'performance indicators', by which individual schools and the system are judged, fail to take account of this varied context and the broader aims spelt out in Chapter 2.

And that is not all. If learners come to their learning with different experiences, it is also true that learning itself is more multifaceted than we sometimes realise, which is why it is worth devoting some of this chapter to looking a little further into it.

Problems, solutions and questions

It is a truism to say that the aim of education is to bring about learning. But truism though this is, and despite the enormous amount of 'measurement' of the learning which consequently takes place, it is surprising how little attention is given to the different kinds of learning or to the quality of learning which schools and colleges are expected to bring about. As we saw in Chapter 2, there is often disagreement about the most appropriate learning for our future citizens. There are questions still to ask: about different kinds of learning, lest some kinds are neglected; about the standards by which these different kinds of learning are to be judged; and about the best ways in which young people, by no means a homogeneous group, do in fact learn.

These questions are given urgency because currently there is a contradiction at work that demands explanation. Despite constant reporting of improved test and examination results (DfES, 2005c, ch.1, states 'We have the best ever results at primary level, at Key Stage 3, at General Certificate of Secondary Education [GCSE] and at A-Level'), there remains general disquiet about the quality of learning. Universities say that young people come ill-prepared for the kind of learning which universities value (Wilde and Wright, 2007).

Employers complain that they lack the skills, knowledge and attitudes which serve business and the economy (Leitch Report, 2006). Many young people drop out of formal learning, bored with what they see to be irrelevant or judged as failures in the all-pervasive testing system (Hayward *et al.*, 2008). Teachers argue that they are constrained by government initiatives, and by the demands of testing, from providing the learning experience they think is needed. And, according to the Chief Inspector, the learning experience is narrowed because of the constant teaching to the test (HoC, 2008). Indeed, even those young people who succeed often feel disillusioned by the experience they have undergone; as one 17 year old wrote to the Review in response to its Issue Paper on aims and values:

> Far too often in education the emphasis is on achieving targets and regurgitating what the exam board wants, as opposed to actually teaching children something. As a sixth form student myself, this frustrates me on a daily basis, especially in history, when we must learn to write to the specifications of the exam board, instead of actually learning about the past
> (NR 2008e)

In England, complaints about the quality of learning are met with an ever more detailed framework of qualifications, each component of which is elaborated through a list of specifications of the learning to take place. For example, dissatisfaction over standards of learning at the lower end of attainment has led to the creation of the Foundation Learning Tier. This is intended to replace the complex range of qualifications below Level 2 and will be created out of units taken from those qualifications (overlapping, for instance, with Level 1 Diplomas) with a view to meeting the needs of the least able learners. So, learning is shaped by the preconceived outcomes of the planners, not by the needs of the learners.

What is the answer?

We should begin where the learners are rather than with the needs of the Qualifications Framework. Programmes should adapt to the learners, not learners to the programmes. Learners begin at different points and often struggle to overcome different obstacles. As one teacher told the Review, 'they do not come to us as blank slates'. This is true across the ability range, but it applies particularly to those with least academic attainment. As Stanton (2008) argues in *Learning Matters*, 'The learning needs of those with below average academic attainment have never been properly addressed, despite the fact that – by definition – they form half the cohort'.

Given, therefore, the widespread concerns about the quality of learning, the Review has questioned the narrow understanding of learning within the system. It asks:

- Are certain kinds of learning neglected which, as argued in Chapter 2, are part of what it means to be educated?

- What does it mean for someone to have successfully learnt in these different ways (that is, 'come up to standard')?
- What connection should there be between different kinds of learning and the assessment of them?

This chapter attempts to answer these questions. Chapter 7 examines the translation of the answers into curriculum development, and asks who should control that curriculum.

Different kinds of learning

In Chapter 2 we argued that, 'Our core task is that of introducing young people to a form of life which is distinctively human, which enables them to be and to feel fulfilled, which equips them to live independent economic lives, and which enables them to participate positively within the wider community'.

All of that has to be learned – inevitably in different ways. Much of it is acquired through living and working in communities which embody these values. In that sense, much learning is a kind of apprenticeship to those (e.g. teachers) who have, and exercise, the desired qualities. It is important, therefore, in nurturing the learning of all young people, to distinguish between the different kinds of learning required of an appropriate education, and of the different standards which are intrinsic to each.

Knowledge and understanding

We don't just 'learn'; we 'learn something' – about the physical, social and economic worlds in which we live. As we learn we come to understand those worlds. So, as we learn biology we begin to acquire concepts – 'organism', 'cell', 'respiration' – which we fit together, which are the product of others' intellectual labours and through which we come to see the world differently. Some of those concepts and ideas we would learn simply by living with and talking to our families or friends. But there is always the possibility of going deeper, of entering into more sophisticated understanding of the concepts. At its best, this is what 'learning a subject' means – the acquisition of a conceptual framework, principles of explanation and modes of enquiry through which we make greater sense of the world and become more able to act intelligently within it.

What does this mean for the learner, and for learning? It is clear, for one thing, that very rarely is learning an all or nothing affair. We can begin to grasp an idea, and then move onto a more and more complete understanding. ('Yes, I'm with you so far, now what about … '.) It is what Bruner (1960) referred to as the 'spiral curriculum' – the ever deepening grasp of a key idea which shapes our thinking. Often it is a struggle. The idea is only gradually internalised.

Importantly, this process cannot be strictly timetabled, which means that learning should be organised in a way that enables learners to progress at their own pace. Hitting targets can get in the way of that, reducing the deeper conceptual development, on which future learning builds, to pre-specified behaviours. The Smith Report (2004) criticised the teaching of maths for so teaching to pre-specified outcomes that the deeper grasp of concepts was not achieved.

Practical learning

What we have just described is 'propositional knowledge' – the kind that can be put down in statements, be verified by reference to experience, give rise to explanatory theories, and be transmitted as such to the learner. It is *learning that* something is the case – and it is different from *learning how* to do something or 'practical knowledge'. This was highlighted in the manifesto, *Education for Capability*, of the Royal Society of Arts (RSA), which for 250 years has striven to bring together theory and practice, thinking and making, intellect and skill. 'There exists in its own right a culture which is concerned with doing and making and organising and the creative arts. This culture emphasises the day to day management of affairs, the formulation and solution of problems, and the design, manufacture and marketing of goods and services' (RSA, 1986).

It is a feature of the way we organise learning that practical knowledge (*knowing how*) is often trapped inside *knowledge that*, even if attempts are made to write about such practical knowledge. A criticism of General National Vocational Qualifications (GNVQs) was that, although intended to provide scope for practical learning, they were assessed by written examination (Capey Report, 1995). Practical knowledge is gained from practising, albeit often guided by an experienced practitioner. It is assessed through the 'successful doing', not through writing about 'doing'. A person knows how to ride a bicycle without being able to describe that knowledge. Indeed, anyone trying to ride, after reading a book on how to, might fall off.

That said, 'knowing how' and 'knowing that' are clearly not disconnected. Practical knowledge provides entry to more theoretical understanding as the learner reflects upon what he or she is doing, or constructs a theory to explain a practical difficulty that has emerged during the day. Many innovative engineers, for example, William Morris – Lord Nuffield – learnt their professional expertise through practical hands-on involvement with problems and through apprenticeship. Intelligent integration of mind and body, of brain and hand, escapes clear formulation in propositional knowledge, but is crucial to every aspect of our lives. And it is learnt.

The Review believed that a tradition of learning based on practical engagement has been lost in schools, reflected in the near demise of Woodwork, Metalwork and Home Economics, in the decline of field-work in Geography (Power *et al.*, 2008), in less experimental approaches to science (caused partly by assessment almost exclusively through written examination), and in the decline of work-based learning and employer-related apprenticeships (Stanton, 2008). Traditions once lost are difficult to revive. Concerned about the lack of healthy eating, the Department for Children, Schools & Families (DCSF) announced that there should be compulsory cooking lessons for all 11–14 year olds, and that £151 million would be spent on 'food technology areas'. But, as teacher representatives pointed out, one in seven schools would be unable to comply because they no longer had the relevant resources, equipment, spaces and expertise (*Guardian*, 12 September 2008). Since the Education Reform Act in 1988, teacher training places in Home Economics have been removed.

The importance of 'hands-on learning' for all was central to the Technical and Vocational Education Initiative (TVEI) in 1983, which did not, however, survive the national curriculum in 1988. To some extent, but only for a minority, it is reflected in *14–19 Education and Skills* (DfES, 2005a). As a result of the Increased Flexibility Programme, thousands of 14–16 year olds now undertake part of their studies in the more practical environment of the local further education (FE) college. These are often pursued through Centres of Vocational Excellence which are judged by Ofsted (2007b) to be generally good and have enabled many to progress to further study and training. Another evaluation also points to the success of this initiative (O'Donnell *et al.*, 2006). But it is mainly directed at those who, unmotivated by academic work, are more likely to be motivated by the practical. This attention to the practical in so-called 'vocational' courses for the less engaged does a disservice both to the importance of practical learning for all and to the status of work-based learning relevant to employment, such as that provided by apprentice-ships. It is vital not to confuse practical with vocational learning.

Such criticism is apparent in the Welsh decision not to advocate the adoption of the Diplomas, as they currently are, because, it is claimed, they put greater emphasis on classroom learning about the world of work than they do on practical learning! Hence, the aim is to enlarge vocational and practical learning choices within the Welsh Bac in a manner appropriate to Wales (Webb Review, 2007).

Experiential learning

Both practical and theoretical knowledge, to be meaningful, need to be related to experience, that is, to the 'lived world', of the young person. Teachers call this, 'starting from where the child is', and it is strongly advocated in official documents as 'personalised learning'. The Gilbert Review (2007) argues for learning to be connected to the learner's experience, including outside the classroom.

Experience contains its own understanding of the world. The experience that the learners bring to class may be wrong or inadequate, but it affects their appreciation of what they have to learn (see Beard and Wilson, 2002 for a comprehensive account of experiential learning). By contrast, learning governed by a prescribed curriculum and directed at pre-arranged targets is often disconnected from those experiences, leaving them untouched and unaffected.

Schools are places set apart – they find it difficult to take seriously, as part of the learning process, experiences which are of significance to the learners and which they bring into the school.

Of course, the importance of experience for learning is recognised. Field-trips in geography, overseas visits in modern languages, work experience, practical experiments in science have long been seen as essential contexts for deeper understanding. But what became evident to the Review was the increasing difficulty schools and colleges have in providing experiential learning (Power *et al.*, 2008). Risk assessment and fear of litigation reduce the number of visits; focus on written assessment in science limits the use of 'hands-on learning'.

Yet research indicates that, especially with 'at-risk' young people, a focus on shared experiences between learner and educator, particularly through out-of-school experiences, and making education a shared experience between family, teacher and learner, make a considerable difference (Frankham, 2007). Perhaps that is also true of colleges, although there were many cases witnessed by the Review of colleges building courses around the experiences particularly of those who came with a deep sense of educational failure.

Social learning

One kind of practical learning is that in which the young learner is inducted into social practices which reflect the value of the group. Social and moral development is like that, and indeed it was because of this that Kohlberg (1975) saw 'the just community school' as an essential framework within which young people might attain, not so much higher levels of moral judgement, but the disposition to be moved by these judgements. It is little good preaching justice if the school or college does not embody those values, or of teaching democracy where the students' voices go unheeded.

This is recognised by schools and colleges which the Review visited. Most display high ideals in their 'mission statements', not a few of which are reflected in the day-to-day situations of the school, in the availability of teachers to learners, or in the care taken of troubled youngsters. This was demonstrated in an interview with a 16 year old student of Ghanaian origin in an inner-city school. He pointed to the school mission statement and said 'they really mean that here – everyone here enjoys equal treatment whoever they are'. This was also a school which had incorporated 'restorative justice' into its daily life – the wrong-doer having to confront and explain to the victim of the wrong-doer. The spread of restorative justice in schools is a significant development, brought to the attention of the Review (Marshall, 1999).

Conclusion: good news and bad news

There is no doubting the increasing recognition of the importance of different, more practical approaches to learning, and of taking seriously the experiences which young people bring to school and college. There is increased recognition of the need to adapt the curriculum to the personal needs or styles or contexts of the individual learner, to take seriously his or her voice and experience (as reflected in an emphasis on 'personalised learning'), and to acknowledge that learning and motivation are enriched by active involvement in tackling problems.

It throws into sharp relief the contrasting approach where learning happens almost entirely in classrooms, with a curriculum divided exclusively into subjects, with the teacher dominating the content and method of learning and with emphasis upon written work. As a teacher reported to the Review of the feelings of one student, 'They make us read a good book, we just get to enjoy it and then we kill it by having to write an essay about why it is a good book'.

But official recognition of that more personalised approach too often seems purely rhetorical. It is rarely allowed, after all, to undermine an assessment regime (a main determinant of how learning is experienced) which scarcely recognises practical, social and experiential learning. Even the Diplomas at Levels 1 and 2, intended to meet the needs of employers, require only 10 days' work experience. An Ofsted (2007b) report on a Centre of Vocational Excellence said that the 'high theoretical content of some Diplomas will exclude students who currently respond well to a more practical approach to learning'.

Words like 'academic', 'theoretical', 'practical' can be heavily loaded against each other – so it is necessary to emphasise that recognition of relevant, practical and experiential learning does not imply criticism of academic work. Academic work can be taught in such a way that it is seen by the learners to illuminate matters of deep concern. Knowledge in science can be acquired through active engagement with problems which interest the learner, under the wise guidance of the teacher, as is illustrated in the Review's Issues Paper on applied science (NR, 2008g). The object of criticism is where learning is understood to arise from the mere 'transmission of bodies of knowledge', disconnected from the interests and experiences of the learner – what the philosopher, John Dewey (1916:4), referred to as 'unduly formal or scholastic notions of education' which 'easily [become] remote and dead – abstract or bookish'.

The voice of the learner

If experiential, practical and social learning are important – if we are to 'start from where the child (or young person) is', then it follows that the voice of the learner should be heard. Issues Paper 11 drew attention to the importance of heeding the learner's voice if those, who are disengaged, are to be brought back into education – working 'on and from young people's territory as determined by their definitions of space, needs, interests, concerns and lifestyles' (NR, 2008i).

Although that paper was written about those who had dropped out of education, the principle is equally applicable to all learners. Informal learning in and out of school, and the learner's aspirations and motivations, need to be the focus of the educational endeavour rather than be marginalised by it. The evidence for 'the learner's voice' in the planning and the development of learning is considerable. Rudduck and her colleagues argued that the maturity and capabilities of young people exceed the assumptions of their teachers to an extent that demands greater attention to the 'learner's voice' (Rudduck *et al.*, 2006; Rudduck and McIntyre, 2007). The review of research by the National Foundation for Educational Research (NFER) points to the growing 'culture of participation' of young people in the development of services and policies which affect their lives and their communities (Halsey *et al.*, 2007). A further NFER study, in its review of learners' experience of the national curriculum, pointed to their want of a greater sense of relevance, requiring more careers advice, and more active and collaborative learning (Lord, 2007).

Indeed, the respect for the learner's voice is a principle in the government's own espousal of 'personalised learning', which speaks of learners as learning resources for other learners, participating in the review of learning programmes, providing feedback on lessons and involved in staff selection (Gilbert Review, 2007).

But respect for learners needs to go further. Learners' experience outside school could provide material for relevant learning. The humanities at their best deal with matters of human concern which absorb the minds of young people, as the Review has argued (NR, 2008f). Discussion of such matters, disciplined by evidence, should be at the centre of learning, not at the periphery. In 1975, the Bullock Report, *Language for Life*, gave an excellent account of the importance of discussion (Chapter 10). The experience which learners bring to school or college should not be left at the gates, but should be part of that 'conversation', taking place in the classroom. Indeed, the Times Educational Supplement Survey of 2000 teachers found that three-quarters favoured involving pupils in drawing up teaching and learning policies (*TES*, March, 2008). There are, of course, 'Schools Councils' or 'Youth Parliaments'. But questions remain about how far 'that voice' should shape the learning programme. Evidence to the Review from the 'detached youth workers' (NR, 2008i), dealing with the most disengaged, showed that learning support for learners should begin with and derive from their voice – from the articulation of how they see the world and their place within it.

This, however, requires concentration upon communicative skills – the ability to articulate ideas, arguments and wants through discussion and interaction with others, and indeed to attend to others' points of view. Here education should learn from the past. The National Oracy Project (1988–91), the discussion-based Humanities Curriculum Project, the Bullock Report's 1975 recommendations, Labov's research on non-standard English, the discussion-based developmental work of Kohlberg and his associates, the pioneering work of the Assessment of Performance Unit (APU), the developmental work associated with the Certificate of Secondary Education (CSE) – all point to the key part to be played by formally organised learner talk and listening. That key role goes beyond the acquisition of 'basic skills'. Giving place to the learners' voice is crucial for their intellectual development – for taking seriously their ideas, testing out partial understandings, and ensuring growth through criticism. 'Students' talk' was once central to the learning experience, encouraged by English teachers, particularly in the inner cities. (See Pring, 2008, for a summary of the research.)

Why then is that so little recognised? Speaking and listening are part of the Key Stage requirements at Levels 3 and 4. But assessing the capacity to speak and listen does not play an important role in the overall grading of a student in the Standard Assessment Tasks (SATs), GCSEs or A-Level General Certificates of Education (GCEs). In the attainment of the necessary grades, for the benefit of the individual and of the school's or college's reputation, the institution might find little room for the development of those skills. And the coverage of the curriculum, as that is laid down, might leave little room for the role of discussion in the shaping of the learning programme.

Enhancing learning through information and communication technology (ICT)

As the DCSF's 'Teachernet' website states: 'ICT can improve the quality of teaching, learning and management in schools and so help improve standards. That is why ICT is at the heart of the DCSF's commitment to improve learning for all children'. The British Educational Communications and Technologies Agency (BECTA) is leading research into effective use of ICT – how the learning process is transformed and how learning outcomes are improved. Its 'ImpactCT2', a study of the impact of ICT on attainment, found a positive relationship between use of ICT and educational attainment.

Therefore, educational use of ICT would be ignored at our peril. Most young people have access to and use internet at home. The *UK Children Go Online Survey* reported that 60% of pupils think the internet is the most useful tool for getting information for their homework – only 21% named books (Livingstone and Bober, 2005:6). They have developed their own on-line community networks through MySpace or Facebook. Davies (2007) reports on 'how assured the great majority of young people questioned were in talking about their uses of technology'. Therefore, something radical has emerged in the last few years affecting how young people communicate with and relate to their friends and acquaintances.

All this has an impact upon the organisation of learning. Learning is embedded in a range of activities outside the formal context of school or college – in the home, workplace, internet café and elsewhere. ICT, to some extent, frees the learner from the authority of the teacher in acquiring knowledge and in being aware of alternative perspectives. Often, the learner is more familiar than the teacher with the technology, and more adept in using or exploring it. Indeed, school students are employed in teaching and mentoring, as in one college in Hertfordshire, where 35 students are employed as 'e-mentors'. Finally, it opens up, through on-line learning communities, a range of informed conversations which transcend boundaries of school, college and family.

Therefore, it is useful, in looking to the future, to be aware of how 'e-learning' is now being made accessible to young people. The following examples were brought to the attention of the Review.

Smartlab Digital Media Institute provides hi-tech after school clubs for children in run-down neighbourhoods: 'It gives them a computer game that requires them to learn some maths and science in order to play'. *Notschool.net* provides on-line community working with disaffected young people outside the system; 98% get a formal qualification, 76% go to FE. *Futurelab: Enquiring Minds* provides ways of bringing informal learning into school; 100 schools attended Enquiring Minds conferences in 2008. *Creative Partnerships* provides support via a website and a national database, which teacher training institutions, museums, etc. are encouraged to join, providing learning outside the classroom. The *National Academy for Gifted and Talented Youth* provided an on-line community network so that learners in different schools might communicate with each other, sharing problems or tackling ones provided by their mentors.

Therefore, future teaching programmes could be transformed by the new technologies. BECTA is researching into what it calls 'e-enabled' institutions – the impact of the new technology on learner access, resource management, work-force skills, and the exercise of management. Indeed, in the light of such research, Livingstone (2007) speculates: 'Many advocate an alternative, even radical conception of learning – a pedagogic shift from a rule-based model of education to an immersive, child-centred model of "learning through doing"'.

Standards

Implicit in all that has been said is the importance of standards. A major aim of government is 'to raise standards'. But the meaning of 'standard' is not self-evident. Standards are the benchmarks by which we judge an activity (academic or practical) to have been successful. To say that someone has learnt something means that their thinking or their performing meets these implicit benchmarks of doing it well. One has not 'learnt fractions' unless one is able to apply certain concepts appropriately and perform certain mental operations correctly.

But there are problems which affect profoundly the pursuit of educational aims.

As was pointed out in the account of system performance, standards too often are identified with targets, as though they are the same thing. If you train a person to hit certain targets in numeracy, then one is told that they have met the standards. This is an elementary confusion. What the students have learnt is to hit the targets, which may bear little relation to understanding the key concepts or being able to apply those concepts in new situations. They may have hit the targets but missed the standards.

Second, standards must be defined in terms of the aim of the activity – in this case, the educational aims we have argued for. Where those aims change, standards change. Where there is disagreement about the aims, there is disagreement about standards. A visit to a Steiner school showed how a different philosophical position about human fulfilment is reflected in a different set of standards by which it would want its 'performance' to be judged – in, for example, its focus on the arts and the aesthetic dimension of learning. The Association of Colleges (AoC, 2006) expressed concern over the publication of league tables which do not reflect their mission to re-engage young people who have failed at school. As the principal of Newham College argued, colleges focus on educational needs of the socially excluded and on meeting employers' needs, as well as raising standards as defined in the league tables. The College has developed its own centre for innovation and partnerships, working with more than 1200 local entrepreneurs and businesses and creating its own Newham College Access Diploma. Its standards derive partly from its focus on social exclusion and economic regeneration in that borough (*TES*, March, 2006).

There is, as we all know, concern about the 'fall in standards'. But much of this criticism fails to identify what those standards should be in the light of the broader aims of what counts as an educated 19 year old in this day and age. Standards relevant 20 years ago might not be relevant today. There have been so many curriculum and assessment changes over the last 10 years that it is impossible to compare performance over time.

Finally, the 'standardisation of standards', reflected in the constant attempt to find equivalences within the national framework of qualifications, runs into all sorts of problems:

- Establishing the 'same' difficulty level between different qualifications, even though difficulty level would vary from learner to learner.
- Stipulating the amount of contact hours for the award of 'equivalent' qualifications.
- Determining the same standard for different awards in the same 'logical area' (e.g. GCSEs and GNVQs in Business Studies).
- Determining the appropriateness of two qualifications for progressing to further or higher studies (e.g. A-Level and International Baccalaureate).

To sort this out is important. Level 2 apprenticeship qualifications (e.g. in engineering and in retail), though seen as equivalent in terms of level, can differ widely in terms of difficulty, study contact hours and appropriateness for progressing to further study (NR, 2008b). Again, an Advanced Diploma is declared to be equivalent to three and a half A-Levels, and a Level 2 Diploma to seven GCSEs A–C. But what this means, or the grounds on which such a judgement could be made, is difficult to fathom.

What follows from this?

First, standards of learning depend on the nature of the many things which we believe are important for young people to learn. To limit the range of standards is unfair to schools and colleges whose idea of the educated 19 year old embraces a wider range of achievements than is recognised in the assessment system – a point developed in Chapter 4 on 'system performance'. Second, the search for equivalences between standards which logically relate to very different activities is generally unintelligible.

Innovative approaches to learning

Despite the generally negative picture portrayed to the Review concerning the narrowing of the learning experience, there is welcome evidence of innovative practices where schools and colleges feel able to break the mould. Indeed, the 2006 Education Act in England allows schools to suspend parts of the education requirements to pursue more radical ways of learning. The official emphasis on 'personalised learning' would suggest more flexible approaches.

Personalised learning is seen as crucial to the fulfilment of the aims of *Every Child Matters*. In practical terms, it means 'taking a highly structured and responsive approach to each child's and young person's learning in order that all are able to progress, achieve and participate' (Gilbert Review, 2007). This can be done through:

- learning which is connected to what the learners already experience;
- learners monitoring their own learning and identifying the next steps;
- shifting the balance from class levels to individual progress;
- recognising and respecting the learner's voice;
- providing out-of-classroom support and advice;
- involving parents;
- recognising non-cognitive factors and high-order thinking skills;
- providing different pathways and more choice;
- developing greater self-awareness.

Indeed, the 'theory' of personalised learning would support the argument of the Review that the learning needs of the young person should shape the learning rather than be shaped by targets and qualifications, and that there is a need to respond more effectively to the different, often more active, practical and experiential modes of learning of many young people.

There are many examples of how more practical engagement by the learner might be achieved, endorsed in principle by the Department for Children, Education, Lifelong Learning and Skills (DCELLS) in Wales, through its *Learning Pathways* programme, and by the DCSF in the *Alternative Provision White Paper* which builds upon the contents of the *Children's Plan*. That is supported by the Innovation Unit established by the Secretary of State. This Unit has a range of projects, in which the Unit supports schools and local authorities as they take forward their own cutting-edge ideas to improve education.

However, it is felt that there is a mismatch between the kind of knowledge and competence needed by young people and that which is promoted within the education system – between encouragement to innovate (to be open to the community, to respond to the personal learning needs, and to set one's sights more widely than qualifications), and emphasis on a rigorous but narrowing assessment regime, the results of which affect profoundly the fortunes of schools, teachers and learners.

The Review examined many examples of how providers of education and training are, despite the constraints of the system, helping young people, often regarded as failures, to love learning, to be highly motivated and to succeed. This so often emerges from a change in the relationship between teacher and learner, and in the style and place of learning.

A little history helps. As Stanton (2008) points out, there have been imaginative attempts in the past to develop learner-centred programmes within broad and flexible frameworks, from which future policy and practice could fruitfully learn – for instance, the City and Guilds (CGLI) 365 courses following the blueprint set out in the FEU (1979) *A Basis for Choice*, or the TVEI, which integrated theory and practice and transformed the experience of learning for many young people across the ability range. What was characteristic of these was the more practical, flexible, cooperative and community-focused modes of learning. But they did not survive the standardised curriculum and assessment regime introduced by the 1988 Education Act, which focused more on writing than on 'doing'.

Nonetheless, despite constraints of a system which focuses on a narrow range of standards, the Review detected a growing advocacy of more active and participative learning where the learner's voice becomes part of the curriculum. The following are but a very few which were brought to the attention of the Review, reflecting this increasing awareness of different approaches. Many schools, colleges and independent learning providers are involved, demonstrating, in a way which is rarely publicised, how there is room for innovation in the system. And there are many more such initiatives.

Many of these initiatives are coming together to provide a powerful voice in transforming the rather narrow understanding of learning which we have inherited.

- *RSA: Open Minds Project.* Recognition of the distinctive quality of practical intelligence was provided by the RSA's, 1986, manifesto 'Education for Capability'. That emphasised the capacity for 'intelligent doing', and this notion of 'practical intelligence', 'capability' or integration of theory and practice has been a hallmark of the RSA throughout its 250 years of history. Such a unity is destroyed where the division is made between 'academic' and 'vocational'. The RSA developed 'Opening Minds: Education for the 21st Century', which is adopted increasingly by schools disillusioned with a national curriculum which does not reflect these practical capabilities (Baylis, 1999; RSA, 2003).

- *Paul Hamlyn Foundation's Learning Futures* brings together the Foundation's long interest in education, the arts and social justice and a different way of engaging young people and questioning what is understood by quality. The emphasis is on a change in pedagogy, illustrated in its *Musical Futures*, now with over 70 schools. The principles which informed *Musical Futures* are being extended across the curriculum, demonstrated in its recent *Learning Futures: Next Practice in Learning and Teaching* (2008).

- *Edge Foundation* aims to raise the status of practical and vocational learning amongst 14–25 year olds of all levels of ability through a number of projects, based on the belief that all young people should experience high-quality practical learning as part of a broad education. Lewisham College of FE and South Bank University are leading partners in teacher training for a more practical approach to learning.

- *Young Foundation*, in partnership with seven local authorities and supported by Edge and the Innovation Unit, launched 'studio schools' in which the curriculum is integrated with running businesses based in schools with a view to better preparation for work. Emphasis is on practical competences, which employers say are lacking in young recruits. Studio Schools will be small schools of around 300 students, incorporating paid work for older students.

- *Futurelab: Enquiring Minds*, funded by Microsoft through its 'Partners in Learning', brings informal learning into schools, starting with the interests and ideas which the learners import and using ICT. Though vilified only two decades ago as the demon responsible for all the problems in our schools (Pring, 2007:3), the ghost of Dewey again haunts those who feel despondent over the constrictions placed on learning by the curriculum and assessment regime. 'Inquiry' – the mind actively involved in solving a problem (theoretical or practical) – rules again. According to a teacher in one school with regard to a project on the environment, 'they had to come with their own topic to research. Top-set students looked at hybrid cars and biofuels, lower ability students did electric cars, bicycles and animals. They were incredibly motivated by it. This kind of work has really fired me up'.

- *SKIDZ* provides motor mechanics and vehicle maintenance courses for young people, sent by their respective schools. It motivated young people not only to re-engage in learning but to want to continue beyond the age of 16. Established in High Wycombe for 10 years, it now has projects in Banbury and Reading and works with other projects in Thames Valley and Milton Keynes. With a donation from Porsche, it is forming a motor project in the London Borough of Hillingdon.

- *UK Youth and the Youth Achievement Award*. UK Youth has entered into partnership with ASDAN to accredit young people's active and experiential learning in informal and wider community settings, focusing on the least measurable but most important qualities and achievements, such as self-awareness and self-esteem.

- *ASDAN* is an education charity for curriculum development and a recognised awarding body. It creates the opportunity for learners to achieve personal development through, inter alia, contributions to local and global communities. Its success is reflected in that the registered learners for its Certificate of Personal Effectiveness (CoPE) number as many as 150,000 in any one year, at 4500 centres.
- *Human Scale Education* has a network of schools committed to the personal relations between teacher and learner as a prerequisite of well-motivated and significant learning. It is based on research into the effectiveness of small schools, especially in the USA and the importance of 'human scale', caring relationships for educational engagement (Tasker, 2003).
- *Learning to Lead*, having worked with around 2000 students over six years, helps young people to create communities by training them to run teams and lead projects themselves to improve any aspect of life in school which they have identified as needing improvement or would be of value to others. Key to this are the school's 'community councils'.

These are but a few of the many innovations brought to the attention of the Review, in many ways encouraged by the respective governments' policies of a more inclusive educational provision. They suffice to demonstrate that there are strong and widely supported voices for a different sort of learning experience. They are real responses to the frequent advocacy of more practical learning, of respecting the experiences which affect young people, of establishing caring relations between teacher and learner, of empowering the learners to take more responsibility, of linking learning with the wider community, and of working collaboratively. They add up to a quite radical understanding of the 'quality of learning' and of the kind of places that schools and colleges might be.

The transformation achieved by a different way of thinking about learning is reflected in the words of the Chief Executive of Michael Jones of Liverpool,

> many ... blossomed in this new environment, with practical skills and abilities coming to the fore and giving pupils the incentive to take ownership of their school work in order to remain on the work related programme ... the environment was so much more conducive to their learning style and/or desires.
>
> (*14–19 Skills Bulletin*, Issue 1, November 2006)

Problems of assessment

Always, though, we return to the contrast between the move to adapt learning to the learner's needs on the one hand, and, on the other, an external and narrow regime of assessment which constricts the learning and overrules teachers' professional judgement. Mansell (2007), in his detailed study of testing and examining, shows many different uses to which testing is put and the unintended side effects it gives rise to. Furthermore, in analysing the difficulties in many recent curriculum reforms, all of which had to be quickly reviewed (national curriculum in 2003, NVQs in 1999, GNVQs in 1995, Modern Apprenticeships in 2001, Curriculum 2000 in 2002), Stanton (2008:20) points out that, 'in each case there was an over engineered assessment regime that was unmanageable, hindered rather than supported learning and, by focusing on the measurement of outcomes, implied that the enabling of learning would be relatively unproblematic'.

It is necessary to distinguish three purposes which assessment should serve, since problems have arisen where these have been confused.

Assessment for learning (AfL) is a way of finding out what the learner knows, understands or can do, so as to plan the next steps. AfL is a major task of the teacher – helped by, but by no means confined to, external tests and certainly not reducible to grades or numbers. The research by Black and Wiliam (1998), and then by the Assessment Reform Group supported by the Nuffield Foundation (Harlen, 2006), provided clear evidence both of the way such assessment might be conducted and of the capacity of teachers, properly trained, to carry it out accurately.

Assessment for accountability (AfA), by contrast, is a way of obtaining reassurance that teachers or schools or local authorities or government are doing their job properly. The Assessment of Performance Unit, established in 1974, developed randomised, stratified and light sampling techniques whereby the performance of the system might be assessed, comparisons made over time, and schools enabled to assess their own performance against national or regional norms, without in any way disrupting the work of the schools. In failing to clarify these different purposes, AfL is conflated with AfA in the tests which dominate learning in schools and colleges (what Mansell refers to as 'education by numbers').

But *assessment for selecting* (AfS) is applied to young people for entry into post-16 education and training or university. Grades at GCSE and A-Level have to bear this responsibility as well as that of recording what the learners understand or can do (AfL). That changes assessment from criterion referenced (i.e. saying what the learner has achieved) to norm referenced (i.e. saying which students are better than others). The former seeks to record what has been learnt; the latter seeks to discriminate between the learners.

Again, it is increasingly clear that the same assessments cannot fulfil each of these functions. In attempting to do so, the examination and testing industry is reducing so much learning to doing well in tests, and encouraging schools to take short-term measures to ensure success in the tests (Tymms *et al.*,

2005). It thereby narrows the range of achievements thought worth learning. It fails to assess those achievements which are less easy to measure – especially practical, social and experiential learning. According to the Director General for Schools, addressing the Association of Directors of Children's Services, July 2007, a decade of pushing the weakest schools to improve exam results has done little for the country's most disadvantaged pupils. It impoverishes the learning experience. It categorises as failures the 50% of young people who fail to meet the targets, howsoever they have struggled to learn and whatever they have in fact learnt and achieved. This was clearly put to the Commons Select Committee on testing (HoC, 2008).

The book, therefore, argues that, in the light of the evidence from Ofsted, the Select Committee, the professional judgement of teachers and research, that quality of learning for all young people requires a radical re-appraisal of testing which takes place in England in almost every year between the ages of 14 and 18. The different functions need to be separated. Light sampling techniques, as developed by the APU, need to be reconsidered for their relevance in relation to accountability. And ways of assessing the wider key skills and personal qualities need to be explored in the light of what, in the not so distant past, was developed through learners' profiles and in the light of exemplary contemporary practice in the work of ASDAN, which has proved so popular in the professional judgement of teachers.

Extended school – and parental involvement

It should be clear that if we are to reach a point where learning is more active and practical, is enriched by external expertise and resources, engages with the community, and takes seriously the experiences and aspiration which learners bring with them to school or college, then there is a strong need for careful appraisal of what this book refers to as 'strongly collaborative learning systems'. No school or college can go it alone. That means links with employers, training providers, voluntary agencies, youth service and the Information Advice and Guidance (IAG) service in order to guarantee to all young people an appropriate education and progression through to further education, training and work.

However, emphasis needs to be given to the role of parents and carers in this regard. Parents play a crucial role in providing encouragement and support and social learning is affected, for good or ill, by the experiences at home. As a comprehensive review of the research literature concluded, 'In essence, parenting has its influence indirectly through shaping the child's self-concept as a learner and through setting high aspirations' (Desforges and Abouchaar, 2003).

There needs to be an integration of home and school, more especially, as pointed out in Chapter 3, in the light of the considerable social changes that are affecting family life. As that review continues, 'The achievement of working class pupils could be significantly enhanced if we systematically apply all that is known about parental involvement'.

There are, however, few examples of the integration of school and homes in the concerted effort to work together. One example drawn to the attention of the Review was that of Family Links which has extended the lessons learnt from its nurturing programmes with early years into secondary schools. In brief, Family Links highlights the importance of developing the social skills for working with and caring for the learners. At the same time, it sees the importance of its work in schools being understood and supported by the parents who themselves will often be in need of that self-knowledge and those social skills. It is not a matter of informing parents but of educating and cooperating with them, so that they too might become learners along with their children (www.familylinks.org.uk).

Distinctive developments in Wales

In 2001, *The Learning Country* was published. Subsequently, there have been several consultation and guidance documents, setting out the vision for different phases of education, including the 'learning pathways 14–19' ('to transform provision for 14 to 19 year olds' – WAG, 2002a) and *Extending Entitlement.*

Progress from the attainments at Key Stage 2 is not maintained as well as it should be in the secondary phase of education; many communities are economically disadvantaged with a relatively low skills base. Hence, there is the need to develop an approach to education and training which is more inclusive and which offers greater flexibility, responding to the different kinds of learning needs and recognising the importance of the experiences and informal learning which the young people bring into the formal learning setting. The 'learning pathways' ensures a wider range of choices and routes (including work based and apprenticeships) from 14–19, albeit within a coherent qualifications structure provided by the Welsh Bac. A 'learning core' emphasises wider key skills, personal and social education and work-related qualities and experiences. 'Learning coaches' (over 200 are currently appointed) will provide individual help to young people as they develop study skills and make choices within the more flexible framework.

Extending Entitlement sets out a basic entitlement to services and support for the young learner ensuring, through the Young People's Partnerships, multiagency activity so that all have access to their full entitlement. And the Children and Young People's Assembly for Wales (Funky Dragon) gives them the opportunity to have their voices heard. Essential to the whole vision are the 14–19 learning networks with their collaboration between schools, further education colleges, work-based learning providers, Careers Wales and employers.

But the significance of all these developments for the quality of learning is best summed up in the words of the recent Webb Review (2007:12) 'Learning opportunities should be as varied as the motivations to learning and the different styles of learning with which learners are most comfortable'. And this requires quite a break from the past as the Review says (para. 1.19).

The UK has a poor record for embedding vocational alongside academic learning, comparing unfavourably with European neighbours. Practical and experiential learning seem increasingly to have been curtailed by a variety of obstacles. Wales must break with its UK inheritance in both these respects if it is to make the promise of entitlement real for all.

Conclusion

There is deep concern over the quality of learning. That concern is not alleviated by assurances arising from measurements of performance based on specific and narrow 'learning targets'. There is a need to recognise different kinds of learning and different standards by which successful learning is to be assessed. The present learning programmes too often fail to acknowledge the wider range of achievements and qualities required of an educated 19 year old in this day and age. Certainly, as is argued in Chapter 4, the 'performance indicators' encourage too limited a view of the quality of learning.

There is increasing support, therefore, for the belief that fundamental to our educational needs is a change in pedagogy rather than a change in content or yet more detailed targets. Such change in pedagogy requires attention to the 'learner's voice', more active participation by the learners in shaping the process of learning, greater emphasis for all on 'learning by doing' and on social learning in relation to the wider community, and the creation of learning environments on a 'human scale'.

This chapter has illustrated how many schools and colleges are taking the initiative, supported by voluntary bodies and funding agencies, and promoted by teachers' own professional commitment to the creation of an educational experience which enhances the quality of life for the young people in their care. Often these are deeply troubled young people for whom school or college is the only place where they will receive such care.

Many of these initiatives were made possible by government policy and interventions, particularly, in England, through its 'implementation plan' that schools, colleges, private training providers and youth services work collaboratively in learning partnerships, and, in Wales, through the promotion of its 'Learning Pathways'. And there is much in the intentions of government to support more inclusive, practical, experiential and personalised learning.

On the other hand, there is a strong tension between these intentions and the narrowing impact of an assessment regime on which the fortunes of schools and teachers depend.

Lord Puttnam summarised it thus in his contribution to Leadbeater (2008):

This means rethinking the National Curriculum to ensure its relevance and usefulness to children. It means reworking our assumptions about how and where learning takes place, whether at school, at home, online or in the community; it means celebrating teachers' and children's achievements wherever and whenever we find them. Crucially, it means identifying the knowledge, skills and responsibilities that must be nurtured in our children.

Both in this and in Chapter 1, there has been an attempt to show that part of the problem we are facing is the failure to learn from the past. The problems are not new. And there are solutions to be found in previous policies and practices which have now been forgotten or rejected, but also in many small but growing practices taking place, often unnoticed, under our very noses.

Recommendations

10.   Greater recognition should be given to practical, active and experiential learning.
11.   *Assessment for learning* should be separated from *assessment for accountability*.
12.   Teacher judgement, suitability moderated, should be integral to summative assessment.

6   Teaching

There are several themes running through this book – the idea of an educated 19 year old, the translation of this idea into a broad curriculum framework, the impoverishment of that framework by the language of performance management, the restoration in such a framework of practical and experiential learning, the pejorative impact on the quality of learning of high stakes assessment, the unrealistic expectation that schools and colleges can 'compensate for society', and the increasing central control of government over the curriculum and pedagogy of schools and colleges.

But all the way through that multifaceted debate there is one constant theme which is that of the central role of the teacher.

Role of the teacher

The teacher mediates what we believe to be valuable in the culture we have inherited and in the traditions through which we make sense of the world to what Dewey referred to as the 'immature minds of the young'. The teacher is both the custodian of a culture and a communicator of it to the next generation. Teachers, therefore, need both a knowledge and a love of the subject matter, or of the practice, which they are to communicate, and a care for and understanding of the young people to whom it is to be communicated. To see a good teacher succeeding in this communication – sharing that knowledge and love, yet adapting it to the capacity and interest of the learner – is a privilege which we have witnessed in the course of the Review. Teachers succeed in circumstances where success seems most unlikely and where the context, as outlined in Chapter 3, would seem to militate against such a relationship.

It is a disservice, therefore, to the role of teaching to see teachers as mere 'deliverers of a curriculum' – something devised elsewhere for transmission to the learners. Rather is teaching an engagement of minds between teacher and learner, as the former draws upon the public traditions of knowledge and skill in order to illuminate the thinking and practices of the latter.

Effective teaching: better management or better pedagogy?

The drive to improve learning has resulted in a more managed teaching force. Performance-related pay and promotion arise out of measured outputs. According to the Institute for Public Policy Research (Margo *et al.*, 2008:6), the 'difference between an "excellent" teacher and a "bad" teacher is equal to one GCSE grade, all other things being equal'. There is an emphasis on 'effectiveness', measured by a limited number of outcomes, as part of the new management by targets and performances.

How we arrived where we are is interesting. In its attempt to transform the teaching profession into a more effective and efficient force, the government in England sought advice from Odden, whose book, with Kelly, *Paying Teachers for What They Know and Do*, provided the basis for doing this. They argued that the traditional way of paying and rewarding teachers is outdated. Teaching should be modelled on the business model of management. Hence, 'the tax-paying public, the business community, and policy-makers still pressure the education system to produce results and to link pay – even school finance structures, more broadly – to performance' (Odden and Kelly, 1997:11). There was a felt need to 'improve productivity', and thereby to manage through precise targets, with appropriate rewards for attaining them. A subsequent Green Paper, followed by a 'technical consultation document' on pay and performance management, spelt out a new pay and reward structure, connected with a 'new vision of the profession', including professional development (DfEE, 1998).

Professional development required the establishment of reasonable targets, and so the government in England invited the American firm, Hay-McBer, at the cost of £3 million, to spell out what constitutes a good teacher, and, in the light of that analysis, to set appropriate teaching targets for the teacher to deliver (Hay/McBer, 2000).

Once again, following what was said in Chapter 2, we need to note the changing language arising from performance management and effectiveness, a language very different from that in which the teacher, rather than being the 'deliverer' of the curriculum, is engaged creatively and critically with the learner in the latter's initiation into new ways of understanding, appreciating and practising. This affects profoundly the nature of teaching as a profession, the initial preparation for teaching, the continuing professional development of teachers and teacher responsibility for what is taught and how it is to be learnt.

What is lacking in these documents is what Brian Simon referred to as 'some problems of pedagogy' (Simon, 1994, ch. 9). The distinctive expertise of the teacher lies, not in delivering a curriculum, but in knowing how to advance the understanding and skills of the learner beyond their present levels of competence – through questioning, explaining and posing problems. That expertise is based on knowing the essential structure of the 'subject-matter' being taught and the next level which the learner might be challenged to reach. It is an expertise developed through constant observation of young learners and reflection on those observations. Teachers, therefore, as experts in pedagogy, are also educational researchers – hypothesising the best way ahead, testing the 'hypothesis', and refining their teaching in the light of experience.

Governments, of course, do have a responsibility to ensure that teachers are doing a professional job. To that end, they established the General Teaching Councils for England in 2000 and for Wales in 2001, and the National College for School Leadership in 2000. In Wales, the Council is setting standards and routes for attaining 'chartered teacher status'. In England, the National College for School Leadership is establishing a post-newly qualified teacher 'ladder' through various leadership programmes, right up to the new National Professional Qualification for Headship and 'Head for the Future'. All these should provide an opportunity for teachers to develop professional practice and policy – and possibly to question the language of 'effectiveness' and of performance management.

Qualifications of the teaching work-force

Teaching in schools and teaching in further education need to be considered separately where we speak of the recruitment, training and qualifications of teachers, despite the increasing interdependence of both sectors in the progression of learners from 14 to 19.

Schools

The main route into secondary school teaching is that of the Post-Graduate Teachers' Certificate (PGCE), a one-year course for graduates, in which the trainee teachers normally prepare for teaching a subject closely connected with their first degree. A second route is through an extended undergraduate course in which there is an integration of subject specialism, educational theory and professional practice. The B.Ed. degree has, in the main, acceded to a Bachelor of Arts or Science with Qualified Teacher Status (QTS). A third, more recently established route, is employment based, as in the Graduate Teacher Programme or in Teach First in England. Here the trainees join a school from the very start, where they are trained by the staff within the school, albeit usually monitored and helped by a University Department of Education. For this purpose, in England, there have been designated 'training schools' which receive up to £90,000 per year for this purpose.

Obtaining QTS by one of these routes is essential for qualification as a teacher. The body responsible for overseeing the standards that these different routes have to meet, and for funding the providers, is the Teacher Development Agency in England. In Wales, the Assembly Government is responsible for QTS standards and also for the standards for accredited Initial Teacher Education and Training (ITET), though the providers of ITET are accredited by the Higher Education Council for Wales. Ofsted in England and Estyn in Wales inspect the quality of training.

In both England and Wales, under work-load agreements, ancillary staff have been appointed to do many of the tasks which took teachers away from the central task of teaching. Twenty-five such tasks were identified (e.g. photo-copying). In addition, there has been the creation of Teaching Assistants (TAs) to assist in the teaching but under the supervision of a qualified teacher. An important extension of this innovation in 2003, in England as part of the *National Agreement* and also in Wales, was the new career path for TAs as they could be promoted to Higher Level Teaching Assistants (HLTAs). Nearly 20,000 support staff have attained HLTA status. Research by the National Foundation for Educational Research has shown what a significant difference TAs and HLTAs can make to the quality of learning (Wilson, 1997).

All this is particularly relevant to 14–19 since it could be a route through which skilled and experienced workers can bring their expertise into schools as these develop the more skills-based and occupation-related courses. But it should be emphasised that that was not the reason for such teacher support, and there has always been the appointment of 'instructors' (e.g. the expert in horticulture) to bring in the necessary expertise for practical courses. But these instructors would not be qualified teachers, would be paid at a lower rate and would not have a career path laid out before them.

The question then is: how can these different workers in the school (TAs, HLTAs and instructors) contribute to the changing 14–19 curriculum fra-mework, and, where desirable from their point of view and that of the school, advance towards qualified teacher status?

Further education

By contrast, until recently, no training or qualification was required for teaching in a college of further education. However, an Ofsted Report (2003) criticised the lack of training in England for many in further education (FE) and the poor quality of the courses which were available for those who wanted them. A government White Paper proposed regulations to support the development of a fully qualified professional work-force in the FE system (DfES, 2006a). Since September 2007, therefore, a new professional status, together with qualifications, has been introduced not only for further educa-tion colleges but also for private training providers if these are funded by the Learning and Skills Council. The body equivalent to the Training and Development Agency (TDA) for schools in the development of the framework for teachers in FE is Lifelong Learning UK (LLUK).

There is a four-tier qualification system instead of the one QTS for schools: Preparing to Teach in the Life Long Sector Award (PTLLS), giving a mini-mum threshold to teach; Diploma in Teaching in the Life Long Teaching Sector (DTLLS); Associate Teacher Learning and Skills (ATLS), licensed to take on a limited range of responsibilities; and Qualified Teacher Learning and Skills (QTLS), licensed to take on full responsibilities of a teacher. For example, the decorator, contributing practical expertise on a vocational course, would not have all the responsibilities for planning and designing the course, and would require only ATLS, to be obtained whilst employed, though having first obtained the PTLLS. All who gain these qualifications have to register with the Institute for Learning (IFL) – the equivalent to the General Teaching Council for school teachers. These qualifications are aligned to the Qualifications and Credit Framework (QCF). The training for these qualifications is essentially 'on the job'. But it is a requirement for all those who attain QTLS to undertake 30 hours per year of professional development if they are to retain the licence to teach.

This important development has not been followed in Wales where it is not a requirement to have a teacher qualification or to undergo continuing professional development in order to teach in further education, a matter which could be of some concern as the future of 14–19 requires greater collaboration between schools and colleges. Under the 'Transforming Education Programme', there will be enforced collaboration but different standards and entitlement for teachers and lecturers.

School and FE mismatch

The arrangements as outlined above create several interrelated problems for the development of a coherent 14–19 phase and for the collaboration between the various providers. First, those with QTLS qualifications are not qualified to teach in schools, even though they, unlike their QTS colleagues, may well have the relevant practical and vocational experience and qualifications for the more occupation-related courses (such as in construction, engineering, hairdressing) which are being developed in schools through the Diplomas and Business & Technology Education Council (BTEC). Second, it is difficult to recruit to schools those who do have the relevant skills and experience (e.g. brick layers, hairdressers, engineers) because they are unlikely to have the degree level background to qualify as teachers. Of course, this may not be a problem where (doubtless in the majority of cases) courses requiring such expertise and skills will be held in the colleges. But that will not universally be the case.

There is, therefore, an anomaly. Teachers qualified to teach in schools can teach in FE with no further training. But qualified college lecturers, though able to teach 14–16 year olds in the colleges, cannot do so in schools.

It would not seem difficult to sort out these problems, that is, to have a qualified teaching status which embraced both sectors, except for two hurdles. The first is that it does not help to have two different bodies responsible for teacher qualifications post-16 (TDA and LLUK) leading to QTS and to QTLS, respectively, especially where the latter, but not the former, is renewable only upon completion of continuing professional development (a minimum of 30 hours a year). Second, and more importantly, obtaining QTS requires a first degree, obtaining QTLS does not – and for good reason since the requirements for much of the teaching are the skills and knowledge gained through apprenticeship training and relevant occupational experience.

Widening access to QTS

Important initiatives to overcome these problems and to widen access to QTS deserve more public support and higher education collaboration.

For example, Barking and Dagenham local authority (LA) enables TAs to progress to part-time Foundation Degrees at East London University, and then to full degrees which enable them to be recommended for QTS. The charity, Edge, is funding teacher training programmes focused on practical learning, led by Lewisham College of FE and South Bank University. There is, therefore, a possible route for those who have the much desired industrial experience and skills to be able, part time and in employment, to attain QTS. This 'widening participation' in the teaching profession needs to be expanded if there is to be a qualified teaching force across the more practice-based curriculum. There are other programmes too. The government's 'Transition to Teaching Programme', school based, offers opportunities for those already in employment, particularly scientists and engineers, to enter the teaching profession.

The system is more flexible than is often realised.

Therefore, as schools increasingly offer more practical and occupation-related learning (e.g. in the Diplomas), it is time to consider what is meant by an 'all degree profession'. Consideration could well be given to regarding certain qualifications and accredited experiences as equivalent to a degree for purposes of QTS in particular curriculum areas. There is a need to develop some institutional mechanism for comparing qualifications and experiences in relation to standards appropriate for teaching particular phases of education and training. More often than not these will include a relevant first degree, but there will no doubt be other qualifications together with relevant experience which, for purposes of QTS, could be seen as equivalent to a first degree.

Recruitment and retention of teachers

The recruitment of teachers through the normal routes to QTS can be seen in different ways. On the whole, there are sufficient teachers for the number of students in schools. Indeed, the ratio of teaching staff to students in secondary schools in England has improved steadily since 2000 (then, 1:17.1; in 2008, 1:16.1). But the development of support staff under the relatively recent 'work-force agreement' has created a much better ratio of adults to learners (in 2000, 1:14.5; in 2008, 1:11) (IoD, 2008). In Wales, the teacher to pupil ratio in secondary education has remained at 1:16.6 for several years.

However, the position may change in the next few years. A large number of teachers are likely to retire within 10 years and will need to be replaced. But in both countries the number of teachers (18.3% in England; 21.7% in Wales) below the age of 40 could compensate for the smaller number aged 40 to 50 and for those soon to retire (44.1% and 42.4%, respectively) (GTC, 2008; GTCW, 2008). The introduction of bursaries in 1997 in England in 'shortage subjects' (and subsequently expanded to all subjects, but with 'golden hellos' to those completing their induction year in science, maths and foreign languages teaching) made a considerable difference to recruitment. Already, possibly due to the recession, there has been a significant increase in the applications for teaching the sciences.

The teaching force in further education is less easy to analyse because of the dependence on part-time staff who bring in skills and experience from industry, and also because the FE sector covers such a broad range of institutions: tertiary, sixth-form colleges, general FE colleges, art and design and specialist colleges (e.g. agricultural and horticultural). Altogether in England there were, in 2006/2007, 378 such institutions, with over 700,000 learners under the age of 19 on LSC-funded further education provision.

Particular issues of recruitment and retention

However, the general picture, though relatively healthy, hides certain shortages.

Recruitment from ethnic minorities

Recruitment of teachers from ethnic minority groups (they constitute just over 5% of the teaching work-force) is not proportionate to the number of students from ethnic minority communities (roughly 10% of the 14–19 cohort and about 30% in Inner London) (DCSF, 2007b). There is a particular problem arising out of the diversity of languages. Over 10% of secondary students do not have English as their first language, mainly in the metropolitan areas (Margo *et al.*, 2008:28/29).

Recruiting for 'challenging schools'

There are growing problems in recruiting permanent staff in what are now referred to as 'challenging schools'. It is estimated that in some the turnover varies between 30% and 40% per year (Smithers and Robinson, 2005). All learners need teachers who know them well and care for them, but even more so is this the case where they suffer from many disadvantages.

Recruiting for practical and vocational courses

As more practice-based and occupation-related courses are promoted in schools (through the Diploma, BTEC and vocational courses), and as school/college collaboration will be required by the Welsh Assembly Government (WAG), with school providing also vocational courses, so too is there likely to be shortages of staff with relevant experience. Routes into teaching for such potential teachers might be: the appointment of instructors with the appropriate industrial experience but also with the possibility of career advancement into QTS, and the opportunities for HLTAs to study part time for QTS. This should be pursued at a regional level to reflect regional or local economic circumstances. Indeed, changing local economic circumstances might make such teaching career opportunities attractive to experienced workers, as well as making such occupation-related courses desirable for young people. The demand for such teaching skills and experience will vary from locality to locality.

Recruiting teachers qualified outside the UK

Within schools in certain regions there is a major dependence on teachers who were qualified outside the UK and who lack the experience and skills to teach in a way that is expected of them (e.g. in the sciences). For example, developments in twenty-first-century science (explained in the following chapter) require a more 'hands-on' approach to the teaching of science. The recruitment of overseas-trained teachers by local authorities, where it is particularly difficult to recruit science teachers, will require an intensive programme of professional development if the new recruits are to absorb the distinctive philosophy of such science programmes – a point made strongly to the Review by heads of science in an outer London borough.

Recruitment for shortage subjects

There are problems in the recruitment of teachers in key areas of the curriculum, particularly in sciences, maths and modern languages, so much so that Education Data Surveys warned that 'it is not too soon to say that, unless firm action is taken, all the good work of the early part of this decade will have been undone: it would be folly to head back into a period of extreme shortages' (EDS, 2006). Or, as the Royal Society (2007) reported, 'the Government has failed to reach its initial teacher training targets for science and mathematics each year for the past decade'. For maths, the target in 2005/2006 was 2350; the intake was 2010. For science, the target in 2005/2006 was 3325; the intake 2930. Of the science teachers, it is estimated that 44% were biology specialists. Hence, there is a serious shortage of physics teachers and chemistry teachers, thereby affecting the number proceeding to higher education in these subjects – and thereby affecting the numbers returning to teaching in the schools. And thereby the vicious circle. One way forward would be for universities to adjust their courses to meet this problem in schools by offering an extended year for those whose maths or science, because of lack of suitable teaching, was not sufficiently advanced for entry to the university courses.

Continuing professional development (CPD)

Teachers are there to help the learners 'get on the inside' of a way of knowing, understanding, appreciating or practising. To do that teachers need both to know the subject or practices they are teaching (the subject-matter of biology or the skilled practice of the motor mechanic or the creativity of the artist) and to appreciate that it is worth communicating. The good teacher has internalised the standards of what counts as having learnt successfully, and he or she seeks to help the learner to appreciate those standards and to perform accordingly. The good woodwork teacher, for example, demands precision in measurement.

It is assumed that qualified teachers already have a basic understanding of, and practical expertise in, what they are going to teach as a result of their completed higher education. But it is wrong to assume that such knowledge and such expertise would be sufficient for the rest of their professional career. It is not just a matter of 'knowledge changing' and of the need to keep abreast of the changes, although that is important. It is much more that teachers, just as much as university lecturers, need constantly to enrich their professional lives through research, scholarship and relevant activities and practices. Teachers of history will on the whole teach history better if they can think, debate and study with other historians. It is necessary to find the time and the opportunity for teachers to enrich themselves and to restore their love of what they are to teach.

But this is complicated. There is a wide range of priorities and needs to be met through CPD – those of central and local government as well as those of the school or college and of the individual teacher. Subject enrichment is important, but so is improved pedagogy – and thus CPD needs to address all these.

In further education, this is partly recognised through the appointment part time of teachers who are practising what it is they are to teach. The car mechanic shares with the learners an expertise which he or she is practising daily. And in England, the FE lecturer now is obliged to undertake 30 hours of professional development a year in order to keep the qualified status.

A little more history is not amiss. There were, not so long ago, 'teachers' centres' owned by local education authorities, but run by teachers for teachers. Teachers were generally in control of their professional development. These centres were particularly significant after the establishment of the Schools Council in 1964, an attempt to democratise decision-making about the curriculum, as teachers were seen as 'curriculum creators', rather than 'curriculum deliverers'. Teachers' centres were a crucial part of curriculum renewal and teacher development in the 1970s and early 1980s. There was, too, an integration of university and schools in the development of a tradition of action research into the advancement of knowledge about the practice of teaching, led in particular by the newly established Centre for Applied Research in Education at the University of East Anglia (CARE – see Elliott, 1991).

Such developments contrast sharply with the later developments of CPD as that has been implemented in the 1990s and reinforced by such documents as *School Teachers Pay and Conditions* with its 'performance management procedures', implemented in 2007, and, in England, based on *School Teacher Performance Management Regulations, 2006*. Nearly all CPD came to be focused on meeting particular targets, determined by 'meeting the standards', and controlled from outside the profession. It enabled teachers 'to deliver the curriculum', but not to engage with and be enriched by the ideas which they wish to convey to the learner.

Furthermore, there is little guaranteed CPD for the 'delivery' of the Diplomas, for the occupationally related courses which young learners will have an entitlement to, or for the changed pedagogy and more active learning approaches described in Chapter 4.

Realising the accumulated experience of the profession

There is a need to learn from history and once again to put more of the responsibility for professional development in the hands of the teacher. If we need patterns or models, we could look to some updated version of the teachers' centres referred to above. These were truly professional centres where teachers of different subjects and practices were able to meet, to discuss issues which mattered to them, to share experiences and difficulties and to link with others in their respective professional associations, creating 'collaborative cultures'. Much of such professional development took place within professional bodies like the Historical or Geographical Associations, or the once highly influential National Association of Teachers of English. The various Nuffield Sciences at both O Level and A-Level were part and parcel of the professional development of teachers. But the Wellcome Trust has recently reported that half the secondary school science teachers had had no subject-related CPD in five years, despite the fact that 73% reported that they would have wanted more subject-related training (Wellcome Trust, 2006).

Such professional development, negotiated between teachers, on the one hand, who identify their needs for subject enhancement or pedagogical improvement, and the school or LAs, on the other, who have a wider picture of what the system needs, requires a professional development framework which reflects what teachers have done and which provides a career pathway. In this, England could learn from Wales. The General Teaching Council for Wales (GTCW), at the invitation of WAG, is developing a programme leading from the induction and early professional development period, retained in Wales, to Chartered Teacher Status, underpinned by professionally owned standards (WAG, 2006c). The two routes to such a status are those, respectively, of an accredited programme and of an accreditation of other professional development undertaken. Both there and in England, the value of action research in classroom improvement, pioneered through the aforementioned CARE, has an important place.

There is a danger, however, as with the recommendations of the Gilbert Review, that the 'programme route', with agreed modules and standards and in focusing upon classroom practice, might provide less opportunity for the teacher to enrich the subject knowledge through further study of his or her own choosing. One lesson learnt from the Sutton Trust support for teacher enrichment courses at the University of Oxford was how valued was that freedom to refresh those sources of expertise, freed from the immediate concerns of the classroom.

Conclusion

Good teaching is essential for ensuring good-quality learning. Another truism. But its significance lies in what one means by good teaching. As we have seen, this has been interpreted as 'effective teaching' – being able consistently to hit certain measurable targets. The science of 'deliverology' takes over (Seddon, 2008). And McKinsey and Company are the authority in becoming effective (McKinsey and Company, 2007). So seductive is this that the Institute for Public Policy Research draws fully upon McKinsey in its report and critique of teachers and teaching (Margo *et al.*, 2008).

However, a main theme of this book is that one needs to see teaching as more than 'effective delivery'. Teaching is that communication of what are considered to be valuable ways of thinking, practising, appreciating and valuing. Teachers are the custodians of a culture through which the physical, social and economic worlds of the young learners are to be illuminated. It requires an engagement of minds, as the learners struggle to understand those ideas and make sense of their experiences. It requires an engagement with the ideas and achievements found in the sciences, literature, the humanities, the arts, the crafts and technology.

To achieve this, the educational system needs to do four things.

First, it must recruit to teaching those who have the relevant knowledge and whose love for that knowledge is something they wish to share with the next generation. We have pointed to the difficulties in such recruitment in areas vital to the success of the 14–19 phase – poor recruitment in the sciences and maths, lack of relevant expertise in the more practical and occupation-related areas of learning, teacher turnover in 'challenging schools' in particular areas. We have also pointed to the work-force reforms which partly address these problems in schools and the reforms of initial training in the further education sector. But the recruitment of sufficiently qualified young people in the sciences, technology and maths (STEM) remains urgent. The Review was impressed with the determination of the Royal Society to address this problem, and urges the government to heed its conclusions (Royal Society Report, 2008).

Second, the initial training of teachers requires a major contribution from the teachers themselves and from schools which should see themselves as 'training schools' – a notion pioneered by the University of Oxford Internship Scheme.

Third, to sustain their knowledge and enthusiasm, teachers need the kind of professional development which meets their professional concerns, is sustained by their professional associations, enriches their subject and craft knowledge, and respects their understanding of the needs of the learner.

They, after all, are the experts, not the government or the policy-makers. But that expertise needs constantly to be respected, sustained and enhanced. Young learners are now given entitlements. But such entitlements can be attained only if teachers, too, are given entitlements. The development of Chartered Teacher Status in Wales is an important move in that direction.

Fourth, the broader vision of learning set out in Chapter 5 requires a change in pedagogy, making demands on teachers for which they need continuing professional support.

Recommendations

13. Recruitment, initial training and professional development of teachers need to take into consideration the practical knowledge required for the changing 14–19 phase.
14. Qualifications for school teaching (QTS) and those for FE (QTLS in England) more closely related.
15. Ways should be found for those with much needed practical and work-based knowledge to acquire QTS.
16. Continuing professional development should be an *entitlement* and located (where appropriate) in professional development centres, run by teachers.

7   Curriculum framework for the twenty-first century

Context

It may seem odd, after what has been written in Chapters 3 and 5, to advocate 'a curriculum framework for the twenty-first century'. The argument so far has emphasised greater responsiveness to the needs and aspirations of learners, to respecting their differences and to taking into account the different social and economic contexts within which young people are to be motivated to learn. One size does not fit all.

Indeed, Chapter 5 pointed to many different initiatives arising within schools, colleges and training providers, which reflect diverse and creative responses from teachers to the learning problems they are confronted with. And the governments of both Wales and England indicate their acceptance of a more flexible approach to the curriculum, albeit within a broad framework.

Wales set the tone in its pioneering consultation paper in 2002, *Learning Pathways 14–19*, and in the development of the thinking within that document in subsequent papers (WAG, 2004; 2006a; 2006b). Emphasised is the 'individual learning pathway', with wider choice and flexibility of programmes – although inevitably the reality remains shaped by the continuation of General Certificates of Secondary Education (GCSEs).

In England, that increased flexibility and decreased uniformity are reflected in the curtailment of the national curriculum in several subject areas, the introduction of different routes to qualifications at age 14, and now the reform of the Key Stage 3 curriculum by the Qualifications & Curriculum Authority (QCA) (now the Qualifications and Curriculum Development Agency; QCDA) with a view to greater school freedom to implement educational aims.

What, then, can be meant by a 'curriculum *framework* for the twenty-first century'?

Curriculum: its different meanings

One sense of curriculum is a detailed *prescription* of a learning programme – objectives, content, teaching method, assessment and evaluation. The teacher 'delivers' such a programme by following the prescriptions. Such an understanding of curriculum has a long history. Its clearest exposition is to be found in Tyler's (1949) *Principles of Curriculum and Instruction.* Subsequent refinements, referred to as 'rational curriculum planning', demanded an ever more precise statement of the objectives (or targets) for purposes of planning and evaluation.

It is a seductive model, attractive to those who wish to exercise control over learning. One saw its application, first, in the national curriculum as it was devised following the 1988 Education Act, and, second, in the precise speci-fication of 'can do's' in the National Vocational Qualifications, influenced by Jessop's (1991) book, *Outcomes: NVQs and the Emerging Model of Education and Training.* More recently the model is to be seen in the design of the Diplomas, namely, the 'end-users' setting out the 'learning outcomes' and the content for attaining those outcomes, the QCA saying how these outcomes are to be assessed and graded, the Awarding Bodies converting the qualifications into how they might be taught, and the teacher trained 'to deliver' the content in order to attain the outcomes which will then be externally assessed. The design process has given priority to the needs of the end-users and the assessment regime, so that the complex specifications are not appropriate, for example, to low achievers. Stanton (2008) provides an excellent critique of the curriculum design.

A second way of understanding the curriculum is that of a set of *proposals* of what and how to teach, which, however, need to be tested in the classroom. Any prescription may be proved wrong in practice. Hence, as Stenhouse (1975:3) argued, the 'characteristic insistence [of curriculum development] is that ideas should encounter the discipline of practice and that practice should be principled by ideas'. Teachers should be seen, not as 'deliverers' of curri-culum, but as ones who test in practice what is tentatively proposed – refin-ing it in the light of their experience of particular learners and contexts. Stenhouse therefore (ibid:3) likened the curriculum to 'an attempt to com-municate the essential principles and features of an educational proposal in such a form that it is open to critical scrutiny and capable of effective trans-lation into practice'.

Curriculum in this second sense specifies the *principles* for educational prac-tice, not the practice itself. The curriculum needs to be written with sufficient clarity that it can be tested in the experience of particular teachers in specific learning contexts – and, if necessary, adapted. In many respects, this is how the reforms to the Key Stage 3 curriculum in England might be seen. The review of the national curriculum by the QCA in 1999/2000 encouraged greater freedom and flexibility within the overall framework – more theme- and enquiry-based learning activities, negotiated with the learners and created by the teachers.

Therefore, testing what is proposed is more than a matter of seeing how content or method achieves pre-established goals. Teachers question, in the light of their experience and knowledge of the learners, the goals themselves – the values which are implicit in the curriculum. Are these the right learning goals for these learners? Professional concerns of many teachers with the curriculum are not so much matters of the effectiveness as of the appropriateness of the goals and of the values implicit within the proposed curriculum. In this view of the curriculum, the teacher comes to the centre of the stage. Elliott (1991) provides excellent examples of teachers testing curriculum proposals and adapting to the 'discipline of practice'.

The question (to be answered by teachers as curriculum developers) becomes:

How can the aims of education, as argued in Chapter 2 (which constitute the broad framework of the curriculum), and how can the principles of learning and pedagogy, as argued in Chapter 5, be implemented in school or college, given the contexts of learning as explained in Chapter 3?

Or, put in another way, how might the idea of an educated 19 year old be translated into particular practices and learning activities?

In thinking through these questions in the light of what has already been said, we need to think about how learners might be more actively and practically engaged, how learning might draw upon the wider resources of the community and be more community oriented, and how connections can be made between this more person-centred (or 'personalised') learning and the inherited way of understanding the world encapsulated within the traditional subjects.

A national curriculum

The experience of most young people, presently in the 14–19 age group, has been shaped in England and (and until recently in Wales) by a national curriculum up to age 16, established by the 1988 Education Act. As originally conceived, the national curriculum was intended to control what was taught in schools. Therefore, it was, intentionally, detailed and prescriptive. The 1988 Act stipulated a 10-subject curriculum, with 10 Levels of attainment in each subject. Four Key Stages were defined, ending, respectively, at ages 7, 11, 14 and 16, with formal assessment at the end of each Key Stage. Curriculum content up to age 16 was specified in detail, through a structure of attainment targets, statements of attainment and programmes of study. So, for example, the first version of the geography national curriculum had five attainment targets, 183 statements of attainment and detailed requirements for each programme of study. Teachers were seen as 'deliverers of the curriculum'.

In 1994, however, in response to criticisms that the national curriculum had become too unwieldy, the Dearing Report (1994) recommended a slimmed down version which would occupy only 80% of school time, thereby providing opportunity for greater flexibility and variety. There was a further review by the QCA, in 1999/2000, encouraging greater freedom and flexibility within the overall framework.

In Wales, after devolution of educational services, a different path was trodden from that of England. 'Learning Pathways 14–19' provided a curriculum framework which is a blend of six key elements described in Chapter 8.

The emphasis was on meeting individual differences, facilitated initially by local Community Consortia for Education and Training and by Young People's Partnerships. Hence, greater scope was intended for developing the curriculum as tentative proposals for teaching and learning, evolving through reflection on these in practice.

The dilution of the original proposals in England was increased in 2002 by the decision to make the teaching of Modern Languages no longer compulsory for 14–16 year olds, thereby freeing time for more practical activities and work experience for those for whom these are thought more appropriate. To this end, alternative courses of a more pre-vocational and vocational nature were actively encouraged with the availability of vocational GCSEs and A-Levels, General National Vocational Qualifications (GNVQs) and Business & Technology Education Council (BTEC) Awards, the Increased Flexibility Programme (IFP) and now the 17 'lines' of Diploma. IFP for 14–16 year olds created 'enhanced vocational and work-related learning opportunities' through partnerships between schools, colleges of further education (FE) and other agencies. Over 300 such partnerships have been formed.

There was also a further review by QCA of the national curriculum at Key Stage 3, for implementation in 2008, together with a revision of the criteria to be met by GCSE at Key Stage 4 in 2009, and of A-Level specifications for 2008.

A curriculum framework

This story of constant review and change, together with our arguments both for greater emphasis on active and experiential learning and for greater scope for teachers to test in practice curriculum ideas, adds up to a clear message. What is required, we conclude, is not a detailed curriculum which teachers have to *deliver*, but a broadly conceived curriculum framework within which teachers work. The different contexts in which learning takes place and the different needs of the learners lead to no other conclusion.

Flexibility creates its own concerns

That said, there are serious arguments on the side of some prescription. So while there is support for a more flexible Key Stage 4, there is also concern by teachers and policy-makers alike over what might be lost along the way – the removal of compulsory foreign languages post-14 raises legitimate worries. Then there is the poor take-up of science post-16, and the state of mathematics teaching. The diminishing importance of the arts and the humanities in contrast with the compulsory core subjects of English, maths, science and information and communication technology (ICT) is yet another cause of disquiet.

So ought not key subjects continue to be part of a prescribed curriculum – the building blocks of the learning experiences of all young people? How is it possible to reconcile an 'entitlement curriculum', determined by a democratically elected government, with the principle of a more student-centred, activity-based, locally related and teacher-created curriculum? Without such reconciliation, the criticism implicit in the Webb Review (2007: para.1.20) no doubt stands. 'Practical and experiential learning seem increasingly to have been curtailed by a variety of obstacles. Wales must break with its UK inheritance in both these respects if it is to make the promise of entitlement real *for all*' [authors' italics].

Flexibility within a framework

The answer must be a curriculum framework that is precise enough to ensure that the agreed educational aims are pursued, that quality assurance can be enforced, and that learners can progress to the whole spectrum of higher level studies, training and employment, and have the knowledge and skills for the 'intelligent management of life'. But, at the same time, such a framework has to be broad enough for implementation through different activities, experiences and content, according to the professional judgements of teachers.

Such a curriculum framework, therefore, must start with aims – what counts as an educated 19 year old in this day and age. Some of these aims leave open a broad range of possibilities, whereas others are clearly constrained by the logical nature of that which has to be learnt. Not anything counts as doing history or thinking scientifically.

Therefore, the framework (and here we refer back to those qualities and attainments which, as argued in Chapter 2, make someone distinctively human and which are enhanced through formal education) would be such as to provide:

- *Knowledge and understanding* in its different forms through which we make sense of the world, namely, the key ideas and principles of enquiry which define each logically distinct way of knowing, and the activities and content through which these forms of understanding might be grasped. The ways in which young people are to be introduced to these ways of seeing the world (e.g. the particular selection of literature, use of experiments, or choice of historical periods) should depend on the professional judgement of the teachers, who know their own strengths as well as the abilities and interests of the learners.
- *Practical capability*, which is too often ignored in an educational tradition which has focused on the transmission of knowledge, for example, technical usefulness and 'thinking intelligently with one's hands', thereby overcoming that disdain for the practical intelligence characteristic of English education (Wiener, 1985). The significance of practical learning was highlighted in Chapter 5 by Fox's (2004) evidence to the Review. It includes the knowledge, skills and dispositions to live healthily, the functional skills in language, maths and information technology, and the social skills in relating to other people.

- *Community-related learning* – learning *how* to live actively within the community, to contribute to its well-being, and to be politically aware and active, all of which was emphasised by the Crick Report (1998). However, the National Foundation for Educational Research longitudinal study of citizenship education suggests there are but few examples of active community involvement or participation in community-related decision-making (Cleaver *et al.*, 2006).
- *'Big issues'* often get squeezed out of a curriculum framework based on subjects, yet are crucial to developing a sense of responsibility to the wider community. For example, environmental change should be addressed in the context of the Brundtland Commission's (1987) *Our Common Future*. Living positively within an ethnically and religiously diverse society, confronting racism in society should permeate the curriculum, as the Swann Report (1995) argued.
- *Moral seriousness* can be developed only within a context of values nurtured within the overall curriculum framework. The Review encountered examples of young people transformed within an educational environment where social context embodies values of justice and respect, and where potential for moral seriousness is nurtured by teachers.
- *Pursuit of excellence.* The curriculum framework should provide opportunities for all learners to extend (or 'to stretch') themselves beyond the immediate and the mediocre and to find interests in which they might seek to excel, whether it be in sport, cookery, writing, music, community action, work experience, historical studies or film making, as, for example, in the UK Skills' pilot project wherein young people at Hackney College of FE created as part of the curriculum a film of growing up in Hackney – the aspirations, the prejudices, the challenges to be overcome.
- *Self-awareness: careers education and guidance.* 'Guidance is the oil that makes the education and training system work effectively for young people' (NR, 2008c:1). It requires matching two kinds of knowledge: that of the young learners (their strengths, interests, aspirations) and that of the possibilities for suitable work experience, further training and progression into higher education and employment. It must be an essential part of the 'personalised learning' described in Chapter 5.

Such an inclusive understanding of an 'educated 19 year old', to be embodied within the curriculum framework albeit in different ways, would emphasise: pursuit of excellence (howsoever modest that activity might appear to some); development of moral responsibility and seriousness; practical capability; understanding (at different levels and in different forms) of the physical, social and economic worlds young people inhabit; social responsibility and commitment (the good citizen); mastery of basic and wider skills relevant to everyday living; and preparation for economic usefulness. One way into much of these would be through a common core of what, sometimes, are referred to as 'wider key skills'. These have been supported and developed by ASDAN and accredited through its Certificate of Personal Effectiveness (CoPE) and Wider Key Skills qualification – as shown and illustrated in Brockington (2004).

The resulting curriculum would be essentially tentative, tested in and disciplined by practice, adapted in the light of experience, as it ensures that all young people, even those who are not intellectual high achievers, are educated in this broader sense. The resulting curriculum, too, would spell out the experiences and activities through which those qualities might be achieved. Finally, it would make possible the caring relations at the heart of learning, because 'the perception of teachers as caring about their students has a direct relation to the students' perceived ability to engage in learning' (Wallace, 1996).

But a word of caution. Should not that framework, in the pursuit of 'knowledge and understanding in its different forms', ensure the continuation of key subjects? Many would argue that there are limits to curriculum flexibility and teacher autonomy.

Developing the framework: subjects or themes as organising principles?

Such a framework is translated into practice (as in the national curriculum) normally through a list of subjects. But the idea of a subject as a 'building block' in the curriculum is contentious. Certain core subjects are seen traditionally to be the basis of an 'academic curriculum', whereas many, who are concerned about the 'relevance' of the curriculum and the need to engage more young people, or about a more vocational preparation for the future, would argue for a curriculum based on practical activities (see Fox's, 2004, evidence to the Review), work-related experience or themes. That is implicit in the initiatives described in Chapter 5 as well as in the proposals from the QCA for the Key Stage 3 curriculum.

But this should not be seen as an 'either–or' debate. There is a danger of creating a 'false dualism' between themes, topics or competencies and subjects.

Subjects at their best represent ways of enquiring into, and of understanding, the world. Having withstood critical scrutiny and the test of time, they provide the resources upon which teachers and learners need to draw. You cannot get far in understanding global warming, say, without a grasp of basic concepts developed within the subjects of geography or science.

However, the particular theme, concern or interest of the learner can give a focus to that understanding, can motivate the learner, and draw together subject areas which otherwise remain quite independent of each other, thereby preventing a balanced understanding of the issues. The art and skill of the teacher lie in drawing upon the cultural resources we have inherited – what Dewey (1902:129) referred to as 'the inherited wisdom of the race' – in order to help young learners make sense of those matters which are of importance both to them and to the society into which they are entering. Often that requires systematic and focused initiation into the key concepts, explanatory principles and interpretations which are organised within subjects.

The tension between that systematic initiation into key concepts, organised within subjects, and the 'theme, concern or interest of the learner' can be illustrated through the teaching of science and the humanities.

Science

The House of Lords Select Committee on Science and Technology, Third Report (1999–2000) and House of Commons Science and Technology Committee, Third Report (2001–2) reflected widespread concern over the lack of interest in science post-16. One reason for this concern has been the lack of graduate scientists prepared for the ever more sophisticated economy – the need for 'skilled personnel' (Roberts Report, 2002). The Royal Society's 'State of the Nation Report' (2008) reveals a worrying participation in science and maths by 14–19 year olds. A-Level entries (as a proportion of total entries) in England in biology fell from 7.2% to 6.5%, in chemistry from 5.5% to 4.9%, in physics from 4.3% to 3.3%, in maths from 9.2% to 8.1%, which contrasts with Scotland entries to Scottish Higher where 13% took biology and chemistry, 12% physics, 28% maths. This means fewer students studying science in higher education and, by relentless logic, fewer science graduates returning to teach in schools. In the last few years, several physics and chemistry departments have closed in the universities of England and Wales because of lack of demand for places – affecting opportunities for potential scientists in some parts of England and Wales.

Hence, the Science, Technology, Engineering and Mathematics (STEM) policy framework (HM Treasury *et al.*, 2004) included policies which would increase the supply of science, technology and engineering skills.

Why are fewer young people choosing science?

They think it is difficult. It was suggested to the Review that students, in choosing A-Levels at 16, see from the statistics that good grades are less easy to obtain in the sciences. Again, there is not enough practical work in the upper secondary years (practical work plays a relatively minor part in the assessment of science at Key Stages 3 and 4) making the subject less interesting to many and less accessible to some. Finally, there is a shortage of suitably qualified teachers in physics and chemistry (Royal Society, 2007).

Why science for all within the curriculum framework?

In 2006 Newsletter No. 2, the Nuffield Foundation gave two reasons:

> One reason is to inspire and educate those young people who will go on to use science professionally in their working lives. ... A second, equally important, is to develop in all students the scientific literacy needed to play a full part as active and informed citizens in a modern democratic society, where science and technology play a key role in shaping everybody's lives, as householders, parents, patients, voters or jurors.
>
> (Nuffield Foundation Newsletter 2, 2006:1)

Scientific understanding, then, is essential for everyone at a certain level for 'the intelligent management of life'.

Tackling the problem

To improve the supply of STEM skills, new targets were, in 2006, aimed at increasing the number of young people ready to move into higher level scientific study, in particular, increasing the number of young people taking A-Levels in physics, chemistry and maths; improving the number getting at least Level 6 by Key Stage 3; improving the number attaining A*–B and A*–C in two science GCSEs; and increasing recruitment, retraining and retention of specialist teachers.

One way ahead, therefore, has been to create more attractive components within the science curriculum before and after 16. Bearing in mind the importance of practical learning (outlined in Chapter 5), such components would need to re-engage young people, yet remain faithful to the basic principles and concepts of science. In this respect, two related developments were brought to the attention of the Review.

First, according to Millar and Osborne (1998:9), 'the science curriculum from 5 to 16 should be seen primarily as a course to enhance scientific literacy'. Emerging from this notion of 'scientific literacy', a suite of courses was piloted by OCR called '21st Century Science', sponsored by Nuffield Foundation, Salters Institute and Wellcome Trust. This, and similar suites of courses offered by the awarding bodies AQA and Edexcel, were introduced as GCSEs in 2006. They offered a flexible structure, adaptable to different levels of ability or attainment, but with a common core which would introduce all learners to basic explanatory ideas in science relevant to the modern world (e.g. gene theory) and to ideas about scientific processes (e.g. distinguishing between correlations and causes). Relevance to the concerns and experiences of the learners, and engagement through practice and discussion, were essential features of 'core science'. For many learners, lack of relevance had been perceived as demotivating (Lyons, 2006). And the evaluation of the '21st Century Science' claimed that students who had been switched off science through the standard GCSE courses were more motivated (Hanley *et al.*, 2008).

Second, '21st Century Science' included GCSE Additional Applied Science. Applied science involves understanding scientific knowledge and methods of scientific enquiry embodied in techniques used by scientists. These techniques cross areas of application (e.g. in the use of microscopes by public analysts and microbiologists). It develops this understanding through authentic work-related contexts (e.g. a doctor or nurse dealing with cystic fibrosis). It focuses on people who apply scientific techniques and knowledge, looking into the thought processes and skills involved (e.g. questioning the theoretical and practical limitations of a given technique). It provides opportunity for practical problem-solving, emphasising ability to use techniques, skills and knowledge for tackling science-related problems (e.g. in the analysis of blood samples in the diagnosis of an illness). Gadd and Campbell (2007) give many examples of the types of relevant enquiry. It engages with contemporary scientific issues, especially the relation between science, technology and society. And it requires high-level numeracy because of the centrality of 'quantity' and statistics in the work-related science; accurate measurement is crucial. Applied Science is proving popular (NR, 2008g), because it emphasises practical and experiential learning, points to the relevance of science to future occupations, and overcomes the dualism between 'academic' and 'vocational'. Whilst providing a basis of a general education for all, it maintains routes into science in higher education.

Yet, despite the success of these initiatives in motivating young people to continue with science, there are warning voices about the emphasis upon 'relevance to everyday life' and to the notion of 'scientific literacy'. These warning voices are reflected in Donnelly's concern that the central importance of science as a distinctive form of understanding might be jeopardised: 'the central argument for the position of science at the core of a statutory curriculum lies in introducing children to science as our best available account of the world, understood materialistically' and that 'the main justification must derive from the distinctive characteristic of science' (Donnelly, 2005:296/7).

That argument agrees with what the Review has promoted as a central educational aim, namely, the initiation into those different ways of understanding the physical, social and economic worlds we inhabit, drawing upon the intellectual and cultural resources we have inherited. They must shape the curriculum framework. On the other hand, those ideas can be understood at different levels and through 'different modes of representation' (Bruner, 1960). Those who have a good grasp of the 'distinctive characteristic of science' can show how they can be embodied in a pedagogy which points to 'relevance to everyday life' and which welcomes practical engagement and discussion. The student of low mathematical attainment, repairing a gear box with a motor mechanic on the SKIDZ work-based learning programme, declared that he now had an understanding of 'ratio' – something he would never have done from a text-book or sitting in a classroom. The 'logical structure' of the subject-matter sets limits to the 'psychology of learning', but it does not determine it.

The challenge, therefore, for those who, to increase motivation and general education for all, advocate 'scientific literacy' and 'applied science' is one of showing how these also introduce the learner to the characteristic ideas and explanatory powers of science and can be the basis of deeper understanding.

Humanities and arts

That tension between traditional subjects and 'relevance', manifested in themes or activities, can be seen in the teaching of the humanities. The Review expressed its concern over the decline in the humanities post-14 and the possible neglect of them in the Diplomas as these are developed under the aegis of the Sector Skills Councils (NR, 2008f). Indeed, as Lambert (2008) states, 'geography as a subject discipline is being sidelined in some schools seeking to establish a "skills-based" curriculum … There are 85 schools in which not one single student sat GCSE Geography last year'.

Why is there this decline in the state sector, if not in the independent schools and schools in more advantaged areas? Subjects, unprotected by SATs at the end of Key Stage 3, and 'disapplied' from the national curriculum at Key Stage 4, are more vulnerable to thematic approaches. They are no longer seen to be important enough to be required in the general education of those who take the more vocationally oriented routes. As economic efficiency becomes the dominant discourse of education, so vocational preparation (e.g. training to be a hairdresser) focuses on the relevant skills – not on the broader historical and social context of employment and the economy.

A more balanced and holistic approach than in England is reflected in the creation of the Welsh Baccalaureate. This is an overarching award at three levels described in Chapter 8. It provides, within an integrated framework, different pathways and options. But it contains within the core studies a requirement for all to study 'Wales, Europe and the World' – assuring therefore a shared humanities-style context throughout 14–19 for the different pathways.

The humanities and the arts (history, drama, geography, literature, painting, music, etc.) are the area of the curriculum where matters of deep personal concern might be addressed, not determined simply by economic and employment needs. They provide the context for political and citizenship education. That is why the national curriculum in 1988 made history, geography, music and art, alongside literature, compulsory until 16. As the then Secretary of State, Kenneth Baker, argued:

> … in this country, as nowhere else, the tradition of humanities teaching has continuing vitality and relevance. I am quite clear that every civilised society, to remain civilised, needs to develop in its citizens the aptitudes and intuitions which flow from engagement with the Humanities. The Humanities are an interrelated effort to give intellectual expression to the significance of what it means to be human
>
> (DES press release, 7 July 1988)

On the other hand, to place the humanities and the arts firmly within the curriculum framework for all does not entail total demarcation between subject disciplines. The issues dealt with by the humanities and the arts – use of violence, relations between persons, an appreciation of beauty and elegance, ambition, the reality of war, moral rights, the prevalence of poverty – were the themes around which the Humanities Curriculum Project and Arts and Adolescence was organised, but the discussion-based consideration of these themes drew upon the evidence found in history, literature, religious studies, science, geography and the arts (Stenhouse, 1975).

Modern foreign languages

In England, modern foreign languages were no longer a compulsory part of the Key Stage 4 curriculum from 2004. That enabled young people, who had little inclination to learn another language, to pursue more 'relevant', practical or vocational studies. The consequence has been a sharp decline in the numbers taking foreign languages. In 2008 entries to GCSE French were 201,940, compared with 347,007 in 2001, and to German 76,695 compared with 135,133. There is a knock-on effect upon those entering university: only 610 students started degree courses in German in 2007 compared with 2288 in 1997, and only 5655 in French compared with 3700 (*Observer Report*, 21 September 2008). The impact of this upon those returning to schools to teach modern foreign languages must be considerable, and thus there will inevitably be a downward spiral (CiLT, 2007).

Does it matter? Is being able to speak more than one language a requirement of the educated 19 year old? According to the EU commissioner for multilingualism, small- to medium-sized companies in the UK are increasingly turning to foreign nationals to fill jobs that need more than one language, and in the global economy there will be an even greater need for such qualifications and talent. Yet fewer than half of UK FE colleges offer languages with vocational courses and fewer than one per cent of all students are taking a language with their vocational courses (CiLT, 2007). But also, even if the mastery of another language is not a necessary characteristic of the education and training of all young people, it is surely a desirable trait – opening the mind to other cultures and ways of understanding the international context which shapes ones life.

To conclude, if education is concerned with the development of understanding in its various forms, then these different forms should be essential components within the curriculum framework. It would be the normal requirement of a general education for all to include science, maths, languages, arts and humanities. But within such broad titles there is room for argument over the balance between practical engagement and theoretical understanding, between response to perceived economic needs (the 'skills agenda') and relevance to personal development. The curriculum of the future has to reconcile these tensions between subjects as organising principles of learning, themes which focus attention on matters of importance across subject boundaries, and the practical engagement of learners. The tension between the three was examined closely in the Review's Issue Paper 7 (NR, 2008e).

Functional skills within the curriculum framework

The Moser Report (1999) pointed to the high number of functionally illiterate young people amongst those who leave school, and who therefore face curtailed opportunities for further learning and fulfilling employment. It is still seen to be a major problem by employers. In a recent survey of nearly

500 directors, 71% assessed young people to be less proficient in writing skills than they were 10 years ago, 46% in reading skills, 52% in oral communication and 60% in mathematical skills (IoD, 2008a:63). Hence, there is felt to be an overriding need to develop what the Tomlinson Report referred to as 'functional literacy' and 'functional numeracy'. It is a problem recognised in England by the then DfES (2005d:30) which promised high standards in the basics as a result of 'specific modules which focus on the functional and practical application of English and mathematics'. Concern also has been expressed about the neglect of 'key skills' of speaking and listening. Therefore, in England there will be a single standard and recognised route for English, maths and ICT from Entry Level to at least Level 3. These will be integrated, from 2009, into English GCSE, and, from 2010, into maths GCSE. They were integrated into the Diplomas in 2008. They are also obtainable as stand-alone qualification.

Defining 'functional'

Without denying the importance of the problem, we need to be careful in isolating 'functionality' from the wider educational goals of teaching English and maths. Within maths, for example, what is now referred to as 'functional mathematics' would supposedly have been contained within the GCSE 'Using and Applying Strand'. Therefore, it is important to understand why, despite that strand, it should have been thought necessary to develop further distinctive modules.

The Smith Report (2004) argued that there was a lack of engagement and motivation for many at Key Stage 4, and a poor transfer of skills to different and real-life situations. And Ofsted (2007a) reports that, although there is an improvement in test results, this is due in part to the better preparation for the tests, but is failing to equip young people well enough for their future. Wake (2005), in his evidence to the Review, questioned the often simplistic and unquestioned reference to functionality in what are too often seen to be self-evidently basic skills. Function must be defined in terms of that for which it is said to be functional, and that requires a detailed analysis of the job or mode of living for which the skills are needed. Functional skills cannot be learnt effectively when disconnected from the deeper conceptual understanding of maths or from the real-life situations in which they make sense. Again we come back to the problems of pedagogy.

Similarly basic skills in English might be lacking because the mainstream curriculum is disconnected from the interests and concerns of young people. As 'ground has to be covered', so there is less room for discussion.

Information, advice and guidance (IAG) within the curriculum framework

From 1998, all schools in England have had a statutory duty to provide careers education in years 9, 10 and 11, but not post-16. In 2003, there was published a non-statutory framework. In Wales, by contrast, careers education is statutory from the age of 13 to the age of 19, but once again supported by a non-statutory framework. More recently, the term IAG has taken over from Careers Education and Guidance (CEG) to indicate a wider concern about the barriers to participation in learning programmes.

However, in England, the government re-directed the privatised careers service to focus particularly on those who had become disengaged. From 2001, the careers services came within the newly established Connexions partnerships. The result was that the majority of learners were not receiving the external support necessary, and were often dependent upon help from teachers who did not have the expertise or training (NAO, 2004). This problem did not arise in Wales where the various careers companies were brought together under Careers Wales. In England, however, yet further changes took place in 2008 as a result of the recommendations of government, namely, the devolving of all IAG from Connexions to services commissioned by local authorities (DfES, 2005c).

Therefore, IAG is firmly within the curriculum framework as an essential part of meeting a key educational aim, preparing young people, in the light of self-knowledge and opportunities open to them, for a more fulfilling future. In some schools and colleges which the Review visited, IAG was fully integrated into the life of the institution with dedicated staff, fully resourced centres and learner-focused courses. But there is still a long way to go for many schools, especially where the number of post-16 learners is relatively small and where there may not be a guaranteed impartiality in the advice given to where studies should be continued. There is need for improvement. Sutton Trust (2008) found that at least half the education and careers advice young people receive is in some way inadequate, especially with regard to the relation between subject choice, university courses and subsequent careers.

Evidence presented to the Review by David Andrews of NICEC (NR, 2008c) suggests the need for:

- a statutory duty on schools to provide careers education from 11 to 19;
- a national professional qualification for coordinators;
- a programme of professional development for all who provide guidance and careers education;
- inspection of all education and training providers and of local authorities on the quality of IAG;
- a strengthening of the links between external guidance service and the labour market to ensure proper understanding of employers' needs.

Young people with special educational needs and disabilities

A major aim of successive governments has been 'social inclusion', following the Warnock Report (1978) and the subsequent Education Act of 1981. One major thrust of the policy has been greater integration of young people with various learning disabilities into mainstream schools and colleges, together with the abolition of the formal labels attached to different kinds of handicap. The view was that all have learning difficulties in various ways and that it is a continuum between those who have few and minor ones to those who have many and large ones. All need to be treated according to their individual learning needs – a forerunner of what is now referred to as 'personalised learning'. Furthermore, that, at the time and especially in later schooling, seemed to give young people a greater opportunity for making the transition into employment or further training.

However, a 2006 report of the House of Commons Education and Skills Select Committee questioned the wisdom of this policy for a wide range of young people. The policy 'is failing to cope with the rising number of children with autism and social, emotional or behavioural difficulties' (p. 12). According to the Report, many young people are being needlessly excluded from school because of behavioural problems. Sixty per cent of exclusions in secondary school are from those who are declared to have Special Education Needs. Many of these join the ranks of the Not in Education, Employment or Training (NEET) or turn to crime. Sixteen to 18 year olds with special needs are particularly vulnerable.

Therefore, there is a growing problem which needs to be addressed within the educational and training system as a whole – the provision of more appropriate learning environments and of teachers specially trained not only in the knowledge of these special needs but also in more practical modes of learning. This might fruitfully include partnership with other educational providers such as the Youth Service and Voluntary Bodies, which, being less constrained by national curriculum requirements or the meeting of inappropriate targets, can develop appropriate learning opportunities and experiences.

The MacBeath Report (2006:12) summarised the feelings of many teachers:

> Practitioners in particular, conceived the educational system to be too inflexible to accommodate a broad range of needs, governed by the demands of the National Curriculum, by high stakes testing, parental choice and the strictures of Ofsted. All of these constrained any radical departure from the 'official' programme of study and its preferred pedagogy, based largely on whole class instruction.

Evidence from Haines (2006), drawing upon a wide and representative reference group on the problems faced by disabled young people in the 14–19 phase, showed how, across a number of indicators, young disabled people experience poorer outcomes: 27% of 16–19 year olds with disability are NEET compared with 9% of the non-disabled; 21% aged 16–19 have no qualifications; and they are much less likely to proceed to higher education. This is despite the evidence from the Youth Cohort Study that aspirations of disabled 16 year olds have risen to the same level as those of non-disabled 16 year olds. As Haines says,

> The greater participation of disabled adults in employment and across society places new demands on the 14–19 system to ensure that young disabled people participate, progress and attain. ... This will require all

those involved with the 14–19 system to rethink the impact of current objectives, culture and practice (p. 2).

The problems seem particularly acute when many leave school: few appropriate courses and a poor curriculum; lack of skill amongst those who teach; the move into non-work options (ALI Report, 2006); age cut-off points in the social services; lack of suitable information and guidance about access to higher education.

The idea of an educated 19 year old embraces those with special educational needs and those with disabilities. At the same time, those same aims need to be reconceptualised to reflect the progress and achievement of young people, who, for whatever reason, are not able to progress as far or as quickly as other young people in some aspects of their learning or require specific support to do so. Alternative approaches to learning should 'embody greater opportunities for them to participate fully in society as adults'. But that is not always easy, for as Haines says, referring to Miller *et al.* (2005):

> The standards agenda depends too much on measures of success defined by summative assessment and external verification. The effect is that there is less incentive to differentiate the curriculum and use formative assessment that can benefit young disabled people's learning (p. 8).

It would be a mistake, however, to think that such an educational ideal, open to all young people, can be attained simply by setting new targets or creating new incentives. Chapter 3 pointed to a wider social and cultural context, too often ignored, which needs to be taken into account. The needs of specific groups of young people get ignored within the mainstream. As the MacBeath Report (p. 25) says:

> As schools widen their intake and as teachers meet more disturbed and damaged children the need for pastoral care increases commensurately. This becomes particularly acute in disadvantaged communities where the issues are compounded by poverty, violent communities and turbulent domestic circumstances.

Conclusion

The current developments 14–19, especially those of the Diploma and of work-based learning, and of the 'learning pathways' in Wales, provide excellent opportunities for rethinking school- and college-based curriculum development. The new Extended Diplomas are intended to cover the whole of the learner's programme. Furthermore, the project within the Diploma and the stand-alone Extended Project appear to give a lot of freedom to teachers and learners to pursue a topic of the learner's choice and could provide opportunities for the curriculum development described above.

But several points need to be remembered if this is to happen.

- Different needs and abilities, and different economic and social contexts cannot be adequately captured in any centrally prescribed curriculum.
- Teachers must be central players in curriculum development within the broadly agreed curriculum framework – critically scrutinising and adapting general principles to their contexts.
- Nonetheless, that broadly agreed framework would benefit from there being independent bodies responsible for curriculum reform – a proposal made by the Royal Society (2008) to protect science education from the 'assault' of politically driven change.
- Designing 'assessment for learning' must be part of curriculum development, adapted to the different kinds of learning (e.g. practical and experiential) and to the particular context.
- Curriculum development (e.g. within the Diplomas in England or the 'learning pathways' in Wales) cannot be undertaken independently of the required expertise, skills and knowledge of the teachers.
- Curriculum development must take place within the collaborative learning systems (see Chapter 11), not an easy matter where Diplomas take place over different sites, and involve different specialists and employers. Perhaps there are lessons from the 'teachers' centres', abolished in the 1980s.
- Since the curriculum is permeated by assumptions about what is worth learning, its development must constantly revisit the question: *what counts as educating this person in this particular social, economic and personal context?*
- Attention in England should be paid to the lessons from Wales as it pioneers its distinctive Learning Pathways.

Recommendations

17. The curriculum framework should introduce all young people to:
  - forms of understanding which enable them to make sense of their physical and social worlds;
  - opportunities to excel and to have a sense of achievement;
  - practical and economically relevant capabilities;
  - issues of profound social and personal concern;
  - an information, advice and guidance for future career, training and education service;
  - knowledge, skills and experience relevant to the wider community.
18. Curriculum should be developed cooperatively and locally between schools, colleges and other providers, albeit within a broad national framework.
19. England should learn from the Welsh attempts to incorporate in its 'Learning Pathways' a broader and more flexible vision of progression.

8 From qualifications reform to a framework for learning

Significance of qualifications

Young people are constantly urged to work hard and to get the best qualifications they can. That way, they are told, they will be better prepared for the future – to get the job or the further training they want. But is it really like that? Are the qualifications we provide up to the task?

In what aspires to be a meritocratic society, qualifications play a vital role in selection, knowledge and skill development, empowerment and personal identity. They also implicitly embody a set of values which tend not to be explicitly discussed, but which fundamentally affect 14–19 education and training. Certain qualifications give access to privileged parts of the labour market (see Chapter 9). Politicians, parents, learners, teachers, universities and employers are obsessed with them, fuelling the ritualistic August debate about examination results and standards. Moreover, over the past two decades, qualifications have been used repeatedly by policy-makers as the vehicles for reform of the post-14 education and training system (e.g. 2000 changes to A-Levels and the broadening of the advanced level curriculum). We cannot ignore them.

The questions are:

- How do qualifications function?
- What effect will current 14–19 reforms have on learning?
- What future role might qualifications have in serving the needs of all learners and ensuring the development of an 'educated 19 year old'?

We argue that qualifications are the main driver of learning in the 14–19 phase. General Certificates of Secondary Education (GCSEs) and A-Levels have a particularly strong shaping role, not only because, as Chapter 4 points out, they are taken by so many learners, but also because of their selective function and the prominent role they still play, in England, in school and college league tables. The dominant culture of learning, in Chapter 5, is thus associated with an examined, subject-based approach, in which attention tends to be focused on performance and selection rather than on the quality of what is learned. In addition, the position that GCSEs and A-Levels have occupied and continue to occupy in the public imagination in both England and Wales and their sheer dominance numerically means that they exert a powerful effect on other qualifications within 14–19.

Reform

Currently, government in England has focused its main qualification reforms on the introduction of the 14–19 Diplomas, a new set of qualifications that co-exist with GCSEs and A-Levels. However, changes to GCSE and A-Level specifications and apprenticeship frameworks are also taking place, and a new Foundation Learning Tier (FLT) is being introduced for 14–19 year olds working towards Level 2 qualifications. In Wales, as earlier chapters have indicated, reform of 14–19 is centred around 'Learning Pathways 14–19' and the development of the Welsh Bac.

This chapter describes and analyses the different approaches to 14–19 curriculum and qualifications reform in England and Wales.

First, we locate in England a number of dominant and subordinate reform themes that contribute to a complex and often contradictory policy landscape that is proving difficult to reform in a coherent way.

Second, in Wales, although GCSEs and A-Levels dominate the educational system, the balance between maintaining the status quo and reforming the system has been tilted more towards the latter. The introduction of 14–19 Learning Pathways and the Welsh Bac offers the prospect of a somewhat more diverse and inclusive qualifications framework. Whilst it is important not to overstate the extent of Welsh divergence from English approaches, these developments in Wales are sufficiently important to warrant close analysis.

Finally, we suggest a move towards future qualifications frameworks in England and Wales that support broader forms of attainment, involve all 14–19 year olds and encourage personal development and innovative learning in order to help the formation of an educated 19 year old.

The learner experience of 14–19 qualifications

Despite the existence of a national curriculum for compulsory schooling to the age of 16, education for 14–19 year olds in England, and still to a large extent in Wales, is primarily defined by two national examinations – GCSEs and A Levels. Since 2002, the national curriculum ensures that all 14–16 year olds follow a course of study in English, maths, science, ICT, physical education, citizenship, work-related learning and enterprise, religious education and health and careers education – a reduction from the original requirement. In Wales, basically the same pattern applies, although with due modification to reflect the teaching of the Welsh language and the particular cultural and historical features of Welsh society. At the age of 16, the vast majority of young people in England and Wales sit one or more GCSEs, with most taking at least five and a significant minority taking 10 or more (JCQ, 2007a).

Furthermore, in 2005/2006, 71% of 17 year olds in England and 68% in Wales remained on full-time courses. Of these full-time learners, about two-thirds (40% of the total cohort) took advanced-level qualifications, with about three-quarters of this group on A-Level traditional and applied programmes, demonstrating the continuing dominance of this qualification. Learners can decide which subjects they wish to study at A-Level. Since the inception of *Curriculum 2000*, which introduced a two-stage approach to A-Levels, most learners take four subjects at AS-Level in the first year of post-compulsory study and continue onto three full A-Levels in their second year, with a very small minority opting for applied subjects (JCQ, 2007b). There is some evidence of increases in the numbers mixing general and vocational qualifications (Hoelscher *et al.*, 2008). But for a large proportion of 14–19 year olds, GCSEs and A-Levels still constitute their experience of the curriculum.

A minority of 14–16 year olds, approximately 12,000 and usually lower attainers, take a more mixed form of learning from the age of 14 with some taking vocational qualifications, such as National Vocational Qualifications (NVQs), Business & Technology Education Council (BTEC) awards and, from September 2008, the first five lines of the 14–19 Diplomas. In Wales, the Foundation Level Welsh Bac is being piloted and may offer a further route for this group of learners. For most of these young people, the vocational experience is added onto their GCSE programme. A few on specifically tailored 'engagement' programmes will spend the majority of their time in further education (FE) college or with a work-based learning provider working towards vocational qualifications. Post-16, however, a minority of 16–19 year olds will have their learning programme determined by a vocational grouped award, such as BTEC Diplomas, the new 14–19 Diplomas or an apprenticeship framework.

Qualifications reform in England

The distinction between academic and vocational learning has broadly been preserved in the government's recent 'tidying up' of the current qualifications framework. It now (DCSF, 2008b) sees qualifications being organised into three main 'routes' or what we term 'qualifications tracks' – GCSE/A-Level, Diplomas and Apprenticeships, with a fourth preparatory or underpinning route, the foundation learning tier.

The term 'track' refers to a qualification-led curriculum, which has a distinctive content, assessment and mode of learning. It thus tends to channel learners in a particular direction, minimising opportunities for flexible movement between different types of qualifications and curricula. We contrast the notion of a 'track' with the idea of a curriculum 'route', which allows learners to progress either horizontally or vertically. This is made possible when qualifications are less distinctive and share common properties in terms of assessment, knowledge and skills.

A-Levels and GCSEs, as single-subject awards, have been retained and the major reform focus has been on the development of a new suite of qualifications related to occupational sectors – the 14–19 Diplomas – along-side revamped apprenticeships.

This new, reformed pattern of 14–19 qualifications, which began to emerge in September 2008, presents a complex picture. In order to describe and analyse it, we have separated out seven themes – four dominant and three subordinate which refer mainly to the first two of the major tracks. The third track – that of apprenticeships – is postponed to Chapter 9.

Four dominant themes

Preserving and strengthening general qualifications

It is possible to see, over the last 20 years, reform of general qualifications moving through successive waves of innovation and preservation. Each wave of reform (e.g. the introduction of the unified GCSE to replace the separate 'O Level' and Certificate of Secondary Education (CSE) qualifications, and the introduction of modular A-Levels) has been accompanied by a period of pre-servation (e.g. the introduction of tiered GCSE papers and the restriction of coursework in A-Levels) (Hodgson and Spours, 2008b, ch. 3). The 2008 chan-ges to GCSEs and A-Levels can be viewed as the latest wave of preservation. The present emphasis is on 'standards', reliability in assessment and increased selection in order to counteract the opening up of GCSEs through coursework and the rise in grade attainment in A-Levels over the past few years. The espoused aim is to 'strengthen' general qualifications and to make A-Levels function better as a selection tool for higher education (DCSF, 2008b).

The changes to A-Level specifications were intended to correct what the government saw as dysfunctional features of the earlier *Curriculum 2000* reforms. University admissions tutors had voiced concerns that the *Curriculum 2000* modular A-Levels had led to a rise in the A grade, making it difficult to select the best candidates; they were not adequately preparing young people for higher education study (Wilde and Wright, 2007). Both learners and teachers had complained about the quality of teaching and learning (Fisher, 2007). The government thus aimed to reduce the negative impact of modular testing on the experience of A-Level learning and to provide 'stretch and challenge for our brightest students' (DfES, 2005a:63). The revised A-Level specifications, introduced from September 2008, have four rather than six units to limit the amount of assessment in these qualifications and to offer more space to study a subject in depth. A related change is the introduction into the A2 of more 'stretching questions' (DCSF, 2007c), which means fewer short answers, more extended writing and more synoptic questions, as well as an A* grade. In addition, coursework is only allowable in a minority of sub-jects (e.g. art and design and PE) and all candidates have to demonstrate a high quality of written communication.

Another consultation paper (DfES, 2002) talked of GCSEs moving from a school-leaving examination to a 'progress check'. This suggested a declining role for a 16+ examination at a time when more young people were remaining in education and training. Associated with this was the idea of 'acceleration', with students taking qualifications early, represented in the slogan 'stage not age'. The 2005 14–19 White Paper, however, emphasised the continued role of GCSE as a 16+ threshold by asserting it was widely recognised by parents and respected internationally and should, therefore, remain. The role of GCSE as an important educational milestone was further strengthened by changes to performance tables which set a higher threshold for the 5 A*–C benchmark by including English and maths GCSEs. This focus on improving basic skills can also be seen in the proposals to incorporate the *functional skills* of English, maths and information, communication and technology (ICT) into the revised GCSEs in these areas. Another important change to these qualifications, referred to as 'toughening GCSEs' (DCSF, 2007c), is the replacement of coursework by 'controlled assessments'. From 2009, all attainments in GCSEs will be measured through controlled assessment in which there will be varying degrees of external control over task setting, task taking and task marking (QCA, 2007).

Introducing an alternative 'applied' route within a four-track system

The development of 14–19 Diplomas at Levels 1–3 of the National Qualifications Framework – the presenting edge of 14–19 reform – implicitly confirms the non-vocational status of GCSE and A-Levels, and so contributes to their preservation and strengthening. The original 14 sector-related Diploma Lines were supplemented by three 'general' lines in science, languages and humanities in 2007, ready for teaching in 2011. Significantly, a Department for Children, Schools & Families (DCSF) press release (23 October 2007) was entitled *Diplomas Could Become Qualification of Choice for Young People*.

The Diplomas are 'composite' awards comprising three elements – *principal learning*, which is related to occupational sectors; *generic learning*, which includes personal, learning and thinking skills, a project and functional skills in English, maths and ICT; and *additional/specialist learning*, which can include other qualifications and units that allow learners to tailor their programme to meet personal aspirations.

According to DfES (2006b) the Diplomas should provide 'an exciting, stretching and relevant programme of learning for young people of all backgrounds and abilities', and should prepare them for life and work. It is claimed that they will achieve this by their blend of general and applied learning in 'real world environments' (e.g. each Diploma has to include at least 10 days of learning in a work setting); that they provide more choice for learners; and that they have been designed primarily by employers.

There have been vocational qualifications before, and it is legitimate to ask whether the Diplomas are different. The answer is: yes they are – to a degree. They are designed from the start as 14–19 rather than 16–19 awards; they require the learner to undertake a *programme* of learning; they are broader and

Table 8.1 Diploma implementation timetable

Diploma area	First teaching
Information Technology	September 2008
Society, Health and Development	
Engineering	
Creative & Media	
Construction and the Built Environment	
Environmental & Land-based Studies	September 2009
Manufacturing & Product Design	
Hair & Beauty Studies	
Business Administration & Finance	
Hospitality	
Public Services	September 2010
Sport & Active Leisure	
Retail Business	
Travel & Tourism	
Humanities	September 2011
Languages	
Science	

Table 8.2 Different types of Diplomas

The Diploma is available at 3 levels
Foundation Equivalent to 5 GCSEs at grades D to G
Higher   Equivalent to 7 GCSEs at grades A* to C
Advanced   Equivalent to 3.5 A-Levels (there is also a Progression Award at advanced level which is equivalent to 2.5 A-Levels)

A new Extended Diploma, designed to extend each of the 17 Diplomas by adding more Generic and Additional/Specialist learning, will be available from 2011. The Extended Diplomas are expected to be equivalent to:
Foundation 7 GCSEs at grades D to G
Higher   9 GCSEs at grades A* to C
Advanced   4.5 A-Levels

potentially more flexibly tailored to individual need, with the possibility of mixing academic and vocational study as well as a strong element of generic learning. It is claimed too that the Diplomas will be more strongly vocational because of the work-related requirements of the 'principal learning'. Taken together, these four differences could be seen as assets in terms of progression, skill development, learner motivation, pedagogy and the promotion of a broader curriculum and it is undoubtedly these factors that excite the policy advocates of the new awards.

However, there are concerns that these assets may not be fully realised and there has been considerable controversy over the introduction of the Diplomas in relation to: their purpose and design (HoC, 2007; Smithers and Robinson, 2008); which learners will take them in the context of the preservation and strengthening of GCSE and A-Levels (Hodgson and Spours, 2007); their role in relation to established vocational qualifications such as BTEC and City and Guilds (CGLI) awards; and whether they will meet learner needs, particularly those below Level 2 (Stanton, 2008). Finally, all of these critics, together with teacher and professional associations, have questioned the rushed timescales for implementation (NUT/UCU, 2008) (Table 8.1).

Breadth through choice

One way to broaden learning opportunities at 14–19 would be to reform GCSEs and A-Level and make them more inclusive of all learners. Such in fact was the advice of the Tomlinson Report.

The government however is committed to the principle of choice in public services (choose your doctor, or hospital, or school) and preferred to achieve the desired broadening of opportunity by adding to the existing menu more qualifications from which learners could choose. The introduction of the Diplomas can be seen as part of this wider strategy by providing 'breadth through choice'. Instead of fundamentally reforming GCSEs and A-Levels to provide a broader programme of learning and curriculum for all learners, as advised by the Tomlinson Report, the government has promoted breadth through increasing learner choice of qualification. Since 2002 and the relaxation of the national curriculum at Key Stage 4, there has been an encouragement for 14–16 year olds to take a greater range of courses, in the majority of cases more vocational and applied options (e.g. GCSEs in vocational subjects, BTEC Explorer and First Diploma, the ASDAN Certificate of Personal Effectiveness and NVQs).

Post-16, the government has actively promoted the use of a wider variety of qualifications through introducing Applied A-Levels and increasing the range of Diplomas (e.g. in humanities, science and languages and the Extended Diplomas). There was even a brief flirtation with the International Baccalaureate (IB) when Prime Minister Blair suggested that all local authorities should make the IB available in their areas (Coles, 2006). Interestingly, this choice-based approach to breadth has also stimulated a 'market reaction' from the awarding bodies and independent sector, who have demonstrated interest in a range of other qualifications, such as the Pre-U and International GCSE, and most recently the IB Careers-related Certificate (IBCC), which threaten to complicate an already complex qualifications system. The Pre-U, for example, has been designed by Cambridge International Examinations as an alternative to A-Levels for 16–19 year olds. The AQA Bac is the latest to join a crowded field of post-16 qualifications (Table 8.2).

Improvement of basic skills performance

'Functional Skills' are the latest in a long line of qualifications initiatives (e.g. 'core skills' and 'key skills'), designed to improve young people's basic skills in English, maths and ICT, because of constant complaints from employers about low skills in new recruits (Frost, 2007; IoD, 2008), and because of the important role these skills play in supporting progression. All young people taking GCSE English, maths and ICT will have to study Functional Skills as part of their course and gaining an A*–C grade will be dependent on their attainment. Functional Skills also constitute a compulsory component of the Diploma qualifications, alongside the Personal Learning and Thinking Skills (PLTS), which are designed to support the development of 'independent enquirers, creative thinkers, reflective learners, team workers, self-managers and effective participators', and are part of the National 14–19 Entitlement. While few would argue against the importance of English, maths and ICT for all, the idea that Functional Skills constitute the only curriculum requirement for all 14–19 year olds is extremely narrow when compared with the breadth of common learning in other successful education and training systems in Europe (Clarke and Winch, 2007a).

Three subordinate reform themes

Alongside these dominant reform themes, the government's 14–19 qualifications reforms also contain three innovative subordinate measures – curriculum breadth, strategies for including all learners, and a flexible common accreditation system – which could potentially support a more creative approach to learning and movement towards a more unified qualifications framework.

Curriculum breadth

For the majority of learners, the 14–19 curriculum remains elective and narrow. This is because, as we have already seen, it is determined by individual qualifications rather than by prescribed combinations of subjects or common learning, as is the case in many other European systems (e.g. French Baccalaureate, German Abitur). In Chapter 7, we saw how this structure led to a decline in the number of learners taking maths, science and modern foreign languages. It also means that there is no assurance that all 14–19 year olds will have access to the knowledge, skills and experience that we argue for in Chapter 7.

The government has supplemented its 'breadth through qualifications choice' agenda with a number of further initiatives.

- *A two-stage A-Level (AS/A2)* encourages learners to take more than the traditional three-subject A-Level curriculum and to broaden their programmes through taking four or more AS-Levels in their first year of study.
- *Functional Skills* have been introduced into all qualifications for 14–16 year olds – though not post-16 except as part of Diplomas and Apprenticeships. But a recent government 'next steps' document indicates an entitlement to 'personal learning, thinking and functional skills' for all 14–19 year olds (DCSF, 2008e).

- *Design of the Diploma* encourages a broader programme of study with a blend of applied and theoretical learning.
- *Three additional Diploma lines* (science, languages, humanities) and their extended versions could be seen as the extension of compulsory breadth into general qualifications, with their requirement for additional/specialist and generic learning.
- *The Extended Project at Level 3* alongside A-Levels could be seen as an opportunity for a broader approach to learning insofar as it encourages a range of research, extended writing, presentation and oral skills – although, in its current form, it is limited by being confined to use within the Diplomas and being a stand-alone optional qualification for students taking A-Levels.

These five initiatives could be seen as employing a weak approach to broadening the 14–19 curriculum, because some are elective and others are confined to certain parts of the 14–19 system.

This approach in England can be contrasted with the idea of an overarching framework for all 14–19 qualifications to ensure curriculum breadth for all learners – a step taken (at least in part) by the Welsh Assembly Government in the form of the Welsh Bac and one recommended by the Tomlinson Report.

Inclusion and the FLT

The government's approach to 'inclusion' in the qualifications system is to ensure that there are different routes to accommodate all learners within what remains a divided system. Apart from the three main routes of GCSEs/A-Levels, Diplomas and Apprenticeships, it is introducing the FLT for those not deemed ready for the other three routes. This initiative has been designed to 'establish an inclusive curriculum offer at Entry Level and Level 1 for learners from age 14 upwards' (QCA/LSC, 2007:1). It consists of a learning programme containing skills for life and work, vocational learning and personal and social development. FLT programmes may be welcomed by practitioners anxious to find appropriate learning experiences and accreditation for those studying below Level 2. There are, however, concerns that it will 'ghettoise' learners precisely because it lies outside the three main qualification routes (National Learning Panel, 2008; NR, 2008h).

A common accreditation framework and changes to qualifications regulation

A further subordinate theme within the government's 14–19 reforms is the proposal that all qualifications for this age group could be accredited through a common credit framework. This arises from the desire to rationalise a very complex qualifications landscape and from reforms in adult learning where the Qualifications and Credit Framework is being used to accredit all forms of learning as part of a UK-wide (or even European-wide) move to a common credit system. Credit has been seen by some (e.g. Tait, 2003) as a major mechanism for breaking down the academic/vocational divide. Until 2008, however, the government resisted the idea of credit in 14–19 education and training and it is still unclear how it will apply to 14–19 qualifications.

Issues arising from the government's qualifications strategy

The government decided to separate qualifications development and specification of standards (now with the Qualifications and Curriculum Development Agency [QCDA]) from an independent regulator (Office of the Qualifications and Examinations Regulator; Ofqual) whose job, as the public guardian of standards, is to 'safeguard standards across all qualification routes' (DCSF, 2008b). Hence, Ofqual reports directly to Parliament (rather than to Ministers) on standards in national qualifications, tests and examinations.

It monitors the work of the over 120 private awarding organisations offering accredited qualifications as well as the National Assessment Agency's delivery of national curriculum assessments in schools. The separation of the functions of qualifications regulation and the monitoring of curriculum and qualifications development is seen by some as bringing much needed political independence into the qualifications and assessment system.

The need to ensure independence arises from public distrust as a result of so many changes to qualifications. This raises the question: 'Is the yearly improvement of measured performance a reflection of improved standards or not?'

General concern lies, according to Lebus (2007), Group Chief Executive of Europe's largest assessment agency (Cambridge Assessment), in the unprecedented control of the examination system gained by the government in the last decade or so, reflected in its interference with, for example:

- the number of units in A-Levels, and the range of grades awarded;
- the use of calculators in and out of exams (changed seven times in 10 years);
- coursework introduced across GCSE, and now being removed;
- approval of grade boundaries for the A* at A-Level;
- complicated Diploma specifications.

All of this makes comparison over years highly problematic. Lebus argues that it is to free the system from such political interference that many schools are coming to value the IB and the Cambridge Pre-U. The problem is that the government has used qualifications as a lever for change not as a guarantee of standards. And that distrust is shared by those universities which, as shown in Chapter 10, are creating their own 'entrance tests'.

In Lebus's view however, the new arrangements would not ensure sufficient independence from government. The qualifications system is still subject to political influence through the QCDA, which retains responsibility for developing the criteria for public qualifications, rather than with the 'regulator [Ofqual] which is accountable for the integrity and stability of the system as a whole'.

The desire of the government in England to preserve traditional qualifications (A-Levels and GCSEs), while at the same time introducing entirely new awards (Diplomas), has a number of implications for 14–19 education and training. The increase in qualifications on offer will provide more choices for young people to participate in different forms of learning. This is to be welcomed.

However, the preservation/innovation approach is likely to affect qualifications recognition and learner progression. Adding 'new' awards alongside 'old' qualifications will produce a greater level of complexity to an already complicated system. Despite attempts to rationalise qualifications into four routes, it is likely that learners, parents, employers and universities may find the system confusing. A survey commissioned by the Department of Education and Skills (DfES) discovered that only 45% of companies had any useful understanding of NVQs – 20 years after their starting; only 1/6 understood the equivalence between NVQs and academic qualifications; 1/20 said they would avoid recruiting people with NVQs – despite employers' involvement in their development. It is the academic qualifications which matter (*TES*, 3 March 2006). Therefore, the jury is still out on whether the new awards will achieve the critical mass necessary to encourage young people to choose them and employers and universities actively to use them in their recruitment and selection.

Moreover, the government's approach to reform reproduces divisions between academic and vocational learning, despite the claim that the Diplomas themselves will lead to more mixed study. These points taken together suggest a repeat of the mistakes of the early 1990s when reform was concentrated on GNVQs, as an alternative to A-Levels and GCSEs, rather than on transforming the 14–19 system as a coherent whole. But in another sense, 14–19 reform is not simply a repeat of history because of what we have termed the three 'subordinate' themes identified above which, as we will see later, could be viewed as steps towards the development of a more inclusive framework for learning.

Current qualifications reform in Wales

Since parliamentary devolution in 1999, the Welsh Assembly Government has followed an increasingly distinctive approach towards education and training policy from that in England (and, indeed, other parts of the UK). This is not to suggest, however, that the nature of the problems confronted in Wales differ significantly from those elsewhere or even that the broad aims of policy are fundamentally different. Rather, given the continuing attachment in Wales to key aspects of a traditional social democratic approach to educational provision, the policies adopted to pursue these broad aims have diverged significantly from those pursued by the administrations in England (Rees, 2007).

A key element in this distinctive approach has been 14–19 provision. As in England, GCSEs and A-Levels still dominate, but, at the same time, the Welsh Assembly Government has introduced new initiatives in the 14–19 Learning Pathways and the Welsh Bac Qualification. Both are intended to produce a much wider range of learning for 14–19 year olds and to improve levels of attainment across all groups of learners. In more general terms, they are aimed both at meeting the needs of individual learners and at combating social exclusion, as well as improving the supply of skills to employers (WAG, 2002a).

14–19 Learning Pathways

The 14–19 Learning Pathways initiative comprises six key elements (WAG, 2004):

- Individual learning pathways to meet the needs of each learner.
- Wider choice and flexibility of programmes and ways of learning.
- A learning core wherever there are learners aged 14–19.
- The support of a learning coach.
- Access to personal support.
- Impartial careers advice and guidance.

The initial intention, therefore, was that each learner is enabled to devise an individual learning pathway, combining – according to her or his own needs and preferences – formal qualifications, non-formal awards (e.g. those offered by the Open College Network and ASDAN awarding body) and informal learning (e.g. community activities, part-time jobs, club memberships). This requires that a wider range of provision is made available, with 'option menus' combining general and applied learning opportunities from Entry Level to Level 4, available in each of the 22 local authority areas in Wales. Support for learners is to be provided by learning coaches and, where necessary, supplemented by personal support. There is also a requirement that impartial careers advice and guidance is made available through Careers Wales, as well as through schools and colleges.

Initially, the emphasis was very much on the delivery of the Learning Pathways initiative at the local level, ensuring responsiveness to the specificities of local conditions. 14–19 Networks were established in each of the 22 local authority areas, bringing together education and training providers, learners and employers. Each was charged with the development of a coordinated programme of provision within their area, reflecting the priorities set out for the Learning Pathways initiative. Perhaps inevitably, the result was a considerable unevenness in progress, with quite different approaches being adopted across Wales (Estyn, 2006b). In response to this, the Welsh Assembly Government announced, as part of a wider *Action Plan*, a more coordinated governance structure, thereby providing a stronger framework for the work of the 14–19 networks (WAG, 2006a).

This *Action Plan* also reiterated very firmly the Assembly Government's intention ' ... further to transform the education and training opportunities available to our young people in the 14–19 age group'. It set key milestones for the implementation of learning pathways: starting in September 2006, there was a major initiative to gain the support of employers and the business community for the reform, including the development of an Employers' Concordat to underpin increased vocational learning opportunities; from September 2009, a revised national curriculum in Key Stage 4, with greater emphasis on skills acquisition; by 2010 at the latest, an entitlement to high-quality learning support and a choice of work-related and general learning options from the age of 14; and again by 2010 at the latest, a new learning infrastructure, which will provide the opportunities for young people to undertake education and training through individual learning pathways.

It is difficult to come to judgements about the impacts of the 14–19 Learning Pathways initiative, especially given its current state of development and implementation. There can be no doubt, however, about its ambition. Its stated goal is that: '95% of young people by the age of 25 will be ready for high skilled employment or higher education by 2015' (WAG, 2006b). Given the current situation in Wales, this implies a very significant transformation indeed in the effectiveness (measured in these terms) of the education and training system for 14–19 year olds. Moreover, it is envisaged that these changes in the education and training system will also have important impacts on the wider economy and society: 'Learning Pathways 14–19 is intended to contribute to enhancing employment opportunities; to supporting the development of equal opportunities; to increasing real Gross Domestic Product (GDP); to reducing poverty, including in Communities First areas; to reducing anti-social behaviour and criminal activity; and supporting improved health' (ibid).

Clearly, it would be an astonishing achievement if these goals were realised, even partially. The Learning Pathways initiative would need to overcome problems that have proved intractable to the multitude of previous attempts to remedy them. In effect, it would need to bring about probably greater changes than any previous restructuring of education and training provision has achieved. Quite apart from questions about the desirability of the goals of the Learning Pathways initiative, there are very real questions as to whether any educational reform can in itself result in these kinds of outcomes.

Less abstractly, it is possible to identify a number of issues that will need to be addressed if the Learning Pathways initiative is to make significant progress. What evidence is available suggests that the coordination of the provision of education and training opportunities and the construction of 'option menus' is by no means a straightforward task. For example, although funding arrangements for 16–19 provision have been somewhat equalised between schools, colleges and training providers through the National Planning and Funding System, relationships between the different providers often remain difficult. Collaboration to share resources and to rationalise curriculum provision appears to be hard to achieve across all the 14–19 Networks (Estyn, 2008b). (These issues are discussed in greater detail in Chapter 11.)

One of the least surprising features of experience with the new initiatives up until now has been the difficulties encountered in engaging employers and the business community more widely. However, there is at least the possibility that what this lack of engagement reflects is something quite fundamental about the nature of the Welsh economy. It may be, for example, that the level and form of economic activity is such that a 'low-skill equilibrium' characterises a much more substantial part of the economy than in other, more prosperous parts of the UK.

There are also real questions as to the extent to which the Welsh Assembly Government can detach the education system in Wales from that in England and the UK more widely. Its continuing dependence on block grant funding from the Westminster Parliament necessarily enforces a financial, bottom-line constraint on what can be done. This is likely to become increasingly significant over time. Furthermore, Wales continues to share the bulk of its qualifications system with England (and Northern Ireland). The impacts of this common system are clearly illustrated in the development of the other major Welsh initiative, the Welsh Bac.

Welsh Baccalaureate Qualification ('Welsh Bac')

The Welsh Bac is an over-arching qualification, which brings together existing awards, such as GCSEs, A-Levels, GNVQs and other vocational qualifications (the 'Options'), with a common 'Core' of skills development and other essential learning. The Core comprises:

- a 'humanities' component for all, 'Wales, Europe and the World', together with a modern language (mostly Welsh);
- personal and social education, including community participation;
- work-related education, including work experience and enterprise;
- key skills at appropriate levels;
- an individual investigation.

Developed at Advanced, Intermediate and Foundation levels, the role of the Welsh Bac is increasing each year. By September 2008, some 80 schools, 17 further education colleges and five work-based learning providers across Wales were offering the Welsh Bac at Advanced and Intermediate levels. This represents about half the schools in Wales that have sixth-forms; and about three-quarters of further education colleges (Estyn, 2008c). In addition, since September 2006, 21 schools have been engaged in a pilot of the Intermediate and Foundation levels at Key Stage 4. The aim is that at least 40% of 14–19 year olds will be involved by 2010 (Davies and Thomas, 2008).

Again, it is as yet difficult to evaluate the impact of the Welsh Bac, with much of the available evidence relating to the Advanced level. Here, after some initial expressions of concern, it is clear that successful completion of the qualification has been rising steadily; in 2007, over 70% of those entered successfully achieved the qualification, with 74% gaining the Core certificate. Most of those undertaking the qualification were relatively high attainers at Key Stage 3 and GCSE; and perhaps not surprisingly therefore, they obtained relatively high grades in their Optional subjects (WBQ, 2006). More generally too, an evaluation indicated that the students undertaking the Advanced Welsh Bac placed considerable value on what they had learned through the programme (Greatbach *et al.*, 2006).

However, it remains to be seen how far the Welsh Bac opens up new opportunities for learners. Some concerns continue to be expressed about how the qualification is being received by the universities, especially outside of Wales. Some evidence suggests that the UCAS tariff of 120 points for the Advanced Core certificate is not, in reality, being accepted, particularly by those university departments which are able to be highly selective in their admissions process, with many requiring three A-Levels *in addition to* the Core (Hayden and Thompson, 2007). Equally, whilst some employers have responded extremely positively to the skills engendered by the qualification, this remains a minority response (Greatbach *et al.*, 2006). Indeed, more generally, the role of employers in the new initiatives being undertaken by the Welsh Assembly Government remains a matter of concern.

The recent Webb Review (2007), which focused on the reform of further education in Wales, made a series of recommendations aimed in particular at those without adequate literacy and numeracy skills and 14–19 year olds who do not have a full choice of learning opportunities. While the Webb Review's recommendations mainly covered governance and institutional organisation, it argued that the Learning Pathways 14–19 strategy had to be strengthened by the introduction of more vocational routes and apprenticeships within the Welsh Bac. It appears, therefore, that the Welsh Bac is moving from a framework model of a Core programme combined with English or UK qualifications, available to a minority of Welsh learners, to a more integrated Welsh Bac System encompassing all Welsh 14–19 year olds.

The Welsh Assembly Government has also been discriminating with regards to the adaptation of recent Whitehall government qualification reforms. The 14–19 Diplomas will not be employed as discrete qualifications in Wales, but individual components, the Principal Learning and Project qualifications, will be available for inclusion in the Welsh Bac. The Extended Project will also be on offer outside the Welsh Bac from September 2009 (DCELLS, 2008a). Wales has not followed England in developing Functional Skills and has, instead, created its own 'versions', not accepting that they should be stand-alone qualifications. Furthermore, rather than phasing out the Applied A-Levels, Wales will retain them within the Welsh Bac. More 'exotic' qualifications such as the IB and the Pre-U have not been adopted widely in Wales. In 2008, only one school and one college offered the IB, and none had adopted the Pre-U.

In Wales, therefore, the balance between preserving the status quo and innovation has been quite markedly different from that in England. The Welsh Bac and the 14–19 Learning Pathways within which it is situated are serious attempts to provide a much wider range of learning experiences, encapsulated within an over-arching qualifications framework. Welsh policy-makers have been largely unimpressed by English 'policy innovation', and have demonstrated that alternative approaches are possible. As the Welsh Bac becomes established, it seems likely that GCSEs and A-Levels will be restructured into components that provide a better fit within the overall framework. In the longer term, there is an expectation that Wales will cease to use GCSE as a stand-alone qualification. Furthermore, according to the Department for Children, Education, Lifelong Learning and Skills (DCELLS') (2008c) Consultation Document, *Proposals for a Learning and Skills (Wales) Measure*, there is an aspiration to have an educational system which has entirely its own qualifications – a full Welsh Bac system – in the same way that Scotland has its *Higher Still* curriculum and qualifications system (Raffe *et al.*, 2007) and its Curriculum for Excellence (CRG, 2004). This would clearly represent a move away from 'versioning', to a clear and distinct Welsh curriculum and qualifications offer for young people.

The Welsh Assembly Government is gradually piecing together a distinctive approach to learning in the 14–19 phase led by a curriculum concept in Learning Pathways and a qualifications framework in the Welsh Bac. The tensions which Welsh policy-makers experience are less to do with the deliberate pursuit of contradictory dominant and subordinate agendas – as in England – and more to do with how a more coherent 14–19 policy approach collides with the effects of the wider socioeconomic realities found in Wales, with its high levels of economic inactivity and wider social disadvantage. Most obviously, the tension between the broadly inclusive policies being adopted and what is seen to be the continuing under-performance (at least as conventionally measured) of Welsh schools and colleges has to be addressed.

These are the contradictions that the Webb Review tried to confront as it sought to recommend measures for combining economic competitiveness and inclusion through raising levels of basic skills; the reorganisation of the FE institutional landscape; the integration of employers into the education and training system; and the extension of the vocational and work-based learning within the Welsh Bac. In effect, Webb was not only arguing for policy consistency, but also for a comprehensive strategy that goes beyond a focus on qualifications alone. How far the Welsh Assembly Government has the powers to address these issues, however, remains to be seen.

Conclusion: 14–19 qualifications and a framework for learning in England and Wales

Following earlier chapters that argue for a curriculum to support the development of an educated 19 year old and the education and training system's need to support this ideal, we suggest four dimensions of an inclusive and challenging framework for learning with a particular focus on qualifications. This chapter indicates that Wales is closer to this goal than England.

Every learner needs a purposeful curriculum and 'learning space'

We have argued that the divided qualifications system in England lacks an explicit set of common values and purposes and does not support the type of curriculum framework of the previous chapter. If, however, general qualifications were to be brought within a Diploma framework with a common core (as with the case of the Welsh Bac), then there is the prospect of a more purposeful curriculum for all. We may even be able to talk about every 14–19 year old being educated, rather than, more narrowly, 'acquiring skills'.

There is a need, therefore, to focus less on examination outcomes and to create 'curriculum space' for more practical, informal and creative learning both within and between subjects and programmes of study. One practical way of addressing this would be to include an Extended Project, and 'personal learning, thinking and functional skills' in the common core of learning, so that all 14–19 year olds would be given the opportunity to develop the capacities to become more independent learners and to progress within education and out into adult life.

The role of a baccalaureate-type curriculum and qualifications framework

Arguments for a more explicit curricular approach to qualifications reform and for the enhancement of 'learning space' point to a baccalaureate-type curriculum and qualifications framework; or what has been termed an 'English Bac System' (NR, 2008h), that draws on the strengths of the IB, BTEC awards, 14–19 Diplomas and Welsh Bac. In proposing such a system, we are not suggesting the abolition of individual subjects, because they are critical sources of knowledge and skills. Rather, we argue for their incorporation into an overall baccalaureate-type qualification framework so they can best contribute to the development of an 'educated 19 year old'. A key issue will be the balance and relationship between theoretical and applied learning, subject knowledge and skill, and the broader competences such as problem-solving and interdisciplinary learning, increasingly associated with developing capacities for the future.

Assessment and awarding arrangements

Assessment plays a driving role in framing pedagogy and learning experience for 14–19 year olds in both England and Wales, and its role in recent years has been almost entirely negative. To make assessment work for the learner, greater weight needs to be given to teacher judgement while still ensuring national standards that give qualifications their currency. A new balance of teacher and external assessment would allow the deployment of a wider range of assessment tools, which do not rely so heavily on written outcomes and are more appropriate to the diverse forms of theoretical, practical and applied learning which young people need to prepare them for the future.

The development of a common credit-based framework to recognise all forms of learning and the establishment of a more independent regulator for standards in qualifications and national curriculum assessment could potentially provide help in moving the education and training systems in England and Wales in this direction. But further steps are needed to ensure independence of qualifications from constant political interference. And, as is shown in the next chapter, the role of qualifications at Levels 1 and 2 in supporting progression into employment needs to be re-examined.

An inclusive system

A new curriculum and qualifications system needs to be totally inclusive with the ability to support the education of all 14–19 year olds. Intended or not, present government policy in England promotes two divides – academic/vocational and above Level 2/below Level 2 – with the lowest attaining learners relegated to the FLT. We think there is a strong case for the further reform of curriculum and qualifications, in both England and Wales, that builds on their existing systems to develop a framework for learning that promotes progression and is simple to understand. However, curriculum and qualifications reform on its own is not sufficient. It has to be part of a wider strategy that recognises the relationship between reform of the education system, institutional organisation and governance, the labour market and the policy process itself. It is to these matters that we now turn in the next three chapters.

Recommendations

20.   England should develop a unified and inclusive qualifications framework that embraces different forms of learning and promotes more effective choice and greater breadth of study.

21.   The Review supports the continued development of the Welsh Bac so that it becomes the organising framework for all 14–19 learners.

---

9 Employers and the labour market

Introduction

Employers want good people who are well and appropriately qualified, and can quickly begin to contribute skills, energy and ideas. Policy-makers invest much faith in this imperative as a driver of educations' aims and practices. Is that fair or realistic?

This chapter, therefore, is concerned with two interrelated issues: the role of employers and their representatives within the governance and operation of the 14–19 phase; and the impact of the labour market and its associated incentive structures on patterns of 14–19 participation, qualification, achievement and progression.

Two aims follow from this:

- To question how realistic or otherwise are current ideas about the development of the labour market – and therefore about the nature and strength of the signals that it sends to young people.
- To probe what can realistically be expected of employers in trying to secure the objectives towards which current 14–19 policies are supposed to be leading.

In addressing these issues, we are, in effect, seeking to turn on its head the prevailing logic about the relationship between education, training and the labour market. The dominant policy narrative is about employers and their demand for skill, and we subject that to critical scrutiny. We suggest, in fact, that the reform of qualifications, curricula and pedagogies – important though they are – will not be enough on their own to take us into the policy-makers' desired high-participation, high-achievement future.

The policy goals

Before embarking on this task, it is worth reminding the reader of the scale of 14–19 policy objectives for which the labour market is expected to act as the motor and with which employers are expected to actively engage. These in England include:

- far higher levels of achievement of Level 2 (General Certificates of Education [GCSEs] and/or Diplomas) at age 16;
- far higher levels of post-compulsory participation, with the aim of reaching 90% in the near future;
- far higher levels of achievement at Levels 2 and 3 (A-Levels, Diplomas and National Vocational Qualifications [NVQs]) at age 18/19;
- Diplomas (at Levels 2 and 3) to have achieved parity of esteem with GCSEs and A-Levels, in terms both of entry into higher education (HE) and of the esteem with which they are held by employers, reflected in the size of the wage premiums they are willing to offer to those who hold them;
- provision of high-quality work experience to all youngsters, and the embedding of such provision within the Diplomas;
- an expanded, vibrant and high-quality apprenticeship system as the sole means of acquiring vocational qualifications for 16–19 year olds;
- an end to jobs without formalised, certified training for young people under the age of 18 as part of the move to raising the compulsory learning leaving age to 18.

It is a daunting prospect. Taken individually, each of these objectives might be deemed ambitious when judged against our performance over the last 25 years. Taken together they represent the expectation that current reforms will deliver nothing less than a step-change in participation and achievement that will enable England to match the kind of performance found in other developed countries and to move us from the lower end to the upper quartile of the Organisation of Economic Co-operation and Development (OECD) league tables on secondary education. At this point, all we will note is that, while willing the ends is relatively easy, willing the means to achieve those ends is potentially a problem of a different order of magnitude – a consideration that policy-makers may not yet have fully apprehended.

Intra-UK variations

Many of the issues to do with employers and the labour market that are discussed below apply across all four of the UK nations. However, it is important to underline the fact that when it comes to government-funded apprenticeship provision (that is, the stream of 14–19 activity that falls within the remit of what is covered in this chapter) we need to remember that there are some variations in nomenclature and structure between the different national schemes. For example, until recently, apprenticeships were only available at Level 3 in Scotland. In England the use of the word 'Modern' in the title for apprenticeships has been dropped, whereas in Wales, Level 2 apprenticeships are still known as Foundation Modern Apprenticeships, and Level 3 provision as a Modern Apprenticeship. These differences notwithstanding, the actual contents or mandatory outcomes within a Welsh and English apprenticeship in the same sector are identical – the real differences occur between sectors and occupations.

Great expectations – the role of employers

Much of the rhetoric around 14–19 policy (and skills policies more generally) emphasises the importance of education, training and skills to business success (at the level of the national economy, sector and individual enterprise). The corollary would be that business leaders are inevitably extremely concerned about skills, and therefore willing to devote large amounts of time, energy and company resources to helping to improve them. It is assumed that they will cooperate with government to redesign education and training (E&T) and participate in the governance of the publicly funded system – Sector Skills Councils, Learning and Skills Council, Regional Development Agencies, and so on. Then they will help to deliver the myriad of often short-lived government schemes and programmes that this system revolves around.

There are good reasons for questioning the assumptions that drive this scenario. For example, when it comes to recruiting people into jobs where qualification requirements are not high, employers have alternatives to consider – students working part time, women returners, older workers and migrant labour. All may offer a more socially skilled and flexible labour force. In other words, why should employers spend time and money on helping to reform 14–19 provision, or focus their recruitment efforts on that sector when they can just go elsewhere? Moreover, for many occupations, the development of mass HE now means that employers recruit for a broad range of jobs at age 21-plus, rather than from 16–19 year olds, and the 14–19 phase matters to them only insofar as it helps equip enough young people to enter the degree courses from which they recruit.

More fundamentally, there is much evidence that skills are not as important to employers as we may assume. In fact, there is evidence that for businesses, skills are a third or fourth order issue (Keep and Mayhew, 1999; Ashton and Sung, 2006; Keep *et al.*, 2006; Grugulis, 2008). If this is the case, then 14–19 issues are but one, often relatively minor, sub-section of what for many employers will be a relatively marginal priority. Acceptance of this reality has tended to be strongly resisted by policy-makers, who have continued to assign to employers a pivotal role in policy-making for the 14–19 phase. We see that working out in a number of ways:

- Delivery of the work-based route as a major (and supposedly growing) stream of provision.
- Activities, supporting a particular pedagogy and curriculum (e.g. work experience and enterprise education).
- A growing role in setting the parameters for vocationally oriented forms of certification – originally NVQs but now also the Diplomas.

The obvious expectation by policy-makers is that employers will be strongly motivated to engage with this agenda – and to the investment of time, energy and money.

But what do we mean by employers?

We have suggested already that the policy-maker's notion of 'employers' as a meaningful and homogeneous collective category is open to serious question (Gleeson and Keep, 2004). Organisations' skill requirements vary across sector, sub-sector, occupational grouping, firm size and product market strategy. It follows that the views they express about these needs will also vary, depending on what level and/or specialism within management is pronouncing on the issue of skill. In other words, the policy-maker's conception of a thing called 'employer demand' for skill, or an 'employer view' about E&T, is an appealing, but ultimately somewhat misleading fantasy.

Can employers' 'representative bodies' make the collective case?

Probably not. We have noted that when policy-makers speak of having consulted employers, or having engaged employers in the process of reform, what they are often talking about is either that they have liaised with the paid officials of a body that claims to represent the views of employers, or that individual managers, usually from large companies, have been involved in discussions. Unfortunately, policy-makers often extrapolate from the enthusiasm of this relatively small band of those who engage directly with the policy process (through activities such as membership of the UK Commission on Employment and Skills, and of Diploma Development Partnerships) and project this onto the attitudes, intentions and prospective actions of employers more generally.

The degree to which these types of representation deliver active support from the broad mass of employers is questionable, not least as many UK employer bodies are relatively weak and poorly resourced (Gleeson and Keep, 2004). What experience suggests is that they are usually unable to deliver any meaningful degree of general employer commitment to either active engagement with E&T innovations or labour market reforms. Keep (2008) illustrates this tendency through his account of the Confederation of British Industry's (CBI's) 1989 Vocational Education and Training Task Force. Certainly in the past this approach has led to endless disappointments, as employers en masse have not acted in the ways promised by those the government has deemed to represent them. It will be interesting to see, for example, whether the employer enthusiasm for Diplomas, which the Department for Innovation, Universities and Skills (DIUS) and the Department for Children, Schools & Families (DCSF) claim has been expressed by those involved in aspects of the Diploma development, will translate into wider active support from the majority of employers in each of the sectors involved.

Moreover, employers may have conflicting needs. Different employers want varied outcomes and outputs from the education system. Insofar as the volume and/or quality of the supply of those requirements are finite at any given moment, they may well find themselves in competition with one another for a limited supply of suitable young people. As a result, the idea of 'meeting employers' needs' may not be the simple and unproblematic goal for 14–19 policy that is assumed. If different employers want divergent outcomes, then to satisfy one set of demands may be to dissatisfy another. A clear example here is engineering apprenticeships. Many engineering employers want a ready supply of academically successful young people who have the requisite skills in mathematics and science and are willing to enter apprenticeship schemes that prepare them for a range of intermediate level posts that require a Level 3. Other employers and government policy are simultaneously demanding that these youngsters complete A-Levels (and/or a Level 3 Diploma) and then proceed into HE to obtain a degree.

The upshot of this situation is positional competition between sectors and occupations for particular segments of the ability range. History tells us that some forms of employment tend to be much less attractive to bright young-sters than others, and sectors at the losing end of the spectrum have a ten-dency to blame the education system – poor or inappropriate careers guidance and teacher bias – for their woes.

There is a strong likelihood that these issues will impact on the Diplomas, in that some of the lines of study will attract those of higher levels of ability and others will not. Lines that are linked to occupations with relatively low pay, weak prospects and poor working conditions (e.g. unsocial hours) may well struggle to recruit students in sufficient numbers and of a quality to satisfy the expectations of some employers.

Yet the CBI has called for the numbers of young people opting to go down each Diploma line to 'match' the size of demand from employers (CBI, 2007). The danger is that, if this expectation is not matched, as has often been the case in the past, employers and government will tend to blame the education system and its staff for failing to meet the needs of the labour market.

Employers and the failure of the work-based route

Having looked at the high and, in our view, unrealisable expectations placed on employers as allies in the creation of alternative 14–19 pathways, we now turn our attention to the related issue of work-based vocational education and train-ing (VET). This area too has had its share of attention from policy-makers. It is seen as a persistent succession of attempts at invigoration, expansion and status raising, going back to 1981, when the Manpower Services Commission published its *New Training Initiative: an Agenda for Action* or even earlier (Perry, 1976).

The desired breakthrough, however, has remained elusive. Despite a succession of institutional reforms and programmes (Unified Vocational Preparation, the Youth Training Scheme, Youth Training, Youth Credits and Training Credits, National Traineeships, 'Other Training', and 'Modern' Apprenticeships – through many sequential iterations), the Manpower Services Commission's original goals for a work-based route, that would rival in quality and scale that found in some other developed nations, have never been realised (Keep and Payne, 2002; Fuller and Unwin, 2003; 2004; 2008).

There are two interrelated reasons for this failure. First, here too, policy has had unrealistic expectations of employers, who have never been committed to this route in sufficient numbers. Second, government has worked against its own objectives in this area by simultaneously urging more young people into further and higher education participation – a route that has asked little or nothing from employers.

At present, in England, we are in another phase of 'one last push', with the government announcing a major expansion of apprenticeship provision to meet the Leitch Review's ambitions (DCSF/DIUS, 2008b), with the added expectation that apprenticeship will form the only route via which youngsters can pursue directly vocational training once the learning age is raised to 18 (DfES, 2007). At the same time, the Conservative party is putting forward their own proposals for re-vamping provision and motivating greater employer engagement (Conservative Party, 2008). In the case of small employers, this is through the simple expedient of giving them a £2000 'bounty' if they prove willing to take an apprentice.

In Wales, the priorities are to improve completion rates so that more apprentices achieve all the different elements within their apprenticeship framework (a competence-based NVQ, key skills, a knowledge-based element, and knowledge of employment rights and responsibilities), integrating apprenticeships into the Welsh Baccalaureate, offering small employers the option of grouping together to provide 'shared apprenticeships', and raising the number of Level 4 places (called Modern Skills Diplomas, and, like apprenticeships generally, open to people of all ages) (DCELLS, 2008d).

The underlying endemic problem

The endless succession of reforms has helped disguise a set of stubborn problems with the work-based route, which, on the whole, policy-makers have dealt with by ignoring. These include (see Fuller and Unwin, 2004; 2008 for details):

- A persistent attempt on the part of the state to combine (a) notions of apprenticeship as a high-status, employer-led route with (b) apprenticeship as a form of universal entitlement and as a social inclusion route to re-engage the disaffected youngster.
- Tension between two conceptions of apprenticeship – one, a contract and relationship between the young person and the employer providing training, and the other, the frequent reality of apprenticeship as a government scheme whose size is dictated by government targets rather than employer demand.
- Limited employer participation in the provision of apprenticeship places (only a small minority of employers offers such opportunities and public services).
- Limited employer involvement in the training element of apprenticeships, with the training and assessment component in the control of separate training providers.

- Large differences in performance between different sectors, although completion rates have been driven up by removal of the weakest training providers.
- Declining proportion of apprenticeships offered at Level 3, who currently form a minority of the apprenticeship places on offer in England – in contrast with most European countries where apprenticeship is almost exclusively a Level 3 route. (Many countries would not recognise many English 'apprenticeships' as such, since lower levels of training are being inflated into apprenticeship, thereby devaluing the overall concept of this form of provision and thus status.).
- Removal in some sectors by employers of the technical certificate (leaving just an NVQ and basic skills), and thereby the narrowing of the training on offer.
- The lack in English and Welsh apprenticeships, unlike in most other European countries, of a meaningful element of continuing general education, beyond numeracy, communication and information, communication and technology (ICT) skills. (In countries such as Norway and Finland apprentices are expected to continue to study their native language and history, a foreign language, and subjects like physics.).

This last point reflects a fundamental difference between English (and probably UK-wide) conceptions of vocational study for the young and those found in many other developed countries (Green, 1998; contributors to Clarke and Winch, 2007b). Elsewhere, the expectation is that choosing a vocational pathway does not mean waving goodbye to general education and focusing solely and narrowly on acquiring the skills needed to undertake a particular job. Indeed, continental traditions of vocationalism embrace the idea of learning as preparation for entry both to an occupation and also to citizenship. Here vocational study has come to be defined, not least by employers via their influence over the specification of NVQs, as learning to perform (competently) a bundle of tasks, the cumulative achievement of which fits the young person to perform a specific job. Such thinking has not only marked the design of apprenticeships, but also been reflected in the structure of the Diplomas, with their lack of any broad-based component of general education. This narrow conception of initial VET that employers are willing to encompass, and the message that this sends about their essentially limited demand for skill, leads us neatly to the issue of the structure of the labour market and of underlying levels of demand for skill therein.

Labour market structures and the incentives they create

The changing labour market

As noted in the introduction to this chapter, English 14–19 policy partly assumes that structural changes in the labour market will make such strong demands for skill that there will need to be a step-change in the rate at which they are fulfilled (Leitch, 2005; 2006; DfES, 2007). From this follows an associated belief that the labour market and employers' patterns of recruitment are creating material incentives (in the shape of reliable positive wage returns to qualifications) that will drive young people to make choices that will enable the desired change in 14–19 achievement to be brought about. Unfortunately, both of these policy 'givens' may be partially mistaken.

One of the most significant general failings of English skills policy over 25 years has been a refusal by those in charge to acknowledge and confront the realities of the labour market as it currently exists and is likely to continue in the short to medium term. The tendency has instead been to take an optimistic view. This means concentrating attention on growth at the upper end of the occupational spectrum, while ignoring the persistence of a large body of low-paid employment at the bottom of the labour market. Along with that goes constant reference to the demand for skills and qualifications generated by the all-encompassing, knowledge-driven economy which has either already arrived or is just around the corner.

The policy-makers' belief in this tale of a smooth progression to the sunny uplands of high-skill – and presumably high-wage – employment has been supported by a narrative produced by various commentators (e.g. Giddens, 1998; Leadbeater, 2000) which contends that globalisation and technological change are inevitably driving all developed economies in this direction.

The illusion of the knowledge economy

In reality, the knowledge-driven economy is, at least in part, a mirage (Nolan and Wood, 2003; Brown and Hesketh, 2004; Thompson, 2004). There are knowledge-driven sectors, occupations and firms, but the effect is not uniform or general across the entire labour market. While there has been and will continue to be growth at the top end in the professions and managerial work, large swathes of low-paid employment remain (and are set to remain) in areas such as personal services, cleaning, retail and wholesaling (which now employs about 15% of the work-force), and hotels and restaurants. At present, about 22% of the entire UK labour force are low paid by EU definitions – that is to say, earns less than 60% of the median hourly wage; with one-third of all female workers being low paid compared with countries such as France and Denmark, the percentage of our labour force who are low paid is relatively high (Lloyd *et al.*, 2008).

Moreover, calculations by the Institute for Public Policy Research (Cooke and Lawton, 2008) suggest that between now and 2020 occupational change will not produce any significant reduction in the overall proportion of the work-force that is liable to be low paid. They also note that occupational projections for the UK tend to point towards a continuing polarisation in the occupational structure, with growth in many top- and bottom-end occupational groups and a relative 'hollowing out' of the overall proportion of middle-tier occupations (and hence demand for Level 3 skills). Finally, the analysis also demonstrates that, at present, those who find themselves in low-paid employment are not easily able to progress out of such work, and for those that do manage to move up the job ladder, the amount of progression (in terms of any improvement in earnings) is often small and the longevity of any upward mobility uncertain.

The other point to make about the labour market is that it is not a uniform phenomenon across the UK. Different countries, regions and localities have labour markets that vary across many dimensions, not least the range of occupational openings that they offer and the proportion of jobs in different sectors and at varying wage levels that they support. There is some evidence (Green and Owen, 2006; Local Futures, 2006) that good, high-paying, high-skill jobs and low-paid, low-skilled work are both becoming more concentrated in certain localities, leading to a polarisation of the employment options facing some communities. This has two implications for 14–19 provision. First, the breadth and quality of opportunities available to young people via the work-based route in areas with a concentration of poor jobs may be attenuated, and similar problems may attend the provision of an adequate number and quality of work placements for those pursuing education-based vocational offerings. Second, in certain places the incentives on offer to youngsters to remain in post-compulsory E&T from many of the openings in the local labour market will be weak – a point expanded on below.

Recruitment, selection and qualifications

The clash between official expectations of the labour market and what are sometimes less glossy realities is made manifest via the recruitment and selection process. Insofar as official policy has a view of how young people move from education to employment, it seems to assume a straightforward 'best practice' meritocratic process based on the possession of formal qualifications. Unfortunately, what evidence we have (and it is patchy and poorly synthesised – see James and Keep, 2008) tends to paint a somewhat different picture.

Where the text-book model does apply, in some cases, it seems to work for jobs at the upper end of the occupational spectrum. In general though, it operates alongside other, less formal procedures. Data from the large-scale Workplace Employment Relations Survey shows that these informal processes include the use of word of mouth advertisement of vacancies (used by 44% of workplaces) and the recommendation of candidates by existing employees (used by 45% of workplaces) (Kersley *et al.*, 2006:72–73). Moreover there is often a strong logic to the use of such 'informal' methods, not least in deploying social networks to secure information on candidates' generic and social skills and work ethic that are poorly assessed by formal qualifications (Iles and Salaman, 1995; Lockyer and Scholarios, 2007).

This in turn underlines the fact that employers are aiming to acquire a range of skills, attributes and attitudes through the recruitment process, many of which bear a weak relationship with formal certification and which often lie outside the spectrum of skill that qualifications assess (Warhurst and

Nickson, 2001; Bowles and Gintis, 2002; Keep and Payne, 2004). These include creativity, physical strength and resilience, manual dexterity, social and communication skills, appearance, voice and accent, effort (e.g. willingness to 'put in the hours'), and a positive attitude towards authority.

There is evidence, too, that employers sometimes appear to harbour doubts about the degree to which some qualifications act as a good indicator of skills and ability, even when defined more narrowly. For example, a Learning and Skills Council (LSC) survey (Bates *et al.*, 2008) of large employers showed that they believed that Level 4 qualifications were generally a more reliable indicator of ability and skill than Level 2 qualifications and were therefore taken into greater account in the recruitment process. More generally, there is a wealth of evidence that suggests that the part played by qualifications in recruitment and selection for many jobs at the lower end of the occupational spectrum is patchy (e.g. EDA, 1997; IFF Research, 2000; Bunt *et al.*, 2005). The CBI claims that its members are often operating a 80/20 rule in recruitment, whereby employers afford an 80% weighting to uncertified generic and soft skills, and 20% to hard skills (CBI, 2007:13).

Do qualifications matter?

None of this is to suggest that qualifications are unimportant, merely that they are one factor among a number in recruitment and selection. For many jobs at the lower end of the labour market the process itself may be relatively informal and may rely upon social networks and forms of skill and job-readiness indicators that lie outside the ambit of formal certification. What it does mean is that lower level qualifications, particularly vocational qualifications, produce weak, complex and uncertain returns in the labour market and that any pay advantage they attract is often limited (Dickerson and Vignoles, 2007; Jenkins *et al.*, 2007), even when measured against the benchmark of the wages of those who possess no qualifications at all.

Moreover, what we know about recruitment and selection throws into stark relief the artificial nature of policy-makers' conceptualisation of qualification levels. For example, the idea that 5 'good' (A–C) GCSE passes represents a Level 2 achievement and that 4 'good' GCSE passes does not (and therefore renders the youngster unemployable or 'unskilled') may make sense to policy-makers who are using Level 2 achievement to assess and manage the performance of the education and training system, but may be a meaningless distinction for many employers when they come to recruit young people.

The somewhat depressing picture concerning the persistence of low-paid work and the nature of the recruitment and selection process has a number of serious but frequently unappreciated implications for 14–19 policy and for E&T policy more widely. These stem from the way in which the structure of labour market opportunities, the pay levels they generate, and hence the returns they offer on the acquisition of various types and levels of qualification produce an incentive structure that may not be particularly conducive to the kind of high-participation, high-achievement future to which policy-makers aspire.

Thinking about incentives

In trying to structure our consideration of the many different forms of incentives that face individuals when they contemplate engaging in E&T, the following typology may be of use (for a fuller exposition, see Keep, 2009):

Type 1 Incentives are generated inside the E&T system and are designed to create positive attitudes towards the act of learning through intrinsic interest. Type 1 incentives are bound up with things such as the curriculum, pedagogies, assessment regimes and opportunities for progression.

Type 2 Incentives are generated in wider society and the economy and the rewards they confer are external to the learning process itself. They include wage returns to particular types and levels of qualification, access to higher status employment associated with higher educational achievement, cultural expectations (including those of parents) about the value of learning, and forms of labour market regulation (such as licence to practise) that make the acquisition of particular qualifications a prerequisite for access to particular forms of employment.

Increasingly, government has noted that neither of these incentive categories has produced signals that are sufficiently widespread or strong to engender the desired step-change in participation. It has therefore increasingly come to rely on Type 1b Incentives, which provide government subsidy to act in lieu of Type 2 Incentives from the labour market – Educational Maintenance Allowances (EMAs) would be a prime example here.

Incentive patterns and their impact on 14–19 participation

The discussion so far leads us to a simple but stark conclusion – that young people who are not on the 'royal route' through A-Levels into higher education are left with Type 2 Incentives (the ones saying in essence, 'work hard, get qualified, get a good job') that are not nearly as strong and certain as policy-makers believe. As we have seen, the evolving structure of the labour market and the recruitment and selection behaviours of employers bear this out. There is further confirmation in the mass of data generated by many studies of the rates of return (in terms of higher average lifetime earnings) that accrue to different levels and types of qualification.

Overall, the message from this research is fairly simple and fairly stark. Having any sort of qualification makes people more likely to be employed than those without any qualifications. But at every level academic qualifications appear to generate higher average returns than their vocational counterparts. In addition, for lower level vocational qualifications, the pattern of wage returns is extremely complex and confusing and often depends on the reputational status of the individual vocational award, the occupation towards which it leads, the form of E&T through which the qualification was achieved, the location (education or workplace) in which it was acquired and who paid for it. In many instances the returns (especially to NVQs) are either somewhere between very low and nil, or in some cases actually negative (having an NVQ Level 2 sometimes appears to be associated with earning less than someone with no qualifications) (Dearden *et al.*, 2004; Jenkins *et al.*, 2007; Dickerson and Vignoles, 2007).

The foregoing suggests two things. First, acquiring at least some qualifications supports employability and this may help encourage young people who have failed to achieve this to continue into post-compulsory education. Second, and perhaps more importantly, the picture on the scale and certainty of wage advantage that lower level vocational awards confer is so uncertain and complex that the signals it sends are weak and confusing, particularly when compared with the rather simpler and more certain story that surrounds A-Levels.

Will the new Diplomas affect earnings?

From the perspective of the current reforms, a key issue is the wage returns that will accrue to the Diplomas at all levels. At the very least, the Diplomas need to appear to be worth studying and to offer positive enhancements to lifetime earnings. Evidence though is thin – none of the earlier attempts to create a set of general vocational qualifications – General National Vocational Qualifications (GNVQs), Advanced Vocational Certificates of Education and vocational A-Levels – has lasted long enough for a significant cohort of its 'graduates' to be absorbed into the labour market and so generate robust data on the relationship with earnings. However, it seems safe to assume that, on average, achievement of such qualifications will have made the young person more employable than someone with no qualifications at all. But if the mantra of 'parity of esteem' with the academic route (i.e. GCSEs and A-Levels) is taken seriously, this means that Diplomas will need to generate broadly similar labour market returns to their academic counterparts – something that the vast bulk of non-academic qualifications have never achieved. Even this test may prove a demanding one where Diplomas are leading candidates towards families of occupations in lower paying sectors of the economy (e.g. retail, health and beauty).

Massification of HE

Moreover, the law of unintended consequences comes into play when we consider the unfortunate juxtaposition of developments in the labour market (growing polarisation in job growth at the top and bottom end, hollowing out of middle-level jobs, poor progression opportunities from low-paid work, and rising geographical concentrations of bad jobs) with policy developments which have placed a heavy emphasis on the massification of HE. This is because as graduates cascade down through the labour market the range of relatively highly paid job opportunities available to those without degrees is gradually being reduced. This means that the incentives to going down the 'royal route' are if anything strengthening (not because the returns to degrees are necessarily improving, but because a whole range of career routes are otherwise closed off), while at the same time the incentives confronting those who cannot or do not wish to enter HE are becoming less powerful in terms of what labour market opportunities non-HE learning routes and qualifications will lead to (Keep and Mayhew, 2004). It should be noted that these opportunities will not only generally offer lower lifetime earnings, but also reflect weaker levels of other Type 2 Incentives, such as opportunities for career progression and development, social status and intrinsic job interest.

In summary, what we appear to be faced by is a situation where the strength and reliability of Type 2 Incentives tend to fade as we progress down both the occupational ladder and the levels of qualification. As the incentives weaken, so does the logic for post-compulsory participation, so that for young people who live in communities where the range of local job openings is narrow and often leads to lower end occupations, and for whom escape via HE entry appears an unrealistic or unappealing prospect, the reasons to stay on and try to achieve a qualification may not appear particularly compelling.

What to regulate: labour market or young people?

In many other developed countries, including the USA, Canada and Australia, as well as North European countries such as Germany, Austria and Switzerland, a very different Type 2 Incentive structure pertains, because of the extensive use of licence to practise labour market regulation. In these countries, youngsters wanting to enter particular occupations (car mechanic, builder, plumber, retail assistant, bank clerk) know that in order to stand any chance whatsoever of pursuing this goal, they must obtain the required Level 2 or 3 vocational qualification. Such expectations are often reinforced by other, wider societal and cultural expectations and norms, and in the case of some countries, by wage systems that mean that even lower occupational category employment secures relatively generous rewards. All this delivers a strong, absolute form of incentive to both participate and achieve. Much of the difference in the levels of post-compulsory participation and achievement that the UK tends to register vis-à-vis other OECD countries can arguably be put down to this absence of labour market regulation rather than to other countries necessarily having more sophisticated and engaging curricula, assessment systems and pedagogies that are delivering relatively more powerful Type 1 Incentives than are found here (Keep, 2005). If this is the case, then it suggests that much of the effort expended on English 14–19 reform over the last quarter of a century may have been, at least in part, misdirected.

The consequences of all this are that for far too many youngsters, the Type 2 Incentives that they face, particularly in terms of pay and career prospects, are fairly weak, especially for those following many Level 2 vocational courses. As a result, the following quote, from a study sponsored by British Petroleum some 16 years ago remains depressingly apposite:

> Much has been made of the need to place greater emphasis on post-compulsory vocational studies. The business community has been particularly vocal. The message is clear: in order to compete, we must improve the skill level of the British work-force. However, financial incentives to pursue these courses contradict the message ... the expected lifetime earnings associated with lower level vocational qualifications. ... generally fall below those of school leavers with only GCSEs. Employers do not seem to place a high value on low level vocational skills and, as a result, young people are acting rationally in not participating in training to the same extent as on the Continent. Quite simply, as long as some employers contradict the message through their pay and recruitment policies young people will continue to spurn such training.
>
> (Bennett *et al.*, 1992:12)

Despite a whirlwind of activity and reform within the field of 14–19 policy, the problem neatly outlined above remains every bit as important now as it was then.

Indeed, it could be argued that the government's decision to compel young people to remain in learning until 17 (and within a few years 18) simply reflects an implicit admission of failure on this point, and, rather than regulate the labour market, they have chosen instead to regulate young people, who are deemed easier to coerce than employers. The most likely outcome of this policy, besides a considerable level of non-cooperation on the part of some young people, is that participation may rise, but achievement may not. In other words, young people will be more or less grudgingly warehoused in some form of 'learning' experience until 18, but without necessarily experiencing any very compelling incentive to achieve anything during their post-compulsory phase.

Conclusions

We conclude – on what we believe is strong evidence – that much of the policy directed at the transition from education to work is based on a rather selective and rosy reading of current and likely future realities. If we are serious about achieving the desired objectives outlined above, then there is an urgent need to come to terms with the deficiencies that exist in terms of the demand for skills from employers. In many occupations at the lower end of the labour market, the fact is that the hold that qualifications have over the recruitment and selection process is often limited, and the returns to many forms of lower level vocational qualifications vary between being weak and being negative. Unless and until this situation changes, and it is by no means certain that the Diplomas will be able to achieve such change, the chances are that the desired level of progress will not be forthcoming.

There are, in essence, two ways of looking at this situation. One is to ascribe the weak, patchy and uncertain returns to many forms of vocational learning to a failure to design high-quality vocational courses and qualifications that employers really value. On the qualification front there is probably some truth in this, in that attempts by government to simplify and improve vocational qualifications through the introduction and subsidy of NVQs have plainly proved a major failure. It is noticeable that earlier forms of vocational qualification (i.e. those that pre-date NVQs) generally seem to demonstrate a higher valuation by employers and hence a higher wage return than NVQs (Dearden *et al.*, 2004; Jenkins *et al.*, 2007; Dickerson and Vignoles, 2007). Adherents to this view of the world, which predominates in policy circles, believe that the answer to the currently unsatisfactory picture on returns is to develop qualifications that employers really value, though in sectors and occupations where pay is endemically low, it is hard to see how this will solve the problem – no matter how well the qualification attests to the required skills, employers may well remain unwilling or unable to pay much for these skills.

The second way of viewing the problem (i.e. the one adopted in this chapter) would suggest that the heart of the problem lies outside the classroom, and that a polarised labour market will produce strong incentives at the top, and weak incentives at the bottom, and the E&T system cannot necessarily entirely compensate for this state of affairs. While further tinkering with qualification design might help to ease problems at the margin, the real obstacles to progress lie in the structure of occupations, their associated wage premiums, and limited ladders for progression. In other words, it is reform of the labour market rather than of education that is now needed.

In taking the line that we do, we are not suggesting that a better curriculum offering and improved forms of pedagogy, coupled with a more nimble assessment system are not worthwhile and valuable goals in their own right. We do, though, suggest that they won't be sufficient to power us towards what is desired. Only in combination with a reformed labour market and more uniform demand for skills across all occupations can they do that.

We have reformed curricula, qualifications and pedagogic regimes for this age group many times since the middle of the last century, and yet world-class levels of participation and attainment have continued to elude us. In a sense an analogy can be drawn with an attempt to design the perfect car, wherein ceaseless efforts are made to perfect the bodywork, upholstery and instrumentation, but with little if any attention paid to the design of the engine – which is small and low powered. The result is something that looks quite nice parked on the drive, but which is unable to travel any great distance at a reasonable speed.

We have seen that so much policy is driven by faith in a universal incentive that should work for everyone. 'Work hard, get the best qualification you can, then you'll get a better job, be happier, and earn more money'. We have seen too that there is abundant evidence of the flaws in that idea at both the supply and demand ends of the spectrum. So why does it hang on so tenaciously? All the way through this chapter, astute readers will have had one persistent thought that at least partly answers that, and which now can be articulated like this.

It is simply that most of our policy-makers, and many educationalists, were themselves good academic students, who followed what we called the 'royal route' through A-Levels to a top university. For them, that is the norm – it is the way things are. They tend towards the assumption that all learners will face the same strong incentives to achieve that they did, and will act in the same way as they did. As a result, the problems discussed in this chapter remain more or less invisible to them.

Recommendations

22.   The apprenticeship brand should be reserved for high-quality employer-based learning.

23.   More employers, particularly in the public sector, need to be encouraged to offer apprenticeship opportunities.

24.   During the economic downturn, however, it may be necessary for further education colleges to offer more strongly vocational full-time courses leading to employment.

10 Progression to higher education

Introduction

The possibility of progression from 14–19 into higher education (HE) is obviously important for individual learners, their schools and colleges and for the future prosperity of society. After all, over 350,000 18 and 19 year olds do proceed to university and other institutions of HE. Schools and colleges are assessed partly on the basis of their success in university entry. And economic prosperity and social well-being do need a highly educated work-force and citizenry. There are, however, questions which need to be addressed in the light of the available evidence.

- Is the school to HE transition as smooth as it might be? It may be impeded for a variety of reasons such as the general unpreparedness of the 'product' of 14–19 for university studies or the wrong choice of course to follow or of HE institutions to attend.
- Are there some 18 or 19 year olds who want to proceed to HE but are prevented from doing so? There may be barriers to progression which need to be addressed such as lack of aspiration and encouragement, or failure to receive good advice and guidance at school or college, or practical difficulties arising from location or finance.
- Does the pattern of entry to HE re-enforce the social inequalities outlined in Chapter 3 – or does it rather have a positive effect on them? Universities have a social role to play within the aims of education, as stated in Chapter 2, which is wider than that of extending the educational opportunities of individuals.

This chapter addresses these questions. First, however, it is necessary to give background information both on the diversity of HE provision and on the pattern of application and entry to those diverse institutions.

Background: diversity and participation

Diversity of HE provision

There has been significant expansion of HE in England and Wales in terms of the total number of institutions, the diversity of those institutions and the courses offered. In looking at both England and Wales a distinction should be made between an increasingly Welsh *national structure of governance* of HE institutions and an integrated *social system* of recruitment and participation which embraces both Wales and England (Rees and Taylor, 2006:371). Within Universities and Colleges Admission Service (UCAS) membership, there are currently 309 providers of HE courses in the UK, of which 265 are in England, and 20 are in Wales. These providers have evolved from the ancient universities of Oxford and Cambridge, the growth of the red brick universities during the nineteenth and the beginning of the twentieth centuries, the expansion of universities in the 1960s to meet the recommendations of the Robbins Report, the granting of university status to the former polytechnics following the 1991 Higher Education Act, to the more recent HE institutions (often former colleges of education). To be added to these are colleges of further education (FE) which offer sub- and full-degree level work.

To add to the complexity, there are 'selecting universities'. By this is meant that, such is the demand for places on some courses, the respective university department selects from applicants, all of whom are suitably qualified. Hence, there has recently been a proliferation of tests outside the normal framework of qualifications.

As we consider possible progression from 14–19 into HE, it is important for those providing information, advice and guidance (IAG) to be aware of this diversity across the HE sector. HE institutions provide different opportunities, offer different courses, relate differently to their local and regional communities and cater for different kinds of learner.

Because of the complexity and diversity, there is a need for each provider to be clear and transparent in setting out its mission statement, the details of its different courses, the requirements for acceptance, and (where they exist) the special links with employers. For some applicants to HE, transition from school or college is well informed; for others, the situation is far less satisfactory. This we shall explain in greater detail below.

Participation

Participation rates have increased exponentially in recent decades, with a large expansion from 1990 onwards. The overall number of UK-domiciled residents *applying* through UCAS to HE for full-time study rose from almost 365,000 in 1996 to 445,000 in 2005, a 30% increase (NR Annual Report, 2005/6). Subsequently, the number increased, but at a slower rate, to 454,000 in 2007. Within those application figures, Wales-domiciled applications rose from 19,390 in 2003 to 21,426 in 2007 (a steady proportion of almost 5% of applications). The overall number of *acceptances* rose from almost 258,000 in 1996 to 360,000 in 2005, also a 30% increase, and then to 365,000 by 2007. Acceptances of Wales-domiciled applications rose from 16,863 in 2005 to 17,366 in 2007. In terms of the age profile, the percentage of accepted applicants aged 20 and under (i.e. those making the transition from 14–19) has remained stable at some 78% between 2005 and 2007 (UCAS website).

Applications and acceptances, therefore, have seen a continued steady rise in absolute figures. In 2007, 93.6% of acceptances were for a full degree, compared with only 4.4% for a foundation degree and 2% for a Higher National Diploma (HND). The age profile of accepted applicants for Foundation Degrees is generally older than for degree- and HND-accepted applicants. The Foundation Degree is not yet a route of significance for the 18 and 19 year olds.

From the overall figures, five emerge which are particularly relevant.

Gender differences

The number of women applying to HE and being accepted has increased faster than the number of men, from 51% in 1996 to 54.1% in 2007. The Higher Education Funding Council (England) (HEFCE, 2005: Section 2.7), charts the growing divide in participation between men and women and confirms a more marked inequality for young men living in the most disadvantaged areas. This is compounded by the fact that young men are less likely to complete their HE courses and gain a qualification than young women. However, such a distribution does not apply equally across subjects. Entries to physics, chemistry, engineering and maths, according to the Royal Society (2008), are heavily weighted to men.

Range of 14–19 providers

Successful applicants come from a range of 14–19 providers – roughly 30% from comprehensive schools, 27% from FE (including the tertiary colleges), 7% from grammar, 9% from independent schools and over 11% from sixth-form colleges. These proportions have remained fairly stable from 2003 to 2007.

Socioeconomic background

Given the drive to widen participation, the socioeconomic background of applicants is important. In 2007, roughly 15.5% of total successful applicants came from the higher managerial and professional socioeconomic status, which includes 11.1% of the total active population, whereas 4.5% only came from the lowest socioeconomic category (routine occupations) and 11% from the next lowest category (semi-routine occupations) which include 9.4% and 9.3% of the active population, respectively (Hall, 2006). Clearly more needs to be done to widen participation in HE as one way of increasing social mobility of the least advantaged in society.

Ethnicity

The proportion of White British has decreased from an 82% share of acceptances in 1996 to 76% across the years 2003–2007, but there is an under-representation of specific ethnic minorities as 9.3% of total acceptances came from those of Asian background but only 5.1% from African/Caribbean.

Unsuccessful applicants

Although, in general, participation in HE is increasing, 19% of total applicants were unsuccessful (Wilde and Hoelscher, 2007) corresponding to some 90,000 applicants in each cycle. For these the system is clearly not working. Some re-apply in subsequent years, and some may enter part-time HE opportunities, but many are 'lost' altogether. Women, Black and minority ethnic groups and older applicants are over-represented in this group.

These statistics give an overview of who is applying to HE, and who is being accepted – an increasing number overall, more women than men, a disproportionately low number of students from certain ethnic minorities and lower socioeconomic groups, and a large proportion from the oft-neglected FE sector. But behind these statistics is a complex set of inter-linked factors related to progression to HE.

Progression to HE: is it as smooth as it might be?

Despite its growing size and complexity, the machinery for processing applications and acceptances is remarkably efficient. Four hundred and forty-nine thousand, four hundred and forty-nine applicants of the 2008 entry had their places confirmed within a day of receiving A-Level results, out of a total of 554,499. For a significant majority progressing from the 14–19 phase, the system works smoothly.

However, in other respects, there are problems. Qualifications and progression to HE are a key issue for politicians, parents, learners, teachers, HE providers and employers. This is evident from the annual debate in the press about A Level results and whether standards are falling. We need to ask, therefore, first, how the range of 14–19 qualifications, and the learning processes embedded within them, function in the transition from 14–19 to HE; second, what effect the proposed 14–19 reforms in England and Wales might have; and, third, what needs to be done to overcome some of the problems identified.

The qualification routes might be divided roughly into three, although any grouping has very rough edges – plus the new addition of admissions tests.

General Certificate of Education (GCE) A-Level route

There is a continued dominance of the GCE A-Level in the English system and Welsh Bac. Indeed, public perception and institutional reality are that GCE A-Levels are the 'gold standard' in providing access to HE. Of the 79% of 16–18 year olds who stayed on in education and training in 2007, roughly 40% were on GCE A-Level traditional and applied programmes.

However, problems have given rise to reforms. One problem is that A-Levels do not discriminate sufficiently between applicants with top grades. Another is that, following pressure to meet high grades for selection to some courses, there has been greater emphasis on 'teaching to the test', rather than on the learning processes. Yet another is the poor preparation, identified by the Review, for the independent learning required of university studies (see below).

Responding to problems

There have been several responses to these problems, namely, the proliferation of admissions tests by selective universities (see more below); a revision of General Certificate of Education (GCE) A-Level specifications from September 2008; the Extended Project as complementary to GCE A-Level; and the introduction of an A* grade to address difficulties experienced by selective universities in differentiating between students.

Extended Project in action

Early indications suggest that the Extended Project will be welcomed by HE as it aims to develop research, synthesis and evaluation skills currently perceived as lacking in new entrants. However, it is not clear how it will be used either by 14–19 centres or by HE. Will it be taken in addition to or in place of the typical fourth Advanced Subsidiary subject? Will HE use it to determine which students are made an offer? Will they specify a grade as a requirement in any offer made? Or will it merely be used for 'near miss' applicants at confirmation? Chambers and Lewis (2008) report that the answer to all these questions is 'maybe', but worry about the impact of its use on those students that HE is seeking to attract in its campaign to widen participation.

The A* grade in action

There is similar lack of clarity about the use of the new grade A*. The decision to use the A* depends on which HE institutions ask for it. Many admissions tutors will distrust predictions of A* in the early years, and some, who are admissions tutors to selective programmes, will prefer admissions tests over the A* grade (Chambers *et al.*, 2008:4). 'There is no evidence yet upon which to assess whether the new A* grade can be predicted with accuracy' (NCEE, 2008). This, of course, illustrates the challenges of introducing any new or reformed qualifications. On the one hand, learners and their advisers need a clear steer from HE on what admissions staff require; on the other, HE needs a minimum of five years to assess the impact upon degree performance, or fully inform admissions decisions.

Vocational routes

General vocational

In the context of widening participation and of the determination to raise the skills and knowledge levels of the work-force, progression to HE cannot be restricted to the traditional school-leaver, who has taken at least three A-Levels. For many HE institutions, A-Levels are but one amongst many qualifications used for entry. Here, we define a vocational qualification pragmatically to include the Advanced Vocational Certificate of Education (AVCE), Business & Technology Education Council (BTEC) and OCR National Certificates and Diplomas (including Scottish Qualifications Authority equivalents), and the former General National Vocational Qualification (GNVQ).

According to TLRP (2008), between 1995 and 2004, the proportion of students entering HE with a vocational qualification increased from 18% to 25%. However, over the same period, for those with vocational qualifications alone, the proportion dropped from 14% to 10%. Any increase is therefore due to students combining vocational and general qualifications, something which in itself may enhance opportunities for progression to HE, but which does nothing to confirm the status of vocational qualifications as entry routes in their own right.

Internal research within UCAS confirms that, whereas full information in respect of entry requirements is provided for GCE A-Level, far sparser information is provided for vocational qualifications. Table 10.1 indicates the position for 2006 entry in respect of BTEC and OCR Nationals, AVCEs and GCE A-Level.

However, according to TLRP (2008) students with vocational education and training backgrounds:

- are more likely to come from a disadvantaged background;
- are under-represented in terms of entry to high-status universities;
- do not progress to 'classical' subjects such as philosophy or languages.

Table 10.1 Number of institutions and courses specifying entry requirements by qualification type

Qualifications	HEI courses	HE institutions
BTEC National Diploma (18 units)	20,913	177
BTEC National Certificate (12 units)	16,692	141
OCR National Diploma (12 units)	6328	68
OCR National Extended Diploma (18 units)	8285	75
Advanced VCE (pre-2005)	30,307	259
Advanced VCE Double Award (pre-2005)	30,776	265
GCE A-Level	42,117	298

Diploma route

Again pragmatically, the new Diplomas might be included within the 'vocational category', for that is how they were first introduced – as successor to GNVQ, as a possible replacement for the equivalent BTEC and Edexcel awards, developed by the respective Sector Skills Councils and occupationally related with relevant work experience. It is too early to say how far Diplomas provide an alternative route into HE. Most HE institutions have prepared statements about the acceptability of Level 3 Diplomas, which are available via Course Search on www.ucas.com. But the time lag between implementation and use for entry to HE means there will initially be limited awareness of Diplomas across the full range of HE admissions tutors. Some institutions will be more reluctant than others to accept Diplomas until they are able to see the quality of learning that they embody. Even the partnerships, which developed Diplomas, are not entirely confident that all lines of learning will align with the needs of HE (Ertl *et al.*, 2007).

Advanced Apprenticeship route

To complete the picture, policy pronouncements support progression from Advanced Apprenticeships to HE, but rates of progression are still very low – at around 2–4% of advanced apprentices (Seddon, 2005). As an entry route Advanced Apprenticeships present considerable challenges in terms of information and, in particular, data on application and participation. This suggests that, despite policy intervention, it is difficult to secure progression from a work-based learning route.

Welsh Bac

The Welsh Bac offers an interestingly different scenario, as was described more fully in Chapter 8. Evaluations by Nottingham University (2006) point to the broadening of the learning experiences of the students. Acceptance by HE ranges from full recognition (Exeter and Aberystwyth Universities) to the demand for three A-Levels in addition to the core elements (University of Oxford). According to the Welsh Bac website, 'the number of centres and learners will increase each year, with the intention that at least 25% of learners aged 16 or over in Wales will participate in the Welsh Baccalaureate by 2010'. The Welsh Baccalaureate Qualification (WBQ) is also effectively taking on board the 'English' reforms as part of its optional component (which, of course, forms the predominant part). The real difference is that the WBQ core attempts to incorporate the 'missing' bits of the curriculum in a way that the Diploma attempts to do, but which is not mandatory in, say, an A-Level programme of study.

Admissions tests

For some years, certain universities and awarding bodies have created a range of admissions tests. These tests lie outside the regulatory framework, and in some cases, as they can be relatively expensive, subvert equality of opportunity. The implication of adopting such tests is that the qualifications and learning at 14–19 are viewed by HE admissions tutors as not providing sufficient information to guide them in their decisions.

The most up-to-date list of admissions tests currently in use in the UK includes the following: Biomedical Admissions Test (BMAT); UK Clinical Aptitude Test (UKCAT); Graduate Australian Medical School Admissions Test (GAMSAT); Health Professions Admission Test (HPAT); National Admissions Test for Law (LNAT); Scholastic Aptitude Test (pilot) (SAT); Sixth Term Examination Paper in Mathematics (STEP); Thinking Skills Assessment (TSA); a generic university admissions test (pilot) (uniTEST).

As well as these national tests, some institutions also run their own. According to Supporting Professionalism in Admissions (SPA), 14% of UK universities and colleges (45 in 2008) use one or more admissions tests. This percentage in itself is not large as it is averaged across the large number of courses and institutions. Its significance lies in the way in which admissions tests are increasingly being used by selecting institutions and courses.

The growth of admissions tests raises many questions relevant to progression from 14–19 to HE. What impact are these tests having on 14–19 provision? How are students and 14–19 institutions preparing for these tests? Where students feel the need for prior coaching, what are the financial implications on widening participation? There is here a lack of transparency on how universities use the tests, on the weight the tests carry, on their relationships to predicted results and to the other information on the UCAS application, and on their validity and reliability. Admissions tests seem to work against the full acceptance by HE of qualification outcomes from the 14–19 phase, and possibly – although there is little published research evidence available – against widening participation.

Progression to HE: are they well prepared?

Joint Nuffield Review/UCAS research (Wilde and Wright, 2007) conducted discussions with some 250 admissions tutors in 21 HE institutions. These revealed perceptions of the mismatch between the forms of teaching and learning in the 14–19 phase and those in HE. The key comment was a variation on the theme of 'over-assessment' and 'teaching to the test' prior to entry to HE. In addition, participants noted not only the level of knowledge held by students entering HE, but also their ability to apply that knowledge. Perhaps the key surprising finding of that research, considering the reliance of prestigious universities on A-Level results, was that the most selective universities also emphasised this issue. Further, the research revealed perceived problems with the extent and scope of students' study skills (including library use, time management, referencing and information technology skills). However, those interviewed acknowledged that some of the problems (such as instrumental approaches to learning, excessive focus on assessment and modular courses) are also problems within HE. They acknowledged the need, in the context of the expansion of HE, to adapt to the students at their institutions. And there are many examples of universities that are making strenuous efforts to work with their local schools and local employers, so that there can be a continuity of learning from 14 to and through HE into employment.

This piece of research calls into question certain assumptions. First, it questions the notion that the 'gold standard' of A-Level is working well. Second, it suggests that current policy initiatives, which focus on differentiation between the highest achieving A-Level students, do not address what focus groups perceived as the more important issues – those of approaches to teaching and learning. They emphasised the need for effective and independent approaches to learning, rather than instrumental approaches to passing examinations. Third, participation as a policy aim requires parallel measures for retention and attainment. All these issues point to the urgent need for greater emphasis on teaching and learning processes in 14–19 and HE.

On the other hand, there may be the need for HE to adjust the content of some of its courses to what is learnt in school. It is clear, for example, from the closure of several physics and chemistry departments that there are not enough young people attracted into science or at the right standard to meet the needs of the university departments. It may be necessary for the universities, rather than see departments closed and regions bereft of opportunities for the further study of science, to adjust their own courses. Schools seek to provide an education in science for all young people. It may be difficult to reconcile this with providing the specialist teaching for those wishing to pursue the subject further. Changes in the science curriculum of schools have encouraged more young people to want to continue with the subject. HE may need to make adjustments so that these students might progress into departments of physics and chemistry.

Progression to HE: is it fair?

The Schwartz Report (2004) stated that 'if we had a fair admissions system, then success will not depend on connections, money or influence, but on talent and motivation. This is a goal worth working towards', one reason being that 'there is an uneven awareness of, and response to, the increasing diversity of applicants'. Such fairness meant admission on merit (not on social class or type of school attended) but that merit needs to be recognised in the light of contextual factors which affect performance beyond the control of the candidate. In other words, merit depends not simply on attainment but also on potential. But there is the problem. Measurement of potential independently of attainment has posed problems ever since the rise and fall of the 11-plus examination.

Nonetheless, steps can and have been taken in pursuit of fairness in ensuring greater social inclusion compatible with the principle of selection on merit, although the picture is mixed. The report of the National Audit Office (NAO, 2007:6) found that, with £392 million given by HEFCE between 2001/2002 and 2007/2008 to institutions delivering HE for widening participation, there had been:

> ... improvements in the participation of some groups, but ... some remain significantly under-represented in higher education. The participation rate for men is currently 10 percentage points below that for women. Those from non-white ethnic groups are better represented than white people. Socio-economic background remains a strong determinant of higher education participation. ... People from lower socio-economic backgrounds make up around one half of the population of England, but represent just 29% of young, full-time, first-time entrants to higher education. Young people living in deprived areas have experienced an increase in participation of 4.5 percentage points since 1998 compared with an increase of 1.8 percentage points in the least deprived areas. White people from lower socio-economic backgrounds, both men and women, are the most under-represented group.

Just as 'education cannot compensate for society', nor can HE. Nonetheless, much has been done by UCAS to make the transition fairer. There is a debate as to whether items of further contextual data (e.g. parental education), as recommended by Schwartz, should be used in the admissions process. But, although some parts of the media suggest that this amounts to social engineering, and the independent sector fears places may be forfeited to students from the state sector, in practice a number of institutions are already taking into account the educational environment from which an individual makes an application.

Finally, from 2009 entry, there is a 'five-day window' after results are received, when those who do better than was anticipated in the conditional offer can make a further application to an HE institution which requires higher entry grades.

Factors affecting progression to HE

Complexity of decision-making

There has been an exponential growth in the numbers of institutions offering some form of HE in England and Wales, and a proliferation of courses available for study at different levels (degree, sub-degree and Foundation). There are also increasingly flexible pathways into HE. Therefore, the applicant is faced with making decisions based on many different factors – the kind and location of the HE institution, type of course, mode of study, financial costs and employment possibilities at the end. And these decisions, wittingly or unwittingly, begin early – especially at 14 with choice of General Certificate of Secondary Education (GCSE) subjects or of a more vocationally oriented programme. Therefore, an effective and well-informed information, advice and guidance service is crucially important.

For example, decisions made at 14 or 16 about the learning pathway affect future choice of HE institution. Nearly 60% of those who enter HE through the GCE A-Level go to pre-92 universities, and nearly 40% to post-92 universities (i.e. HE institutions given university status after 1992). The proportions are reversed where entry is through vocational qualifications (13.5% and 76.5%, respectively) or through a mixture of academic and vocational (36% and 58%, respectively) (Hoelscher *et al.*, 2008).

The UCAS form allows applicants to make five different choices. The choice, however, may be constrained by various factors: availability of courses or the need to attend a local HE institution or the perceived social and cultural environment. The choice of course, too, is influenced by different factors, including gender, and this in turn affects future life-chances in terms of earnings and career. Opportunity for part-time study could be important for those facing financial constraints, and the Open University, for example, now accepts applicants direct from school or college. But there is a dearth of information about part-time in comparison with full-time HE provision, and a current lack of financial support for part-time learners (Pollard *et al.*, 2008).

Financial worries will increasingly be a factor in decisions taken. Callender and Jackson (2005) found that those from lower social classes are more likely to be deterred from going to university because of a fear of debt. Garner (2008) claims that first-year students have annual debt levels of £5563 a year, and that the average debt across all years is £14,161. And, as Langda-Rosada and David (2006) claim, 'While upper and middle class male and female students live their university lives with a clear feeling of entitlement, lower middle class and working class students need to justify their economic dependence on the family and so their university status'. Variable tuition fees, together with loans, have indeed been in place for three admissions cycles, and in fact application figures have risen in England, whilst those for Wales and Scotland have remained stable or dropped. But social differences in attitudes to borrowing money to learn are crucial in this context. Hesketh (1998) and Hutchings (2003) argue that those from low-income families are more cautious about borrowing. This has an influence on the desire to live close to home or at home. Increased part-time working patterns on the part of students aiming to limit their level of debt may have a negative impact on their academic performance and psychological well-being (Marriott, 2007). Indeed, the National Union of Students (2007), reporting the UNITE student experience survey in 2007, showed that 43% of students believe that paid work adversely affects their studies.

Finally, for some, but not all, young people applying to HE, their intended progression to employment will be a key feature of their decisions. This is most clearly apparent in occupationally oriented courses such as engineering, medicine and law.

The effects of decisions and attainment at Key Stages 4 and 5

GCSE subject choice and level of attainment influence learners' decisions about the type of qualification and the subjects they progress to post-16. These decisions are significant for later progression to HE. The choice may be determined as much by what a school or college can offer as by individual preference. For example, difficulties faced by some HE institutions in recruiting enough students for single-science honours courses (particularly physics and chemistry) can be traced back partly to changes in Key Stage 4 choice patterns, and the decline of single-science provision in the state-maintained sector. A shortage of qualified science and mathematics teachers has meant fewer pupils taking single-science subjects as an option at GCSE and A-Level (UCU, 2006a). With regard to modern foreign languages, the government's decision to make languages voluntary from the age of 14 has sent out a signal to youngsters that it is not an important subject. The Dearing Report (2006) warns there may be further language course closures as a result of this. For many learners, therefore, decisions at 14 are constrained by what is on offer at school (including collaborative arrangements with the local college). And attainment at 16 influences subsequent decisions which set the learner onto one of the several HE entry routes. Hoelscher *et al.* (2008) report important differences in progression from different categories of qualification to different types of HE institution.

Perceptions of HE as 'not for people like me'

Educational histories shape HE choices. The decision to participate in HE is nurtured over many years, and cannot be conjured up in the final stages of compulsory schooling. Aspects of that history, which both constrain and enable choice to participate in and complete HE, include the economic and social conditions but in particular the enduring influences of family, peer group, institutional and class culture. These influences interact and have a pervasive and subtle influence on choices. Reay *et al.* (2005) highlight the narratives of choice of a variety of young people. Family culture is part of the interconnected network of factors that influence HE choice, including the 'deeply ingrained system of perspectives, experiences and predispositions family members share'. The educational experience of parents is central to this culture. Established middle-class families with parental experience of HE provided contexts of 'certainty and entitlement', 'in which going to university is part of a normal biography, simply what people like us do, and often too obvious to articulate'. By contrast, working-class families with no parental history of HE were 'characterised by uncertainty, unfamiliarity, lack of knowledge and often confusion in relation to the field of higher education' (ibid:67). The particularly active influence of mothers also emerged in the study. Parents have a significant influence and involvement through 'interest, influence and support, investment and intrusion', and for this reason IAG is important not only for young people, but also for their parents or carers.

Non-traditional qualifications

Hoelscher *et al.* (2008) argue that recognition of qualifications, which have not traditionally been considered by HE, is a problem. Admissions and academic tutors remain unaware of them. Some qualifications may be recognised as 'tickets' to a limited type of HE institution or course. Further, some qualifications, such as the Welsh Bac core, may be recognised by HE institutions, but as additional qualifications rather than as qualifications that, in themselves, fulfil entry requirements.

Progression routes from work-based learning (Advanced Apprenticeship) – for example, in engineering and nursing – into HE should be relevant. But rates of progression are still very low. Seddon (2005) puts it at 2–4%. Connor and Little (2005) say that it is 0.7% of successful Advanced Apprentices for 2002/2003 with a further 0.8% who have not completed the full framework. But there is lack of reliable data on these progression rates. Unfortunately, such possible progression receives little attention in the Apprenticeship Strategy document.

There is, therefore, need for greater understanding and recognition of non-traditional qualifications (i.e. qualifications other than GCE A-Level). This requires admissions staff to engage with the full range of qualifications, in order to ensure that applicants' prior learning can be fully recognised. This puts pressure on UCAS to ensure that qualifications are integrated into the UCAS tariff points framework. UCAS research shows that applicants with qualifications other than A-Level are more likely to be non-placed at the end of the application cycle. In particular, there is an increased risk of non-placed applicant status for those with 'only vocational courses' (Wilde and Hoelscher, 2007:3). Furthermore, the debate about differentiation between top-graded students at A-Level has distracted attention from the problems associated with progression to HE from vocational routes (Wilde and Wright, 2007).

Pre-HE institutions

Differences between and within institutions can lead to inequality – schools within the independent sector, for example, may offer more focused support for the transition to HE, particularly 'selective universities' at an earlier stage than other institutions. There is, however, increasing influence of the 'coupling' of 14–19 providers with HE institutions. But there are differences in the nature of that coupling. FE colleges' advice is shaped by the necessity 'to think local', while prestigious institutions may have strong links with Oxbridge, through teachers and former students (Bathmaker *et al.*, 2008:46).

Therefore, there would seem to be new forms of inequality. The question of 'who goes where and who does what' becomes more important within the context of widening participation. The number of young people participating in HE has increased, but there are enduring social inequalities within the highly differentiated field of HE that now exists. Ethnic minority students are concentrated in the new universities. More working class are participating, but in different Higher Education Institutions (HEIs) from their middle-class counterparts. In general, the expansion of HE has been of greatest benefit to the middle classes.

Strategies for improving progression to HE

For many applicants progression routes from 14–19 to HE may be smooth, with applicants facing relatively few obstacles. For others progression is more difficult. This is created partly by a lack of awareness by HE of vocational learning pathways in the 14–19 phase and also by the sense held by some learners that HE is 'not for them' (Archer and Yamashita, 2003). Therefore, various initiatives are attempting to improve that progression. The following are examples.

HE in further education and Foundation degrees

Two recent policy and subsequent institutional developments are inter-linked: the expansion of the provision of HE in FE colleges, and the introduction of Foundation degrees. This 'dual-sector' provision is also relevant to the widening access agenda: '... dual-sector establishments were seen to offer extended opportunities for access, progression and transfer, particularly for working class and non-traditional students who were the target of widening participation policies' (Bathmaker *et al.*, 2008:127). Furthermore, progression taking place within the same FE institution could be beneficial for students who might otherwise not make the progression to HE study. This could provide the vehicle for progression from apprenticeships to HE, which, as noted above, is very low, a point commented on by the House of Lords Select Committee (2007:34) in their assessment of apprenticeship. UCAS has attempted to extend the UCAS tariff to cover Advanced Apprenticeship frameworks, but the variability of those frameworks presents a considerable challenge to this process.

UCAS tariff

UCAS introduced the tariff to help bring about a fairer and more transparent system and to help HE institutions give guidance on admissions to those who seek to enter through vocational routes. The tariff is a points system, used to report achievement for entry to HE in a numerical format. It establishes agreed comparability between different types of qualifications and provides comparisons between applicants with different types and volumes of achievement. Its importance lies not simply in reflecting the range of practice relevant to entry to different kinds of course, but also in creating awareness of the kind of learning which otherwise would go unnoticed. It has had a positive impact on HE institutions accepting qualifications in addition to GCE A-Level (http://www.ucas.com/students/ucas_tariff/). In practice, however, there are outstanding issues, such as the fact that apprenticeship frameworks have not yet been fully incorporated into the tariff. And there is an inevitable time lag between the introduction of new qualifications and the accumulation of reliable evidence to support the tariff points ascribed to them.

Collaboration between the 14–19 phase and HE

In pursuit of wider participation, there have been many initiatives to over-come difficulties associated with a lack of smooth progression. Some of these have been initiated by government, and many have involved partnerships between universities, schools and colleges.

Aimhigher

The Aimhigher national programme, started in 2004, targets interventions at regional and local levels. The summer school programme is mainly funded by HEFCE. It offers a taste of university life to Years 10, 11 and 12 students, many of whose circumstances might lead them to consider only a limited range of subjects or institutions, or not apply for HE at all. Activities supported by the programme include visits to university campuses, residential summer schools, master classes and open days, and mentoring schemes.

Outreach

Outreach activities such as summer schools have been run by Aimhigher, as well as other charities and government initiatives such as Sutton Trust, Action on Access or by the Gifted and Talented Youth Scheme. Sutton Trust Summer Schools offer an opportunity to try university life for over 800 young people every year. The programme consists of lectures, seminars and tutorials but also various social activities. The programme started in 1997 at Oxford and the Trust has subsequently expanded it to Bristol, Cambridge, Nottingham and St Andrews Universities. Another example is the Dick Whittington Summer School at University College London, for Year 11 students based in London attending non-selective secondary schools and interested in studying Medicine.

It has been argued that programmes such as Aimhigher adopt a 'deficit position in relation to the attitudes and expectations of non-participating groups' and that ' ... a middle class standard is in place relative to which working class students are perceived as failing' (Baxter *et al.*, 2007:267/269). Again, the process of selecting students to participate is seen to lack transparency, a problem which HEFCE has addressed in guidance to Aimhigher Partnerships. Teachers often decide which pupils will be invited to participate, and this, so it is argued, may perpetuate rather than alleviate disadvantage and inequality of opportunity. However, no doubt such criticism could be levelled at any attempt to widen participation. Aimhigher certainly offers positive opportunities for young people to engage with HE, and to become better informed, and case studies would bear this out.

Compact schemes

Compact schemes are arrangements between HE institutions, schools and colleges that provide special conditions or consideration for entry into HE. Research by HEFCE (2008) confirms that 51 institutions offer some form of compact, most of them by single institutions, but some of them collaborative. They engage up to 60,000 learners in around 1700 schools and colleges and help at least 8000 people enter HE every year. The diversity of compact arrangements is arguably a key strength. They reflect the varying require-ments of the participating HE institutions and schools. However, HEFCE has called for more effective record-keeping and greater clarity by HE providers regarding the target groups and purposes of a compact. There is danger of *ad hoc* arrangements, without the necessary transparency for schools and young people to utilise compact schemes effectively. It is difficult to assess exactly how the compact schemes support learners in the absence of reliable data, but, as the HEFCE report claims, there seem to be clear benefits. The compact schemes support learners prior to entry, learners are better prepared and have a familiarity with HE that stands them in good stead on entry.

Partnerships

A variety of partnerships has been established between universities and their local schools. Hertfordshire University, for example, is an integral part of the Stevenage partnership with a college of FE, comprehensive and special schools – providing an accessible route from 14–19 vocational courses and Diplomas. Keele University through the Keelelink programme has enabled 123 schools and colleges to access activities such as homework clubs and e-mentoring. These partnerships have potentially positive benefits for all students in those schools, and not just for those who are considering applying to HE. The Russell Group of universities has a commitment to such partnerships. Its statement on partnerships (10 October 2007) says that they are:

> constantly improving and accelerating the raft of initiatives they already undertake to widen participation including bursaries, access courses and summer schools. We are particularly determined to help to tackle the root cause of the problem of the under-representation of students from poorer backgrounds at Russell Group institutions – the fact that they do not apply due to low aspirations or most importantly, under-achievement at school.

Subject associations

Subject associations have promoted a range of activities and networks to ensure that young learners will see the point of pursuing those subjects to and beyond A-Level. For instance, the geographical community has had a number of initiatives throughout the 1990s and 2000s aimed at extending the dialogue between schools and HEI: joint seminars run by the Council for British Geography (Rawling and Daugherty, 1996); 'Geography into Teaching Project' at the University of Northumbria, where geography education modules are part of a degree course; Qualifications & Curriculum Authority and Geography Association piloting, in 2004, a GCSE which encouraged work with universities; Action Plan for Geography – the Ambassadors programme where undergraduates and post-graduates act as ambassadors for the subject in the classroom. Other subject areas have opted for Ambassador schemes, for example, Science and Engineering and Modern Foreign Languages.

The importance of IAG

The Secretary for State for DIUS said that 'all prospective HE entrants need clear and accessible information about the lifetime benefits of HE, the financial support available, the choice of university and courses, and simply about what the experience of HE is actually like'. Yet time and again this chapter has pointed to where that is still lacking, though much improved.

Of course, the internet has, in the last few years, helped young learners enormously to find the different courses and institutions they would be happy with – most necessary because of the increase in courses, institutions and kinds of course. UCAS has played an important role in this through its request that all HEIs provide detailed and transparent entry profiles for all courses.

Chapter 7 gives details of the changes to IAG in the schools and colleges, and the way in which increasingly IAG is integrated into the curriculum rather than seen as an 'extra' to a crowded timetable. The up2uni project, funded by Aimhigher North West, is in its third year of providing HE guidance-related support to staff with responsibility for advising learners. They suggest that the best help government might offer to students and staff alike is to revive the concept of entitlement to effective IAG, guaranteeing staff the time necessary to deliver it and to profit from what HE institutions have to offer. There is a need for what has been referred to as 'compatibility of choice', that is, matching, in the students' choice of institution and course, their expectations with those of the HE institution (Ozga and Sukhanandan, 1998:322).

Hence, as stated in the government's IAG checklist (www.dcsf.gov.uk/14–19):

> good quality, comprehensive and impartial information, advice and guidance about these progressions routes is key to the programme's success. Poor choices of learning/career options or unresolved personal issues will lead to under achievement and/or drop out. Diplomas and other 14–19 options cannot be delivered effectively unless they are underpinned by effective local arrangements for the delivery of IAG.

Therefore, it is proposed that schools should appoint senior staff with responsibility for IAG, with staff undertaking HE-related professional development. HE institutions, as part of the collaborative partnerships with schools and colleges, should incorporate timely advice and guidance in all strands of their engagement. And schools, for their part, should encourage the ambition in students from lower socioeconomic groups to study at the most selective HEIs, and improve the advice given about 14–19 curriculum choices.

Conclusion

The chapter began with three questions. First, is the transition from school or college as smooth as it might be? Second, are there 18 or 19 year olds who would wish to proceed to higher education but are prevented from doing so? Third, is the pattern of entry to HE re-enforcing rather than ameliorating the social inequalities outlined in Chapter 3?

In many respects the answers to the questions coalesce into a general response. For many learners, there is adequate provision and few obstacles for them to progress to HE. However, some groups of student are hampered in their progression by some of the choices they find themselves making and the lack of IAG for specific groups. That in turn means that social inequalities are re-enforced. These specific groups include:

- *Young people applying to competitive institutions and courses where all applicants have the same predicted high grades.* Some of these applicants are required to take an additional (and sometimes expensive) test to provide a layer of differentiation over normal qualifications in order to facilitate selection. Current uncertainty about how the new A* grade will be used by HE makes such choices even more problematic in the short term.
- *Students taking qualifications other than A-Level, particularly vocational qualifications.* These are disadvantaged because of a lack of full information about entry requirements, the reduced opportunities for progression because of a lack of articulation with some HE provision, and, in some instances, academic snobbery.
- *Young people from backgrounds currently under-represented in HE.* Despite significant investment in widening participation, participation remains low for specific groups.
- *Students who go through the application process but remain unplaced at the end of the cycle.* It is not known exactly what happens to many of these, although some re-apply and are placed in subsequent admissions cycles.

Decisions made at 14 and 16 are crucial in determining the choices which will be available for the future if students subsequently wish to apply to HE. Choice of 14–19 qualifications, choice of HE institutions, and choice of HE courses will all affect future opportunities and it is critical that young people understand fully the potential consequences of the choices made. For all these reasons, IAG is critical for ensuring that all make the most informed and best possible judgements.

Recommendations

25.   All education and training providers, in conjunction with Connexions, need to develop more effective IAG services to ensure an appropriate match between student, provider and course.

26.   The growth of independent entrance tests needs to be curbed and the selection needs of HE institutions incorporated into the qualifications framework.

---

11 Institutional arrangements and the wider governance landscape

The organisational landscape in England and Wales

The institutional and governance arrangements for 14–19 education and training in England and Wales are complex and evolving. While the incoming Labour Government claimed that it would focus on 'standards not structures', in fact there has been continuous organisational transformation since 1997.

First, however, a word of explanation. By 'governance' we refer to the way in which government operates through a range of national, regional and local agencies in an era of what has been termed, by Kooiman (2003) 'policy steering'.

In England in particular, new types of education and training providers have been encouraged by central government (e.g. City Academies, Trust Schools, Skills Centres and 14–19 Consortia). These have been overseen by a fast-changing array of national and regional agencies (e.g. Learning and Skills Council [LSC], Quality Improvement Agency, Regional Development Agencies), together with new configurations of local governance (e.g. Children's Trusts). Even the title of the national ministry responsible has not remained the same throughout successive Labour Administrations – it began as the Department for Education and Employment, changed its name to the Department for Education and Skills and then more recently went through a more radical transformation by splitting into two Departments – the Department for Children, Schools and Families and the Department for Innovation, Universities and Skills – neither of which retains the word 'education' in its title.

In Wales, by contrast, institutional changes have been predominantly in the organisation of central government: most significantly, of course, the creation in 1999 of the National Assembly for Wales and the Welsh Assembly Government. More recently too, in 2006, the 'democratic deficit', which played a considerable part in the debates leading up to parliamentary devolution, has been addressed by the absorption of a number of 'quangos' into the Welsh Assembly Government itself. These included a number of organisations with responsibilities for education and training matters, including, most notably, Education and Learning Wales (ELWa) – the Welsh equivalent of the LSC – and the Qualifications, Curriculum and Assessment Authority for Wales (ACCAC).

In all of this change in the organisational and governance landscape, there are a number of underlying features of this aspect of the 14–19 education and training system in both countries that have remained constant. The majority of 14–19 learners in England and Wales still pursue their education and training in schools and colleges, with only a minority in work-based learning. Schools, including those in the independent sector (especially in England), dominate the political arena with further education (FE) colleges and independent learning providers playing a much less important role in the minds of most political figures and the general public as a whole. This is despite the fact that in 2007 the majority of 16–19 year olds in England and Wales were *not* studying in schools (as pointed out in Chapter 4). While policy documents stress the need to increase the role of vocational qualifications and apprenticeships (e.g. DfES, 2005a; DCSF, 2008c), employers still play a marginal role in this phase of education in comparison with countries such as Germany, Austria or Switzerland (Clarke and Winch, 2007a).

Different localities have varying combinations of providers offering 14–19 learning opportunities, depending on their history and political complexion. However, in all parts of England and Wales, local authorities (LAs) have been exhorted to provide a strategic plan for 14–19 provision in order to give learners more choice of institutions and qualifications (DfES, 2005b; WAG, 2008b). This has involved the encouragement of partnership between providers. National policy levers, such as funding, inspection and targets, drive provider behaviour in both countries and encourage institutional competition for learners, albeit in somewhat different ways in the two countries (Coffield *et al.*, 2008).

Beyond this, there are a number of additional features that characterise the English 14–19 organisational and governance arrangements, which are not prevalent in Wales. These include the government's active encouragement for diversification in school type (DfES, 2004) and its policy of 'sixth-form presumption' in the Education Act, 2005, which supports 11–16 schools and academies in founding sixth-form provision. Its continued, or even heightened, reliance on performance tables is used as a way of 'driving up standards' and increasing competition between institutions.

There is also a top-down approach to governance, which relies on unelected arm's length agencies, policy-steering mechanisms and institutional autonomy to shape the organisational landscape and 14–19 provision (Coffield *et al.*, 2008). An integral part of this centralised and marketised governance framework has been the role of quangos and private organisations as regulatory and implementation agencies. Of particular importance in the area of 14–19 education, where, as Chapter 8 indicated, qualifications play a leading role, have been the Qualifications & Curriculum Authority and the private examination and awarding bodies. These continue to be a site of controversy and organisational adjustment as the government seeks both to regulate the curriculum and, more recently, to make key national agencies (e.g. Ofqual) more directly accountable to Parliament.

The privileging of the national and institutional levels of governance over the regional and local levels has also been changing since 2004, with the introduction of a regional management tier in the LSC and, since 2006, with a reassertion of the importance of LAs as 'strategic commissioners' in relation to 14–19 education and training (LSC, 2004; DCLG, 2006). It is possible to see a strengthening of this trend towards devolution of power to the local and regional levels in the recent White Paper (DCSF/DIUS, 2008a), although, as we discuss below, powerful control will still be exerted from the centre.

Wales, on the other hand, has pursued a more traditional social democratic agenda in this area of policy since parliamentary devolution in 1999. For example, it has retained the concept of community-based, comprehensive schools as the basic mode of secondary provision. The power of competition between learning providers has been further limited through the abolition of performance 'league' tables. Moreover, the LAs have remained central to the system of service delivery, not least as the channel through which funding has been directed to schools, albeit on a formula basis (Rees, 2004).

This chapter describes in more detail the current and intended 14–19 institutional and governance arrangements in England and Wales, identifying the problems they face and analysing their strengths and limitations in tackling them. The conclusion debates the future for both systems and suggests that a devolved social partnership approach, together with strongly collaborative local learning systems, may help to build a more equitable and effective 14–19 phase in both countries.

14–19 institutional arrangements

While the governance and organisational arrangements in England and Wales differ to some degree, nevertheless, from the perspective of schools, colleges and work-based learning providers, both countries face similar challenges in terms of 14–19 education and training. As earlier chapters have indicated, post-16 participation and attainment rates remain a concern in both countries and, since the early 2000s, policy in both has stressed the importance of introducing a more diverse curriculum, with greater opportunities for young people to opt for vocational and work-based qualifications from the age of 14.

Taken together, these challenges of increased performance and new curricula highlight the need for institutional change. In both instances the national policy steer has been towards collaboration between schools, colleges and work-based learning providers (see DfES, 2005a; WAG, 2008b), rather than more radical reform, such as tertiary reorganisation or 'middle school' systems. Thus, a tertiary reorganisation would require all schools to relinquish their sixth-forms for a tertiary college to provide all forms of full-time 16–19 education and training. The last stage of a middle school system would begin at 14 (or 13 in a minority of cases) – possibly seen to be more appropriate where we are thinking of a 14–19 phase.

To date, however, in both countries, LAs and 14–19 Partnerships have been given considerable latitude in the model of collaboration chosen. This has meant that quite different institutional configurations have arisen in different local areas, as we discuss below. Whether these developments will adequately tackle the common challenges the two countries face is an issue we return to later in the chapter.

England – strongly competitive, weakly collaborative

Mosaic of providers

As Chapter 4 recalls, Fletcher and Perry (2008:8) describe the current configuration of 14–19 providers in England as 'a collection of bits and pieces' rather than a 'system' that operates collectively to meet the needs of all young people. This graphic description is used to highlight the diversity of the institutional arrangements in different localities across the country.

The situation is compounded by the fact that, despite the government's desire to drive national reform from the centre, its measures are mediated through the actions of a range of providers and agencies, thus resulting in varied patterns of responses. All LAs have been given the task of providing a Strategic Plan for their area, which ensures that all young people have access to the full 14–19 Entitlement. That Entitlement was confirmed by the 2005 Education Act. It entitles all young people to have access to Functional Skills up to Level 2 and all the Diploma lines in a local area. The institutional configurations they have inherited vary considerably. National figures about the proportions of 16–19 year olds studying in different types of institutions (see Table 11.1) give some indication of the range of institutional settings involved in initial post-compulsory education and training. What is striking is that, despite the prominence of schools in 14–19 policy documents, they only cater for 23% of 16–18 year olds. The largest provider for this part of the 14–19 phase is FE colleges. Independent schools, which enjoy a high public profile and are politically influential, cater for less than 5% of 16–18 year olds. Nevertheless, they are key providers of high-achieving students to prestigious universities.

Within this diverse national picture there are several configurations of partnerships in different localities. Some areas will have a majority of 11–18 schools with sixth-forms, others will have a more tertiary system with 11–16 schools feeding into a sixth-form, general FE or tertiary college and many will have a mixture of both types of arrangements. Moreover, the geographical area that an LA covers will vary considerably both in size (compare, for example, Lancashire with Tower Hamlets) and in socioeconomic make-up (e.g. inner-city Manchester versus rural Devon). Of necessity, therefore, LA Strategic Plans are diverse and a range of 14–19 collaborative arrangements has emerged in different parts of the country.

Table 11.1 Institutional diversity: where 16–18 year olds study

Type of institution	Participation in 2006/7
Further Education Colleges (general and specialist) Largest type of provider Wide range of full-time and part-time courses at all levels With particular focus on vocational and occupational provision Cater for adults as well as young people Often accommodate learners other providers reject Funded via LSC and private sources	27.8%
Maintained schools (e.g. community/specialist schools, academies, faith schools, grammar schools) Primarily offer A-Levels Smaller number of applied/vocational qualifications at different levels Varied size of sixth-form and, therefore, qualifications choice for learners Often selective in the sixth-form Funded via LAs, directly from DCSF or an element of private funding	18.6%
Work-based learning (e.g. Apprenticeship, Independent Training Provider, Employer Funded Training) Providers vary in size, type of provision offered and form of governance (e.g. large companies offering apprenticeships, not for profit organisations working with vulnerable groups of learners) Funded via LSC and private sources	11.5%
Sixth-form colleges (including a few tertiary colleges) Cater primarily for 16–19 year olds Wide range of A-Levels, fewer vocational and applied courses Often selective Funded by LSC	7.1%
Independent schools (e.g. fee-paying day and boarding) Have more freedom with regard to their curriculum and use of qualifications Primarily offer GCSEs and A-Levels Some experimentation with International Baccalaureate, International GCSE and Pre-U qualifications Wide range of extra-curricular activities Mainly selective in the sixth-form	4.4%

Source: Derived from Fletcher and Perry, 2008

Partnership development

A recent Department for Children, Schools & Families (DCSF) (2007a) publication has provided guidance on the definitions, roles, membership and functions of 14–19 Partnerships and has highlighted three current working models – 'county' (e.g. Gloucestershire), 'city' (e.g. Sheffield) and 'cross-border' (e.g. Hull and East Riding).

The county model

In this model, the formal commissioning role for provision rests with the LA and the LSC at county level through a Strategic 14–19 Partnership. Beneath this, a number of Strategic Area Partnership Groups are responsible for developing provision in their district or 'travel to learn' area and their plans inform the county Strategic Plan. The benefits of this model are seen as supporting the LA in its overall 0–19 role; effective links to post-19 provision and a degree of autonomy at the local level. The disadvantages are that it is resource intensive because of the different levels of management and will only work if the whole 14–19 Entitlement can be provided within the county.

The city model

Here the City 14–19 Partnership has the formal commissioning role for 14–19 provision, guided by a number of sub-groups (e.g. curriculum, information advice and guidance, learner progression, vulnerable children). This model works well if the whole 14–19 Entitlement can be delivered within the city and there is a strong FE college, but there is limited scope to commission provision outside the city and a potential for conflicts of interests because the Partnership is made up of competing providers and the LA may find it difficult to maintain a sufficiently neutral position.

Cross-border model

In this case more than one LA is involved: each has its own 14–19 Partnership and retains responsibility for commissioning for the young people in its area, but there is joint working between the LAs to develop compatible delivery systems across the different areas. This model is particularly pertinent for small unitary authorities, which need to work with others to ensure access to the full 14–19 Entitlement, possibly on a sub-regional basis. The advantages of this model are that LAs are able to plan provision to meet 'travel to learn' patterns, because there is a strong likelihood in a small authority that learners will want to cross borough boundaries to access relevant provision. However, it is potentially burdensome for providers having to deal with more than one partnership and LA and economies of scale are not always achieved because areas make separate arrangements with schools, colleges and work-based learning organisations.

While these models are useful as working examples, they only provide guidance at a high level of planning. Behind all of these lies a number of well-documented and considerable practical issues, including funding, quality assurance, information, advice and guidance, data management, employer engagement, work-force development and transport (Higham and Yeomans, 2006; O'Donnell *et al.*, 2006; Hill, 2008) which make partnerships working highly challenging. Moreover, as Hodgson and Spours (2008a) point out, of the five major policy levers used by national government to effect institutional behaviour – targets and performance tables, inspection, funding, qualifications and policy initiatives – the majority focus on individual institutional performance and support competition between providers rather than collaboration.

Hence the Review's conclusion that 14–19 institutional relationships remain strongly competitive and weakly collaborative (NR, 2007b). In this climate, it is still an up hill struggle for 14–19 Partnerships to build the 'trust' between providers that so many of the studies on collaborative working see as vital to success.

Perhaps it is not surprising, therefore, that the National Audit Office (NAO) commented that, while three-quarters of the partnerships claimed that they had been in existence for two or more years, 'there is a bit of a difference between setting up partnership structures and accountabilities and getting them working well to produce specific improvements in education for young people' (NAO, 2007:18). One-third of consortia still saw themselves as in the early stages of development, 40% bemoaned the fact that not all institutions in their area were participating in the partnership, often as a result of concerns about the relevance of the 14–19 qualification reforms to their institutions. This was particularly the case with grammar schools and other highly selective institutions. And collaboration with work-based learning providers and higher education institutions was still undeveloped in most areas. One of the conclusions of the NAO report was that a gap was likely to develop between those consortia that had been successful in the Diploma Gateway bidding process and would receive funding to support them in offering the 14–19 Diplomas and those who had not and would, therefore, not receive extra resources. More recently, Ofsted (2008b) has produced a report on 14–19 developments in 16 LA areas, in which it paints a more optimistic picture of the progress of 14–19 Partnerships. Most had improved access to a wider range of provision, particularly pre-16, but with gaps persisting in work-based learning post-16 and for Entry and Level 1 programmes.

Performance, equity and cost

Two other studies raise bigger questions for 14–19 institutional arrangements in relation to learner performance, equity and cost. Schagen *et al.* (2006), in a national study for the National Foundation for Educational Research, sought to assess the role of institutional patterns on the performance of 16–19 learners in England. They concluded that when social background and ability were taken into consideration, there was no significant difference in participation rates between areas with high numbers of school sixth-forms and those with none or very few, despite the popular perception that 11–18 schools encourage post-16 participation.

Fletcher and Perry (2008:21) bring together evidence from this and a number of other studies to demonstrate that 'the more selective the local system the more participation is depressed'. They use this as part of their argument against the government's policy of 'sixth-form presumption', referred to in Chapter 4. They also show how the existence of a variety of institutional types in an area leads to inequity because school sixth-forms and sixth-form colleges contain more White and middle-class learners than general FE colleges and the latter receive less funding for equivalent provision. Inequity is compounded by the fact that learners on lower level programmes are less well resourced than those on Level 3 programmes.

Fletcher and Perry are also sceptical about partnership working. 'The overall, but not universal, pattern is one of limited and tactical involvement where participants' engagement is sustained by external funding and qualified by institutional self-interest' (ibid:30). They express concern about partnerships' lack of focus on both outcomes for all learners and value for money, which is exacerbated by the government's policy emphasis on institutional choice in a time of demographic downturn in numbers of 14–19 year olds. For this reason they conclude that 'there is little prospect of partnerships tackling difficult issues where institutional interests strongly diverge' and argue, therefore, for LAs (either individually or in clusters) to have strengthened powers to create 'managed tertiary systems' (ibid:46/47).

So how do we square the government's enthusiasm for 14–19 collaboration with researcher scepticism for partnership working? Is it just, as government publications and pronouncements imply, something that will be resolved with the passage of time and by newer partnerships learning from more advanced ones, or are there more fundamental limitations to a 14–19 system based on institutional collaboration? In the final part of this chapter we suggest that 14–19 partnership alone is not a panacea but that, together with changes to policy on qualifications, governance and accountability, it may constitute part of the solution.

England – complexity and the difficult role for the LA

The governance arrangements for 14–19 education and training in England have seen major shifts over the last two decades. From 1988 and the Education Reform Act, local education authorities (LEAs) took a back seat, as central government played a more interventionist role in curriculum and organisational matters and increased autonomy was given to individual providers. The downgrading of the role for LEAs in education and training was compounded in 2001, when the LSC was given the major responsibility for planning of all post-16 provision at the local level. In 2005, however, the 14–19 White Paper (DfES, 2005a), the 14–19 Implementation Plan (DfES, 2005b) and even to some extent the Schools' White Paper (DfES, 2005e) appeared to recognise the importance of LAs, as well as local LSCs, in guaranteeing the 14–19 Entitlement across an area. The apparent rehabilitation of LAs was further reinforced with the publication of the DfES (2003b) *Every Child Matters* in which they were charged with coordinating local services for children and young people, and by the local government White Paper in 2006 (DCLG, 2006), which emphasised the importance of this tier of governance. The most recent White Paper in this area, *Raising Expectations: Enabling the System to Deliver* (DCSF/DIUS, 2008a), follows this trend by proposing to give

LAs primary responsibility for the 14–19 phase, although it still does not fund some of the providers (e.g. work-based learning and voluntary organisations or the majority of FE college provision).

These are still proposals, however, and the overall effect of policy on governance over the past 20 years has been a hollowing out of local government, as the national and institutional levels have become more dominant. Nevertheless, over the last couple of years, the present Administration, and more particularly under Gordon Brown, has come to realise that it cannot do without local government. Its answer has been to mould LAs into its 'modernisation' agenda with their roles as 'commissioners' and 'integrators' of services. Even the Local Government Association (LGA) has adopted the language of modernisation by describing LAs as 'community leaders' and stating that it does not want to 'regain old or lost territory' (LGA, 2007). It is within this new and more contested context that LAs are being expected to provide a strategic lead at the local level. There are, however, a number of potential difficulties with LAs playing their new role in relation to 14–19 education and training.

Over the last few years, as their responsibility for 16–19 education was reduced, LAs shed many (sometimes all) of their post-16 specialists or in the words of the LGA: 'Over the past decade, staff, skills and resources have been stripped out' (LGA, 2004:16). Many unitary LAs are very small and simply do not have the staff to carry out the kind of functions envisaged for them. Moreover, LAs in 2008 are very different from LEAs in 1988. Whereas LEAs were dedicated funders, providers and planners of education, education provision is now only part of the brief of the new Children's Trusts. Hodgson and Spours (2008a:x) cite a policy-maker as saying:

> They're (LAs) undergoing great changes at the moment into Children's Services and so what used to be a LEA with teams that had education as their centre, has now become part of a much larger structure and smaller units. 14–19 development has got lost in that change and what we're finding is that 14–19 teams are disappearing in terms of status and clout and you do have to have clout to bring about change.

In their new role as 'strategic commissioner', LAs will be required to produce a local commissioning plan for the education and training of young people, which will form 'part of the integrated regional strategy for economic development' (DCSF/DIUS 2008a: para. 2.5). In recognition of the fact that many young people will be in non-school learning environments and may wish to travel beyond LA boundaries in order to study or train, it is suggested that there should be a role for decision-making at sub-regional, regional and national, as well as local level. This will be important with regards to the involvement of FE colleges, work-based learning providers, youth services and voluntary and community organisations that often work at the sub-regional or regional levels. LAs will be expected to cluster together in sub-regional groupings to commission provision. At regional level, LA clusters will be expected to work with the Regional Development Agency, the regional Government Office and the new Skills Funding Agency, which will fund adult skills, to develop a regional strategy.

In addition, a new national organisation, The Young People's Learning Agency, will be given responsibility for funding local plans and for arbitrating between LAs. A further new agency, the National Apprenticeship Service, which will be under the Department for Innovation, Universities and Skills (DIUS), will be established to provide apprenticeship places to ensure that all suitably qualified 16 and 17 year olds have access to their entitlement of an apprenticeship. These new organisations replace the LSC and will come into operation from September 2010.

As we have just seen, below this increasingly complex and evolving governance landscape lies a mosaic of institutions, many of which are funded by LAs (e.g. community schools), some of which are funded directly by the DCSF (e.g. academies), colleges funded by the LSC (in future by a mixture of the Skills Funding Agency and LAs) and independent learning providers supported by a range of government and non-government sources (see Chapter 4 and Chapter 9 for more details). All of these providers have a high degree of autonomy and are primarily responsible to their individual governing bodies. Moreover, recent policy has stressed the importance of a 'self-regulating' FE sector (see Foster, 2005).

So, while LAs have been given a statutory responsibility for delivering the 14–19 Entitlement, it is not clear what powers they will have to enforce it or to ensure the introduction of all Diploma lines within a local area. As we argued earlier, schools, colleges and work-based learning providers have considerable incentives to pursue their own agendas and specialisms. Strong national policy levers and drivers, which encourage institutional competition (e.g. performance measures and funding), remain in place while, as Perry and Simpson (2006) observe, there are few area-wide mechanisms that impact directly on schools and colleges, and the ones that do exist are weak.

The ability of LAs, therefore, to provide a level of governance above that of the individual institution is still limited. Furthermore, whoever is leading 14–19 at the local level in the future is going to face three tough decisions over and above the practical issues we have raised so far. First, what balance is to be struck between young people's choice of institution and their choice of provision in a period of declining numbers of 14–19 year olds? Second, how possible is it to reconcile choice and cost-effectiveness (Stanton and Fletcher, 2006)? Finally, is voluntary collaboration between providers sufficient to ensure that the needs of all young people in a local area are equitably served? Might there need to be stronger policy steers at local, regional and national levels to build the strongly collaborative local learning systems the Review has argued for (NR Annual Report, 2005–6; NR, 2007)?

Wales: trying to be strongly collaborative

In Wales, as we have seen, the approach to provision for 14–19 year olds has followed a different trajectory from that in England. In some key respects, the Welsh Assembly Government has attempted to adopt a more strongly collaborative system for delivering learning opportunities at the local level. It is important not to overstate the case here; what central government in Wales has set out to do is only imperfectly reflected in actual developments on the ground (at least, up until now). Nevertheless, Welsh experience does provide a useful comparison with that in England, and offers the prospect of casting new light on the potential of collaborative approaches in general.

The commitment to managing the delivery of learning opportunities for 14–19 year olds by means of collaboration between schools, FE colleges and training providers has been a key element in the strategy of the Welsh Assembly Government almost since its inception (WAG, 2001a; WAG, 2002a). As we have seen in Chapter 8 and elsewhere, the principal embodiment of this collaborative approach has been through the 14–19 Learning Pathways. The Pathways are seen as a vehicle for making available to learners a wide range of learning opportunities, which extends substantially beyond the 14–19 Entitlement in England. In Wales, it is intended that learners have access to local 'menus' that embrace not only academic and vocational programmes, but also a range of forms of learning, including formal, non-formal and informal modes. This, in turn, is seen to be key to raising learners' engagement and levels of participation post-16; and to producing the school- and college-leavers who are equipped to enter higher education and to meet the needs of employers and of the Welsh economy more widely (WAG, 2006a; WAG, 2006b).

In practical terms, for each of the 22 LA areas in Wales, 14–19 Networks are required to produce an Annual Network Development Plan that shows how the requirements of the Learning Pathways are actually being put into effect in their area. These Plans are subject to approval by the Welsh Assembly Government. It can be seen, therefore, that each Network has a strategic role in policy delivery; and, as such, the Networks are required to secure appropriate representation of the various providers of learning opportunities, as well as of other groups with a stake in the effective delivery of education and training, such as Careers Wales, learning coaches and other statutory agencies such as youth offending services.

What is most striking in terms of governance here is that the delivery of a broad set of curriculum choices to each *individual* learner is clearly seen to imply forms of *collective* provision that necessarily depend on close cooperation between schools, colleges and private training providers. This collective provision has to be effective at a *local* level, in order to ensure that access to the range of learning opportunities is realistic for the overwhelming majority of 14–19 year olds. In part, this reflects a rather deep-seated *ideological* commitment to collaborative forms of public service delivery in general; indeed, this approach is embodied in the Welsh Assembly Government's 'Making the Connections' policy on services delivery as a whole (Beecham Review, 2006). Welsh politics continues to be dominated by a broadly social democratic consensus, into which the competitive models favoured by New Labour – let alone neo-liberalism – have made only very limited inroads (Drakeford, 2005).

Equally, however, the emphasis on collaborative strategies for 14–19 provision is an essentially pragmatic response to the specific circumstances that characterise contemporary Wales. More so than in England, demographic shifts mean that many schools in Wales have falling pupil numbers. Estyn recently estimated that, in consequence, over 23% of schools had significant numbers of surplus places; whilst only 47% of sixth-forms in Wales were operating at or above the level of 150 pupils, which the Audit Commission has identified as the minimum size for effective operation (Estyn, 2007a). Similarly, many of the FE colleges in Wales are relatively small – especially when compared with those in England – with some 25 institutions providing for almost 30,000 full-time and 8000 part-time 16–18 year old students.

What all of this implies, therefore, is that it has proved extremely difficult for individual institutions to provide a full range of learning opportunities. In particular, access to vocational programmes has been restricted in some areas and this has been reflected in relatively low participation rates after 16. This has been recognised as a significant problem for some considerable time, especially given the poor performance of the Welsh economy in relation to the UK average (Rees, 2002).

There can be little doubt as to the Welsh Assembly Government's commitment to achieving the rather strong forms of collaboration implied by the 14–19 Learning Pathways, with, for example, significant investment (some £74 million over the three years up until 2008) in the piloting and facilitation of the initiative, in addition to the 'normal' funding going to 14–19 provision – which itself is estimated to be well over £500 million annually (NAWFC, 2008).

Moreover, there are some grounds for arguing that achieving such strong collaboration is likely to be easier in Wales than in England (although the latter has presumably benefited from the collaborative planning associated with the development of the Diplomas, which are not being adopted in Wales).

The institutional configuration of Wales is much simpler than that of England. For example, the independent schools sector does not play a significant role; secondary schools are predominantly 11–16 or 11–18 community-based comprehensives. There is a single funding system for sixth-forms and FE colleges, namely, the National Planning and Funding System, which has progressively moved towards a common basis of funding for both types of institution. And the LAs have retained throughout a significant role in the organisation and delivery of educational services to a much greater extent than in England (although, of course, as in England, the FE colleges in Wales are independent and responsible directly to the Welsh Assembly Government).

Despite these favourable circumstances, however, fulfilling the collaborative agenda of the 14–19 Learning Pathways has proved difficult. Undoubtedly, there has been very significant progress in some areas, where, for example, common timetables and effective transport arrangements have substantially increased the range of learning opportunities available, especially to 16–18 year olds. However, such developments remain patchy. Indeed, it was the unevenness of activity between local areas which prompted the Welsh Assembly Government to adopt a more regulatory role at the national level in 2006 (WAG, 2006a).

Moreover, research by Estyn in 2006 suggested that only 36% of schools with sixth-forms in Wales were collaborating actively with FE colleges; and this collaboration was confined mainly to the provision of a small number of A-Level options for some 5% of sixth-formers. The implication of this is that the provision of vocational options has continued to be difficult, with little evidence of increased numbers of learners combining general education with vocational options. Whilst levels of participation post-16 have been rising in Wales (as in England), it is not as yet clear how far this is attributable to changes brought about through the 14–19 Learning Pathways. Similarly, it is not clear the extent to which collaboration has improved the quality of learning or the levels of attainment achieved by learners (Estyn, 2006).

It is reasonable to expect that there has been further progress towards more effective collaboration across a wider range of local areas during the period since this research was carried out. Nevertheless, the Webb Review (2007) recommended that it was necessary to establish new, more powerful consortia at the local level that would ensure that effective collaboration would be achieved by linking funding to the achievement of this objective.

Moreover, whilst the Welsh Assembly Government recently announced that it will not be accepting this recommendation fully (DCELLS, 2008a), it has nevertheless made clear that it continues to seek ways of *ensuring* that effective collaboration does take place. The Government of Wales Act of 2006 provides powers to the National Assembly to enact its own legislative measures in those policy areas delegated to it by the Westminster Parliament. Accordingly, the Assembly Government is currently progressing a Learning and Skills (Wales) Measure, which will not only provide a legal entitlement for 14–19 learners to choose a programme of study from an extensive local curriculum, but will also require LEAs and the governing bodies of schools and FE colleges to consider cooperation in order to maximise the availability of courses of study within local curricula. Clearly, then, there is a recognition that there remains 'unfinished business' with respect to achieving effective collaboration; but equally, there appears to be a continuing commitment to resolving this.

In order to achieve this, however, some fundamental issues will need to be addressed. Firstly, as the Webb Review recognised, it is not easy to devise structures of collaboration which are able *both* to provide a range of curriculum options sufficient to fulfil the preferences of individual learners *and* to supply the skills necessary to meet the needs of employers and those of the Welsh economy more widely (Webb Review, 2007, ch. 6 and 7). In part this is a matter of scale. Given the small size of the LAs in Wales (22 to serve a population of only some 3 million), it is already recognised that significant collaboration across LA boundaries will be necessary to enable the provision of an adequate menu of learning options, despite the travel difficulties that this will pose for learners in some areas – the 'cross-border model' referred to earlier in the chapter.

However, even combining across LA boundaries in this way will not guarantee that the forms of provision necessary to meet the skills demands of employers will be available in each local area or even across Wales as a whole. This disjuncture is likely to be especially acute where specialised skills are required; or where economic development entails increasing demand for skills necessary for jobs that will only become available at a future date as a result of new economic development. Equally, however, whatever the scale at which the delivery of learning opportunities is planned, the Welsh experience highlights the fact that there is a general tension between responding, on the one hand, to students' preferences and, on the other, to employers' demand for skills or some other measure of wider economic needs (Rees *et al.*, 1989).

Secondly, again as the Webb Review recognised, the balance between local autonomy and central regulation needs to be drawn very carefully. As we have seen, wider circumstances in Wales provide an environment which, in key respects, is more conducive to fostering collaboration in the delivery of local learning opportunities than that in England. Nevertheless, it is clear that, at best, progress towards achieving effective collaboration between learning providers at the local level has been uneven and patchy. It remains to be seen how far further progress towards effective collaboration can be made, whilst maintaining what remain in Wales – as in England – essentially voluntaristic arrangements for cooperation between schools, colleges and training providers.

Future institutional and governance arrangements in England and Wales

It is clear, therefore, that institutional and governance arrangements in England and Wales diverge in some significant respects and are arguably becoming more distinctive. Nevertheless, the very practical problems 14–19 Partnerships face, such as working towards a common timetable across a number of providers, organising transport to move young people around to access specialist provision and deciding which courses should be offered by which partnership institution, are the same for schools, colleges and work-based learning providers in both England and Wales, although the Welsh Assembly Government's approach has been more coherently focused on doing so. Moreover, most significantly, neither country can legitimately claim they have successfully tackled the participation and attainment challenges that the different 14–19 curricula reforms in each country require.

The fundamental debate for this area in both countries remains one of institutional autonomy and markets versus a more planned 14–19 system. Within this, there are decisions to be made about the role of the various agencies involved in governance at the local, regional and national levels. In this final section of the chapter we explore a possible model for the future. In doing so, we bring together two related concepts – 'strongly collaborative local learning systems' and a 'devolved social partnership approach' to governance, in order to provide an analytical framework for building more equitable and effective 14–19 governance and institutional systems in England and Wales.

Strongly collaborative local learning systems

The Review 2006 Annual Report characterised 14–19 partnership arrangements in England and Wales as 'weakly collaborative' and contrasted them with a model of strongly collaborative 14–19 local learning systems, developed from ideas and practices advocated in the Tomlinson Final Report (2004) and evidence from practitioners, policy-makers and researchers gathered as part of the Review (see Table 11.2).

The Review concluded that some progress had been made in England in relation to Dimensions 1 (vision), 3 (planning and organisation), 4 (pedagogy and leadership) and 5 (learning environments and communications systems). Less progress, however, had been made on Dimensions 2 (qualifications and assessment) and 6 (accountability frameworks including league tables). These latter two dimensions, arguably, are the most powerful because, in combination, they have a major influence on the competitive relationships between institutions. As we have discussed in Chapter 8 and earlier in this chapter, neither is fully within the control of local consortia. Even where partnerships develop a stronger local strategy, it has been constrained by national qualifications and accountability policies (Hill, 2008).

The Welsh profile is somewhat different. The 14–19 Learning Pathways policy is quite explicitly aimed at achieving something very close to the strongly collaborative model. Moreover, this is consistent with the Welsh Assembly Government's wider strategy on public service delivery and engaged citizenship, which, in turn, reflects its continuing commitment to quite traditional, social democratic forms of governance. However, it is salutary to reflect that, even with this degree of commitment from central government, it has actually proved difficult to implement this sort of model. As we have seen, whilst there has been progress on all of the Dimensions outlined in Table 11.2 in some areas of Wales, none of the 22 LA areas could claim to meet all of them and in some areas developments have been rather limited. It remains to be seen how far new central government regulation – through, for example, the envisaged Learning and Skills (Wales) Measure – will succeed in effecting a more consistent and enhanced implementation of its strongly collaborative agenda.

Table 11.2 Dimensions of weakly and strongly collaborative 14–19 learning systems

Dimensions and examples of local actions	Weakly collaborative	Strongly collaborative
1. *Vision, purposes and underpinning principles* e.g. Vision statements for the curriculum and for 14–19 partnership Learner entitlement statements	Vision statements and learner entitlements largely confined to the government agenda of providing 'alternative' learning experiences.	Vision statements and learner entitlements cover all aspects of 14–19 learning, including GCSEs and A-Levels, and attempt to take a more unified and integrated approach to learning.
2. *Curriculum, qualifications and assessment* e.g. Mapping provision Building progression routes Deciding on a Diploma offer Strengthening vocational provision	Development of vocational pathways and programmes from 14+ for some learners. A primary goal is motivating disaffected 14–16 year olds, using college and work-based provision.	Developing holistic programmes across all types of learning with a focus on more flexible, applied and practical approaches for all learners from 14+.
3. *Planning, funding, organisation and governance in 'a local area'* e.g. LAs, LSCs and Connexions working together to deliver the Entitlement Forming partnerships and clusters Developing local prospectuses Making decisions about funding collaborative learning opportunities	Confused or contested relationships between LAs, LLSCs and providers, with lack of clarity about local leadership. Partnerships and clusters are under-developed, dependent on external funding and easily destabilised (e.g. by institutional competition or changes in key personnel).	Clear and accepted local governance arrangements with a high degree of collaboration between LAs, LLSCs, local providers and wider partners (e.g. Connexions, employers, voluntary and community organisations), thus increasing governance capacity and leadership.
4. *Professionalism, pedagogy and leadership* e.g. 14–19 pathfinders Learning visits Development networks and joint CPD	Conformity to government reform agenda without a strong professionally informed sense of what is required at the local level. Limited leadership and CPD, with a dependence on nationally generated support and key local individuals.	Strong sense of local professionalism, leadership and a shared knowledge of the area; a more reflective, longer term, planned and locally generated approach to capacity building using pooled local and national funding and locally agreed tariffs for learner programmes.
5. *Physical learning environments and communications systems* e.g. Building new skills centres Building Schools for the Future ICT infrastructure Pooling funding for shared resources or specialisms	New infrastructure arrangements are driven by institutional self-interest and incentivised by national funding (e.g. vocational and ICT facilities developed on a competitive basis and dispersed across schools, colleges and work-based learning providers).	The development of institutional infrastructure, physical learning environments and communications to meet the needs of all learners in the local area. Institutional self-interest is subordinate to area-wide agreements.
6. *New accountability framework* e.g. Performance measures Progression targets Local quality assurance and improvement systems	National government steering mechanisms and policy (e.g. performance tables, targets and funding) continue to drive institutional self-interest and inhibit collaboration. Little development of local accountability mechanisms.	New government mechanisms (e.g. 14–19 Entitlement, prospectus and progression targets) used to strengthen local accountability frameworks. Development of agreed local quality assurance systems and area-wide performance measures.

As the Welsh experience illustrates, while Table 11.2 contrasts the features of weakly and strongly collaborative approaches to partnership working, these are not opposing models. They suggest a continuum with the possibility of movement along different dimensions at varying speeds. From the evidence discussed earlier in this chapter, there are clear grounds for arguing that local partnerships in both England and Wales will need to be further strengthened if they are to meet the needs of all the learners in their area in an equitable and cost-effective manner.

In the current climate, local partnerships cannot be expected to achieve this by themselves. The extent to which they have the scope to determine their actions is clearly constrained by national factors. In particular, as we have argued above, Dimensions 2 and 6 are strongly determined by national policy. Movement towards more strongly collaborative arrangements has to involve tipping the balance of institutional incentives to ensure that potential partners are able to focus attention not only on their own institution and their own learners, but also on the 'learning area' and the attainment and development of all 14–19 learners within it. Potential measures might include:

- area-wide performance indicators for participation, achievement and progression that are monitored by Ofsted/Estyn;
- shared quality assurance and improvement systems between partners;
- local area targets, developed on a 'bottom-up' basis by partnerships;
- funding incentives for collaborative provision and practices and greater clarity about funding learning which takes place across more than one site;
- local area inspections and reviews against specified criteria on collaboration;
- 14–19 qualifications reform that focuses institutional attention and collaborative practice on all 14–19 learners in a locality – achieved to some extent in Wales through the Welsh Bac;
- expanding the area of collaboration between practitioners in schools, colleges, youth service and work-based learning providers, for example, by increasing their involvement in local curriculum development and assessment of provision, based on national processes of validation and institutional licensing;
- changes to 'rules of governance and accountability' (e.g. for governing bodies) that actively promote collaboration and reduce competition;
- greater powers of governance at local and regional levels and a reduction in those at national and institutional level (discussed at greater length in the Webb Review);
- encouraging the links with HE institutions illustrated in Chapter 10.

The development of strongly collaborative local learning systems does not preclude post-16 rationalisation and reorganisation. In fact, many of the measures above could push 14–19 institutional arrangements in the direction of the 'managed tertiary systems' that Fletcher and Perry advocate. These would have the advantage of containing larger institutions able to offer a greater range of provision more cost-effectively without unnecessary journeys to learn. However, tertiary institutions in themselves are not the total solution because of the sheer diversity of provision, both full time and work based, required to meet the needs of 100% of 14–19 learners in a locality.

A devolved social partnership approach – a new balance between national, regional and local governance

Although national policy initiatives in England now provide greater encouragement for local 14–19 collaboration, the arrangements remain essentially voluntary and tied to specific national government funding streams. Evidence suggests that their success still depends very much on the enthusiasm and commitment of all the providers and the calibre of the local coordinators (Higham and Yeomans, 2006; Hill, 2008). Current government policy stresses the responsibility of localities to deliver the national 14–19 Entitlement in England. However, effective practice cannot be achieved simply by a strong practitioner response to national policy. Equally, however, Welsh experience suggests that there are clear limitations to central government's capacity to engage organisations at the local level in creating strongly collaborative systems for 14–19 provision. Earlier chapters stressed the importance of much greater local and professional responsibility for curriculum planning in relation to local and regional contexts. Accordingly, the full realisation of 'strongly collaborative local learning systems' will require new balances of power between national, regional, local, consortia and institutional levels, based on the principle of subsidiarity, so that decisions are made as close to the learner as possible (Coffield *et al.*, 2008).

A key question, therefore, is at what level key decisions should be made about 14–19 education and training. We suggest that there are five interrelated levels.

National government should set the broad narratives and frameworks for policy to indicate the direction of change and to guarantee equity and national standards. This is not just about creating more 'space' for decision-making lower down the system, but also involving a wider range of social partners, including educational practitioners, in the framing of national policy. Moreover, there is a case for the creation of organisations more independent of government – not just Ofqual, for example, but also an inspectorate, more closely modelled on HMI than Ofsted and a teacher training body that genuinely represents those working in the 14–19 field as a whole.

The regional level, particularly in metropolitan areas with small LAs, is arguably best placed to make decisions around specialist vocational facilities, community-based projects with voluntary organisations, employer and higher education engagement strategies. It would also be logical for regional government to oversee the funding of general FE colleges, and larger work-based learning providers, who often play a sub-regional or regional role.

Local – this would leave LAs, working on a smaller scale, to coordinate the planning of provision in the locality, to bring together local providers including Connexions, youth and voluntary organisations, to oversee funding and admission arrangements for schools and sixth-form colleges, to support curriculum development and to assist with the creation and operation of area-based accountability arrangements.

14–19 consortia, as they do now, should be given the power to make day-to-day decisions on collaborative working to expand provision in order to meet learner choices and to aid progression.

Individual institutions would remain at the heart of a local learning system, but would need to see themselves as part of a 'local ecology' recognising that their decisions affect the 'health' of other providers in the area and thus the overall opportunities available for learners (Stanton and Fletcher, 2006; Spours *et al.*, 2007a).

While 14–19 Partnerships have made progress, particularly in helping to diversify provision at Key Stage 4 and to offer more choices for learners, they are doing so at a high cost, both financially and in terms of professional time. Moreover, the wider policy context, with its tensions between competition and collaboration, will constrain their further development. In this chapter we have argued that policy levers, governance arrangements and incentives will have to shift markedly to favour collaborative activity. In some areas tertiary reorganisation also needs to be considered. These will be important steps in the direction of creating cost-effective and inclusive strongly collaborative local learning systems. But we also argue that any new local formations will also have to be empowered. This we link to a new balance of national, regional and local relationships, in which the new partnerships have what Pratchett (2004) calls 'freedom to' bring about real and sustainable change, rather than simply 'freedom from' central control. For this reason, in Chapter 12, we explore how a devolved social partnership approach to governance requires a new type of policy-making and wider politics.

Recommendations

27.   14–19 education and training should be organised through 'strongly collaborative local learning systems' involving schools, colleges, work-based learning providers, higher education, the youth service, voluntary organisations and employers.

28.   Policy levers, such as funding and performance measures, should focus on collective action rather than promoting institutional competition.

12 Policy and policy-making in 14–19 education and training

The need for 'devolved social partnership'

Previous chapters in the book have identified a number of problems related to policy and policy-making in 14–19 education and training. This chapter draws these together and suggests approaches to the policy process that might be more effective in moving us towards an education system that encourages the formation of an educated 19 year old.

As we have seen in earlier chapters, the English and Welsh governments have adopted increasingly divergent approaches not only to the content of policy in the reform of education in general and 14–19 in particular, but also in the style of policy-making. Accordingly, we reflect too on the implications of these divergences for thinking about developing more effective policies for 14–19 provision.

In general terms, we suggest that in complex democratic societies, success-ful system-wide reform cannot be carried out effectively simply by imposition from above. Clearly, the central state has an important part to play in insti-gating such reform. However, it also requires the participation of all relevant parties, not only in implementing policy, but also in shaping it. This applies particularly to the creation of inclusive and effective education systems that, by their very nature, need high degrees of participation by various social partners – policy-makers, teachers, learners, parents, end-users and researchers. We argue that the success of education reform is not simply based on the content of policy, but equally on how policy is made.

We see social partnership operating within a wider democratic strategy, which changes the style of national policy-making and devolves greater powers to the regional and local levels. Recent research by Coffield *et al.* (2008) has termed this a 'devolved social partnership' approach that combines power-sharing at the national level between employers, trade unions, profes-sional associations and community organisations, as practised in the Nordic countries and the Republic of Ireland (as explained by Boyd, 2002), with the civic republican ideal of positive freedom and self-government (as explained by Devine *et al.*, 2007). This fusion could create a more democratic set of relationships between national, regional and local governance with the accent on devolution and subsidiarity: 'that unless there is a strong counter reason (usually with regard to the need for equity and consistency) democratic institutions should be located as closely as possible to the people they represent' (Lawson, 2005:28). In Chapter 11 we applied the concept of devolved social partnership to institutional organisation and governance. Here we focus on its application to the process of policy-making more broadly.

Policy-making over the last 30 years

Looking back over the last 30 years, it is possible to see several broad changes in the way in which policy, particularly in England, has been made across different aspects of public life, in what some refer to as an era of neo-liberal politics (see, for example, Newman's, 2001, *Modernising Governance: New Labour, Policy and Society*). Policy has become more ideologically driven and less pragmatic, policy-making more centralised, the voice of professionals weaker, the power of arm's length agencies has grown and the role of local government has diminished. Moreover, as Ball (2007) demonstrates, private agencies now play an increasingly important role in shaping and delivering policy.

This shift began under the Conservatives in the early 1980s and, in important respects, has been continued by the Labour Government since 1997. Distinctions, however, can and should be made between pre- and post-1997 Administrations. Labour has demonstrated a greater commitment to government intervention than its Conservative predecessors, albeit tempered by an ongoing belief in the market to deliver efficiency gains. Indeed, the combined strategy of both performance management and markets was articulated in a key document from the Prime Minister's Strategy Unit (PMSU, 2006). Despite having gained a reputation for micro-management and command and control (see Chapter 2), the British government has, nevertheless, delivered devolution to Scotland and Wales and more recently has suggested that local authorities and the regions should play a stronger role in the policy process.

The government's approach to policy and governance is, therefore, complex. Moreover, according to Larsen *et al.* (2006), the mix of policy approaches or policy styles appears to differ according to the particular area of policy. Education, due to its prominence in the New Labour project, its high costs and its impact on the life chances of young people and families has, arguably, been more centrally controlled and ideologically driven than other areas of policy. On the other hand, as explained below, we can now detect changes which suggest a more favourable climate for the way forward suggested by this Review.

The context of 14–19 education and training

This and the next section focus particularly on England. There has been, since devolution, sufficient divergence in the process of policy-making that we felt it better to examine Wales separately before drawing out more general lessons.

In England, education as a whole has proved to be a politically charged area since the 1980s. The emerging 14–19 phase has proved to be no exception. The future of A-Levels, in particular, has been a delicate issue in the reform process because of their role in selecting young people for university (see Chapters 8 and 10). It was this area that, unsurprisingly, became the focus of debate when the government asked Tomlinson to review the future of 14–19 curriculum and qualifications. The government's rejection of the Tomlinson recommendations for a unified Diploma system, and statements from teachers' professional associations as they set out their position since the publication of the 14–19 White Paper in 2005, suggest the lack of a 'settled will' in England as to how to reform 14–19 education and training.

As we saw in earlier chapters, disagreements go further and include debates about different approaches to institutional organisation (Chapters 4 and 8) and the work-based route (Chapters 4 and 9). This underlying lack of consensus has been a contributory factor to a highly controlled approach to policy-making by government; since 2005, the Department of Education and Skills (DfES) and now the Department for Children, Schools & Families (DCSF) have concentrated on implementing the government's 14–19 strategy. There has been little inclination, as is clear from the fifth report of the House of Commons Education and Skills Select Committee, in national policy circles to reflect on the overall direction of policy or to question its underlying assumptions.

Dimensions of policy-making

The development of a distinctive approach to policy-making in England can be explored further through a brief analysis of several interrelated dimensions: policy narratives and language; centralism and the level of policy decision-making; the pace of policy; policy memory and policy learning; and organisational change and complexity. We deal with each of these in turn.

Policy narratives and language

Policy aims and narratives communicate the underlying assumptions of policy-makers. They are also used to craft consensus and to exhort various social partners to cooperate with implementation. In the area of 14–19, the government in England has, since the publication of its Green Paper in 2002, *14–19 Education: Extending Opportunities, Raising Standards*, used several interrelated narratives that link choice and opportunity to standards and performance. The underlying argument has been that the offer of a wider range of alternative applied and vocational learning opportunities and contexts for learning will allow some learners to perform better than if they were to continue to struggle in academic education and in schools.

In the wider learning and skills sector, increases in attainment and skills have been linked to two other policy 'drivers' – economic competitiveness and social inclusion. At the same time, policy documents contain key words with which education professionals would find it hard to disagree but, as Chapter 2 suggests, there has been a gradual shift in language with the virtual disappearance of the terms 'education' and 'lifelong learning', and their replacement by the language of skills, performance management and business. These shifts may be producing a 'language gap', as sections of the education profession and government interpret policy words in different ways or even talk different languages.

In the context of the language gap and a relatively controlled policy process, the government has attempted to win hearts and minds in other ways. A major strategy has been 'co-option'. Key individuals, such as university vice chancellors, and even Tomlinson himself, have been recruited as 'Diploma Champions'. At the local level, influential practitioner innovators have been paid large sums to promote collaborative delivery. So how should we understand the process of co-option? On the one hand, it can be seen as a way of excluding some voices and carefully sifting others, which will prove more useful in the implementation process. On the other hand, it may also reflect the dependence of national government on practitioners who have knowledge of implementation processes and some control over local implementation environments.

Centralism and the level of policy decision-making

Over the last two decades, policy-making in England has become more centralised. A process that started under Conservative governments in the 1980s has been broadly continued under successive Labour Administrations. However, the centralisation of policy has become more complex and extensive under New Labour, due in part to its belief in interventionist government. Centralisation can be illustrated by the use of 'remote policy steering' which has directly connected national government and institutions, but which has bypassed local government and marginalised the professional voice in policy-making. The Conservatives used policy steering, largely through funding mechanisms, to exercise control while allowing the market to play a strong role at the local level. The use of policy levers has grown under New Labour and in learning and skills, they include funding, targets and performance measures, inspection, planning and national initiatives (Steer *et al.*, 2007).

Recent research in the school and post-compulsory fields suggests that while national policy-makers assume certain outcomes from central policy steering, these do not always occur. At various levels of the system, policy is contested, mediated and translated, as policy actors and practitioners, coming from different perspectives and speaking different languages, apply their professional values or engage in gaming activities far from the source of the policy itself (Lumby and Foskett, 2005; Hoyle and Wallace, 2007). The result has been unpredictability, complexity and the lack of reliable intelligence from the ground. In Chapter 11, we raised the issue of the kind of decision-making that should take place at national, regional and local levels. We suggested that a new balance of national, regional, local and institutional governance involving a wide range of social partners was more likely to provide a more effective and inclusive policy process that minimises the errors that arise in a centralised system that relies on remote policy steering.

The pace of policy

It is common to hear complaints from practitioners and their representatives about the rapid pace of the policy process and the sheer amount of policy itself. On this, representatives of the teachers have spoken with some force, witness NUT/UCU (2008), ASCL (2008) and NAHT (2008). Coffield and colleagues (2007), in surveying the evidence, referred to the government's desire for 'permanent revolution' in the area of public service reform. Since 2002, there have been numerous Green and White Papers in this area, together with a plethora of other documents – enumerated and analysed by Hodgson *et al.* (2007). 14–19 education and training in England has been very much part of this trend. The intensity of policy activity is in part to do with the real complexity of the post-compulsory education and training system, reflected in the different themes of this book – curriculum and qualifications, institutions and organisation, youth policy, the work-based route, skills and the relationship to the labour market.

The government's approach to reform, however, has made a potentially complex area more complicated still. Its 2005 14–19 White Paper rejected a more system-wide and gradual approach to 14–19 reform, embarking instead on a rapid piecemeal reform strategy. In addition to the flagship Diploma programme, as we saw in Chapters 8 and 11, there have been policy announcements on A-Levels and General Certificates of Secondary Education (GCSEs), institutional collaboration, a new secondary curriculum strategy, a separate Foundation Learning Tier, the Qualifications and Curriculum Framework, Apprenticeships, the Raising of the Participation Age and Machinery of Government changes, to name but a few. The result has been complexity and the displacement of professional energy. Teachers and college lecturers feel as if they are on the receiving end of endless change in which they spend a great deal of their time responding to the reforms and being involved in new initiatives, rather than slowly consolidating good practice. All this is argued at length by Edwards *et al.* (2007) and Coffield *et al.* (2009).

Policy memory and policy learning

How far have policy-makers been able to learn from the past and the experience of others in order to exercise what the Review refers to as 'policy memory'?

Policy memory, as Higham and Yeomans (2007) explain, has been described as the ability to learn from an 'awareness that similar issues and problems to those currently being addressed had been addressed in the recent past and an appreciation that they might yield insights into contemporary policy'. This book has, on several occasions, but particularly in Chapter 1, reminded us of times in the past when solutions were tried to similar problems. What lessons have been learnt from the highly popular Technical and Vocational Education Initiative (TVEI) or from the short lives of successive pre-vocational qualifications or from the brief but impressive life of the Assessment of Performance Unit? And can we, as we look to the future, learn from the curriculum creativity of teachers in the past, working together and with university colleagues, to create vibrant and motivating courses in science (think of the Nuffield Science courses in physics, chemistry, biology), in 'school technology', in geography for the young school-leaver and in the humanities? How might we unleash that creativity in the profession to address the problems which have been identified by the Review?

Policy-makers can also learn from the experience of other countries within the UK (from what has been termed by Raffe (1998) as 'home international comparison'), and from local Pathfinders. Researchers have suggested the government has failed to engage sufficiently in policy learning of this kind because of the increased mobility of policy-makers and an emphasis on policy innovation, spurred on by the political project of modernising public services (Higham and Yeomans, 2007; Raffe and Spours, 2007). As Chapter 8 points out, one notable effect of a failure to learn from the past has been the 'recycling' of past policy solutions in the area of vocational qualifications. The introduction of the 14–19 Diplomas, for example, looks in many respects like a replay of the fated General National Vocational Qualifications (GNVQ) and Advanced Vocational Certificate of Education experiments, as was pointed out in Chapter 1.

The government in England has inevitably been selective about what it is prepared to learn and to whom it is prepared to listen. No doubt that is the case with most governments, though, in education, it contrasts with a previous era when the professional advice of Her Majesty's Inspectorate had much greater influence on political thinking and decision-making. But, as we suggested earlier, government appears less interested in forms of learning that question the underlying assumptions of policy – the kind of 'double-loop learning', explained by Argyris and Schon (1978), as when error is detected and corrected in ways that involve the modification of an organisation's underlying norms, policies and objectives. This is arguably the reason why there is little interest in England in the experience of other countries, such as Wales and Scotland.

In addition to the failure of Whitehall departments to learn from the devolved administrations, there is a more fundamental perception that these countries are following a different policy trajectory. On the other hand, the government has engaged in 'single-loop learning' (that is, back to Argyris and Schon, when the error detected and corrected permits the organisation to carry on its present policies) in order to address problems that inhibit policy implementation. For example, criticism of the early versions of the 'specialised' Diplomas led to a change in their name to Diplomas. However, even here, the commitment to learning is limited, as local experience (e.g. from the 14–19 Pathfinders) is used less as a source of reflection and more as a means of legitimating national policy implementation.

Organisational reform and the problem of complexity

The conduct of policy is closely tied to the structures that policy-makers use. As Chapter 11 illustrated, in England recent organisational changes, resulting from the 'Machinery of Government' proposals (DCSF/DIUS, 2008), appear to have added yet another layer of complexity to systems of governance with the emergence of two ministries – the DCSF and the Department for Innovation, Universities and Skills (DIUS) – with a number of mediating organisations to straddle the organisational and policy divide between 14–19 and 19+. Clearly, no government actively strives to produce complexity. The key motives of this organisational change were to create a system capable of integrating education and social services pre-19 and skills and higher education post-19. However, these changes have been grafted onto already complex arrangements and may undermine the organisation of an all-through lifelong learning education service.

And yet, there are interesting signs of a change of climate, many of which were detailed in Chapter 4, namely, the removal of Key Stage 3 Standard Assessment Tests combined with a less restrictive curriculum framework, the creation of the Innovation Unit, the consequences of the Children's Plan in freeing up the system, the insistence in the Gilbert Review (reflected in Ofsted reports on schools) of a more 'personalised' response to perceived learning needs, and the broader understanding of worthwhile learning as reflected in recent Ofsted Reports (e.g. Ofsted, 2008b; 2008d).

The Welsh experience of policy-making

As we have seen in earlier chapters, since parliamentary devolution in 1999, policy for education and training in Wales has developed in distinctive ways. It is not surprising, then, that when the First Minister, Rhodri Morgan, in a speech to the National Institute for Public Policy Research at the University of Wales, Swansea, in December 2002, wished to demonstrate his claim that there was 'clear red water' between the policies of his administration and those of New Labour in Westminster, it was to educational initiatives that he frequently turned (Drakeford, 2005).

As this suggests, the rationale for pursuing this 'Welsh route' in educational policy is as much about ideology as efficiency; it expresses profoundly held beliefs about how the education system and the learning opportunities it provides *ought* to be organised in Wales. The commitment here is to what in many ways can be interpreted as deep-seated social democratic virtues, albeit in changed and unfamiliar circumstances: equality of opportunity through universal provision; the necessity of the state's role in ensuring this; the rights and obligations of citizenship, expressed through the notion of the 'entitlements' of children and young people; partnership between the central state, local education authorities and professional groups; and so on.

Crucially, here, Welsh distinctiveness is not so much over the goals of educational policy, but rather over the means of achieving them. Hence, for example, in Wales as elsewhere, there is a widespread acknowledgement of the need to improve levels of attainment, thereby contributing to economic development, and to widen educational opportunities. To these ends, the Welsh Assembly Government has pursued an extremely active agenda of policy initiatives, especially within the compulsory sector of education in schools. However, in contrast with what has happened in England, Welsh policies, such as the abandonment of published 'league tables' of test scores for individual primary and secondary schools, are intended to soften the competitive edge of relationships between schools.

Equally, the promotion of higher standards of pupil attainment through enhanced support and continuing professional development for teachers, rather than through centralised and competitively driven approaches being pursued in England, reflects an emphasis on partnership and collaboration between the Assembly Government, the local education authorities and the teaching profession and other employee groups. Similarly, the strong commitment to the maintenance of comprehensive schooling in Wales, ruling out the adoption of the English pattern of specialist secondary schools, academies and even partial selection, is an important re-affirmation of a traditional Labour principle (Phillips, 2003).

With respect to 14–19 provision, too, the distinctiveness of the Welsh approach is striking. As we have seen, central government policy – especially the 14–19 Learning Pathways and the Welsh Bac – has moved significantly towards a model of provision which the rejection of the Tomlinson recommendations prevented from developing in England. Crucially, the effective delivery of a wide range of learning opportunities to individual students, increasingly within the single, over-arching qualifications framework of the Welsh Bac, is seen to depend on meaningful collaboration between schools, colleges, private providers and others at the local level. Moreover, again unlike in England, there is a substantial consensus of support for such a model of 14–19 provision, embracing not only policy-makers at central and local level, but also the professional groups responsible for implementing policy and actually delivering learning opportunities to young people. It is significant, for example, that the recent Webb Review (2007) of further education in Wales records no significant dissent from these broad principles of provision.

However, this is certainly not to suggest that there are no problems in Wales. Again as we saw in earlier chapters, there is a considerable gap between the agreed aims of central government policy and the actual implementation of policy at the local level. Whilst there is general agreement about the essential contours of what is required to make effective provision for 14–19 year olds, it is much more difficult to secure agreement from schools, colleges and other bodies to accept the sacrifices necessary to make the required collaboration at the local level a reality, especially in a wider context of falling student numbers, highly restricted public expenditure and straightened economic conditions.

Accordingly, there is a pressing need to *ensure* that schools, colleges and other providers do actually collaborate meaningfully in local areas so that students really have access to a wide range of different types of learning programme. The Webb Review recognised this and recommended that funding be made conditional, in effect, on the development of what the Review has termed 'strongly collaborative' local systems. It is striking, however, that the Welsh Assembly Government has not felt able to move beyond an essentially voluntaristic approach to securing local collaboration.

Of course, at one level, this reflects nothing more than the well-established difficulties of achieving *national* policy goals in the face of *local and other special* interests. However, there are also particular difficulties that arise because the Welsh Assembly Government remains so firmly wedded to the kind of social democratic consensus that we sketched earlier. Crucial to this consensus is securing collaboration with local authorities, professional groups and so forth. And this remains integral to the form of policy-making which has been adopted in Wales during the era of parliamentary devolution. Certainly, it is very difficult to conceive of central government in Wales lurching towards the kinds of 'remote policy steering' which have been adopted by successive New Labour administrations in England, for reasons both of ideology and, in truth, governmental capacity.

In some regards, therefore, the Welsh experience of policy-making for 14–19 provision provides a salutary reminder of the complexities that arise in balancing national policy goals against local interests. It should certainly not be thought that because Welsh policy and policy-making are different from England's, this implies that they are more effective. Indeed, as we saw in Chapter 4, if we accept the conventional measures of system performance, there is considerable evidence to suggest that the English system is improving at a substantially higher rate than the Welsh one. And this is a problem that policy-makers and other professional groups in Wales have to take very seriously.

Improving policy-making and governance

While England and Wales appear to be following somewhat different models of policy and policy-making, they share an important common characteristic – the multiple expectations of education reform. In the case of the Labour Government in England, it could be seen to start with Tony Blair's mantra 'education, education, education'. The reliance on education reform might be viewed not only as a commitment to education as a social good, but also as part of a reluctance to fundamentally reframe the relationship between the education and training system and the labour market.

In the case of Wales, as Chapter 8 vividly illustrates, a daunting range of expectations has been heaped onto Learning Pathways, which extend far beyond the scope of education and training themselves. Here too, it may well be that the emphasis placed upon education reform reflects the extent to which government is able to change policy in this area. Certainly, as we have seen, there is little indication as yet of profound impacts on educational attainment in Wales, let alone on economic and social conditions more widely.

One of the conclusions we draw from an assessment of policy-making in both England and Wales is the need for a slower but more comprehensive approach to reform that makes more realistic demands of education and that links education reform to wider changes in the economy and society. It is to the future of the reform process that we now turn.

Future of the policy process

We have shown that policy-making in England and Wales has important similarities and significant differences. However, the challenges facing both countries are relatively similar in building effective and inclusive 14–19 education and training systems. If we want to see an improved 14–19 phase, it is not only important to have the right kind of policies, but also to develop a more reflective approach to policy-making and a more open policy process. We conclude, therefore, by outlining a number of dimensions of the devolved social partnership approach to policy-making and governance, defined earlier, in the context of 14–19 education and training.

Vision as the 'glue' of policy relationships

At the heart of the reform of policy should be a vision of what policy itself is for. In the case of 14–19 education and training, the Review has stated its aim as the formation of an 'educated 19 year old'. A clear vision around which a broad consensus can be forged is essential because it provides the possibility of a more collective view and actions that do not require control from the centre. The vision can be elaborated at different levels of the system as it provides a framework for creative interpretation by different agencies nationally, regionally, locally and at the institutional level.

A new national style of politics

We have argued that 'fast politics' and policy busyness is essentially manipulative, in that it tends to exclude, frustrate and demoralise social partners whose efforts are needed to shape and deliver effective educational reform. There is, therefore, a strong case for a new style of politics from the perspectives of both equity and efficiency. There is a role for a slower politics based on a regard for professional experience and judgement and the perspectives of different social partners.

A new balance of relationships between national, regional and local decision-making

A different approach to policy-making will depend on the development of governance relationships founded on a process of 'de-centring'. This is not an argument for the abrogation of national leadership, but rather the exercise of real leadership as opposed to micro-management. Leadership within a devolved social partnership model would mean outlining broad policy frameworks which also offer considerable space for interpretation at lower levels, balanced by consideration for equity and securing national standards. Genuine national leadership is also about distributing power within the centre of national politics, including a greater role for Parliament and the Select Committee system in Westminster, as well as to the National Assembly for Wales and its committees (Lawson, 2005; Heald, 2006, address to the Conservative Party, *Giving Responsibility to Local People and Local Communities*).

Collaborative local and regional ecologies

Devolved governance structures can be viewed through an 'ecological' perspective, in which regional and local governance and policy-making relationships are conceptualised as ecological systems. An ecological perspective in education and training attempts to think about the multidimensional nature of learning beyond schooling (e.g. decisions about where to learn and how to get there; inter-dependent relations between providers and the influence of wider community, social and labour market factors). It thus recognises the complexity of educational decisions and relationships that have become more complicated as a result of market reforms.

A bonfire of the quangos?

Non-departmental public bodies or quasi-national government organisations (quangos) have become an integral part of the governance and policy-making landscape in England. However, there is a strong case (exemplified in Ranson's, 2006, critique) for their democratisation, which could include their realignment, and in some cases their abolition. Some could be absorbed into local and regional tiers of government and others made more directly accountable to democratically elected bodies, as in Wales, and to a wider range of social partners.

Developing feedback loops to empower social partners

We have argued that government is prepared, to a degree, to engage in 'single-loop learning'. A devolved social partnership approach with the full involvement of different parties could lead to 'double-loop learning'.

However, this is only likely to occur if space and structures are created for feedback from social partners – teachers, college lecturers, parents, voluntary bodies, employers, youth workers – to senior policy-makers. The ability to create a variety of 'feedback loops' is intimately tied to the slowing of politics, increased time for deliberation, the emphasis upon independent professional advice through Her Majesty's Inspectorate, and the creation of independent and representative networks for curriculum development. This was once the case and was well argued for by Morrell, the 'architect' of the Schools' Council for Curriculum and Examinations – a victim of the very centralisation described in this chapter. It has been a constant theme of this book that there should be a greater respect for professional judgement and expertise in education delivery and on the constraints on how far politicians can intervene in areas of practice.

Capacity building and the development of mutual understanding

A devolved social partnership model will also require a concerted effort to increase the effectiveness of all who are involved in policy-making and implementation. This will include improving the capacity of policy-makers to utilise evidence as well as the ability of teachers and researchers to engage in the policy process. After all, it is their professional judgement and expertise through which policy is translated into good practice. Capacity building, as explained by Nutley (2003), involves bridge-building between different communities to ensure that each party recognises the distinct concerns and problems of the others.

We recognise that these proposals would represent considerable change in national politics and policy-making, particularly in England. But as we indicated above, there are already signs of it beginning to happen. It is not, therefore, utopian to argue for this modest approach real steps in this direction have already been taken in Wales and Scotland. Moreover, the seeds of these changes can be found even in recent government legislation related to local government (DCLG, 2006). Devolved social partnership simply takes these ideas to their logical conclusion. As we have argued throughout this book, the successful creation of an inclusive and effective 14–19 phase requires the commitment and expertise of all the social partners. Further progress in this direction cannot take place without important changes to the style of policy-making.

Recommendations

29. Initiatives by central government should be scaled down and changes (particularly in curriculum and assessment) made only after full consultation with representative professional bodies and democratically elected representatives at local level.

30. Agencies responsible for quality assurance in curriculum, assessment and qualifications should be independent of government.

31. More decision-making over curriculum and professional development should be devolved to the local or regional levels of governance.

13 Looking to the future

The central question

Every parent of a 19 year old knows how much their young person has changed since 14. These are crucial, life-determining years that once gone cannot be recaptured, which is why, over the last 25 years or so, 14–19 has been identified as a distinctive phase in the education and training of young people. The whole of the journey through school and college is perceived, rightly or wrongly, in such phases, all of which are crudely drawn, with continuities that cross the boundaries. This last leap, though, takes a young person from relatively early adolescence to the responsibilities of adulthood, independence and citizenship. Given that it is a transition accompanied by other pressures – of adolescence itself and of social and economic changes in society (described in Chapter 3) – it is unsurprising that this phase has become a magnet for policy-makers, anxious to make the most of what they see as a last chance to secure the future of the nation.

All of the consequent mix of influences and interventions impinges on those who provide education and training to young people. Accordingly, we see a clear need to re-examine not only the content of that education and training, but also the manner in which it is conducted and the institutional arrangements through which it is provided – that is, *content*, *pedagogy* and *provision*. Above all, however, it is necessary to question the aims, whether explicit or implicit, which determine the priorities and the values which underlie the policies and the practices. What sort of person and community do we want to see as a result of the massive investment in education and training?

The question, therefore, which was posed in Chapter 2 and has shaped the investigations of the Review, is:

What counts as an educated 19 year old in this day and age?

Why a Review is important?

What, then, has been happening in the last few years which makes this Review relevant?

- There has been a lot of talk about 'global competition', 'knowledge economy', and 'skills shortage' which has led to the conclusion that greater responsibility should be placed on education and training to find a solution to our economic needs. More 'vocational education', at least for some, is one solution.
- The worrying sight of many young people without employment, further education (FE) or training has provoked the search for new education and training initiatives.
- The apparent failure to 'stretch' and 'select' the most able young people has made it seem necessary to reform the qualifications framework.
- Concern about 'standards', exacerbated by international comparisons, has caused successive governments to proliferate targets for the sake of public accountability – and an equal number of 'levers' and 'drivers' to make sure those targets are met.
- At the same time, there have been many responses in schools and colleges to the perceived learning needs of young people – and these 'bottom-up' innovations struggle to survive the 'top-down' interventions and targets.

We could go on. But it would be wrong to see the drive for change in such purely utilitarian terms. There is a genuine desire for greater social inclusion. There is the belief that such social inclusion can, at least in part, be achieved through a reform of education and training and through a more productive relationship between schools, colleges, employers and others in the community who have a stake in the outcomes. Both in England and in Wales, steps have been taken to link together a range of services to ensure a more holistic approach to the well-being of each young person.

The Review has recognised and welcomed this drive for a more inclusive system – for extending opportunities and hope to many young people who were too easily dismissed by a system that had a very narrow understanding of success. It has recognised, too, the wider responsibilities of education to serve economic well-being and to enrich the wider community of which it is part. Further, the Review has recognised the more radical thinking which, through its *Learning Pathways*, Wales is pioneering in order to ensure a learning experience for all young people which links to, and serves, their respective communities and yet which supports individual aspiration and progress. It is, of course, early days for seeing how successful this and other innovations in the two countries will be, but they clearly indicate imaginative ways of thinking about the problems and finding solutions.

But three grounds for caution arise from the previous chapters.

Words of caution

First, what constitutes 'success' depends on the answer to the basic question of the Review: 'what counts as an educated 19 year old in this day and age?' Answers to that question are implicit in all that happens: in the selection of subjects and their content; in the manner of teaching or pedagogy; in the mode of assessing learning; in the qualifications framework (whether or not it should perpetuate divisive tri-partite tracks); in the ethos of the different providers and selection processes for entry; in the degree of cooperation between providers and other bodies (or 'stakeholders'); and in the degree of control over the content and manner of learning. Education is not ethically neutral. Values matter. We cannot avoid the tricky question as to what values and whose aims should prevail.

Second, the Review has underlined the fact that, often unrecognised by the policy-makers, these questions are not new. Nor are many of the solutions to the problems identified. We have been there before. And maybe some of the problems, which stubbornly resist solution, are rooted in the failed solutions of a forgotten past. What seem to be new are often in fact the inheritance of past problems, past diagnoses and past remedies. There is a need to stand still awhile and to reflect. How, for instance, do the Not in Education, Employment or Training (NEET) solutions differ from those of the Youth Opportunity Programme (YOP) and of the Youth Training Scheme (YTS)? Can we learn from the Technical and Vocational Education Initiative (TVEI) – and from its demise? Why do the 40 years of continuing qualification reform still need reforming?

Third, perhaps we are just asking the impossible, but may there not be a fundamental misjudgement in the political expectation of so much from the education and training system? Basil Bernstein's statement that 'education cannot compensate for society' has appeared before, but it bears repetition here. As Chapter 3 pointed out, there have been social and economic changes affecting the lives of many young people and militating against the very best efforts of school and college. There is a connection between poverty (and the widening gap between very rich and very poor) and educational aspiration and success. Good schooling, adequately staffed and resourced, and with an appropriate curriculum, can make a difference. But educational reform must be accompanied by more radical measures of social and economic transformation.

The Review, therefore, has tried to make sense of an ever moving, ever being reformed system. Chapter by chapter, it has asked questions about the underlying values and assumptions, the quality of learning, the appropriateness of the assessment procedures and qualifications, the progression into higher education and employment, the institutional provision and the need for changes in the making of policy. And throughout it has examined the different ways in which England and Wales are responding.

Key messages

These then are the key messages arising from the previous chapters.

Establishing aims and values

Chapter 2 argued that education and training should be guided and inspired by aims and values which are relevant to all young people, irrespective of background, ability and talent. Such aims respect the young person as a whole, in need not only of intellectual development, but also of a wider sense of fulfilment, self-esteem and hope. They recognise and nurture 'moral seriousness' – a sense of responsibility for their future lives, for others and for the wider community. But more than that. The social and economic conditions, described in Chapter 3, which impinge upon the lives of many young people, make many schools and colleges the main, if not only, providers of that care for the well-being, resilience and self-esteem of young people. This broader responsibility of school or college, though recognised in theory and though pursued by countless teachers, too often goes unrecognised in the narrow 'performance indicators' by which schools and colleges are judged.

Therefore, within local curriculum development networks, or the collaborative learning systems described in Chapter 11, aims and values, in terms of which schools and colleges believe their performance should be judged, should be a constant focus of deliberation.

Watching your language

Language matters, as we argued in Chapter 2. The words we use shape our thinking. The Orwellian language of 'performance management and control' has come to dominate educational deliberation and planning, namely, the language of measurable 'inputs' and 'outputs', of 'performance indicators' and 'audits', of 'customers' and 'deliverers', of 'efficiency gains' and 'bottom lines'. There is a need to recall the essentially moral language of education as we try to help young people find value in what is worthwhile, lead fulfilling lives, gain self-esteem, struggle to make sense of experience and become responsible members of the community. Perhaps George Orwell's *1984* should be made essential reading for all trainee teachers.

Creating system performance 'fit for purpose'

The overall conclusion, arising from Chapter 4, must be: poor rates of participation, high rates of attrition and low levels of attainment remain endemic features of the English and Welsh 14–19 systems – reflected in the relatively large NEET category of young people. Furthermore, there is a continuing divide in attainment between socially advantaged and disadvantaged groups – not surprisingly, except that the divide seems greater in the UK generally than in most other developed countries. Successive initiatives to increase participation and progression have not had the hoped-for impact. Perhaps the fault lies not so much with the education and training programmes (constantly blamed and then 'reformed'), as with other factors such as the wider social and economic context and the weak incentives for low attainers to participate. Many qualifications have little 'market value'.

But the present indicators are no longer 'fit for purpose'. They too often fail to reflect the broader aims and values as set out in Chapter 2, and consequently the broader vision of learning, achievement and assessment, as well as the new partnerships between providers (although, more recently, Ofsted reports have sought to correct this). Such indicators should recognise variations within a system which responds to different conditions affecting young people. The performance indicators should be partly determined by local or regional networks, or the collaborative partnerships, in the light of agreed aims. They should reflect, too, the achievement of the learning partnerships, not of their often competing members.

Alleviating the negative effects of diversification

But the sheer variety of arrangements in England, though not in Wales, makes the local region, through which the system as a whole is to achieve success, more difficult to operate. It embraces comprehensive alongside grammar schools; local community schools alongside academies, specialist and trust schools; schools with sixth-forms alongside sixth-form and FE colleges; tertiary systems alongside 11–18 school systems – all governed and funded differently and often inequitably.

From this, three points in particular stand out from the analysis of Chapter 4. First, the baleful effect of this diversification is to be found in the so-called 'sixth-form presumption'. But expansion of post-16 provision in schools through development of small sixth-forms will reduce choice, lower attainment and raise costs. Second, the most needy learners – the NEETs – and the voluntary sector that helps them (e.g. 'detached youth workers') receive least money, typically in the form of short-term initiative-led funding. Third, the FE sector, despite the provision it makes for the majority of post-16 learners and despite its crucial role in giving a 'second chance' to those who have not succeeded earlier, rarely gets due recognition or (in England) equitable funding.

Having a broader vision of learning

Too often, as argued in Chapter 5, learning programmes are purely academic exercises, failing to acknowledge practical and experiential learning. The Royal Society of Arts (RSA) was right to emphasise in its 1986 Manifesto the importance of practical capability – for all young people and not to be confused with 'vocational'. The Review has discovered many initiatives building on a broader vision of learning, valuing the practical and the experiential, though needing to reconcile (with difficulty) this with an assessment regime which prioritises 'transmission of knowledge' and attainment of pre-conceived objectives. Attention should be given, too, to the quality of work-based learning which is the way ahead for many but which requires cooperation from more employers. The key question is: how might the many exciting innovations, pioneered by voluntary bodies, charitable trusts, youth service teachers and independent training providers enter the mainstream of education and training?

Responding with a broader vision of assessment

Too often the system of assessment, as described in Chapter 5, fails to reflect the different kinds of learning and achievement, and focuses on that which is more easily measureable. It encourages 'teaching to the test', thereby impoverishing the quality of learning. One problem is that the same assessments are used for distinct purposes: finding out what has been learnt, selecting for different progression routes and different providers, and accounting for the performance of the school, college or system. These all require different assessment tools. Therefore, *assessment for learning* should be separated from *assessment for accountability*, which itself should be conducted on a light sampling basis, building on the experience of the Assessment of Performance Unit. Teachers' appraisal, suitably moderated, should play a much more important part in public assessments.

Respecting teachers: training and professional development

Teaching quality is central to successful education in both schools and colleges. That requires a respect for the profession of teaching – of the role of teachers as the custodians of what we value and as the experts in communicating that to the learners. Teachers should be central to curriculum development, not the 'deliverers' of someone else's curriculum. But, as we argued in Chapter 6, there is a need for recruitment, initial training and professional development to reflect the more practical skills and knowledge required of them for the changing 14–19 phase. First, because 14–19 learning crosses the divide between schools and colleges, the distinction between qualification for school teaching (QTS) and qualification for teaching in FE (QTLS in England) should be bridged. Second, ways should be found to enable those with the much needed practical and work-based knowledge to acquire QTS. Furthermore, continuing professional development is all the more important and needs to be reflected in an *entitlement* at regular intervals, and located when appropriate in 'teachers' centres' run by teachers in their cooperative effort to develop curriculum, pedagogy and assessment.

Providing a curriculum framework for the twenty-first century

There has been too much central direction of what to learn and how to teach. Part of the expertise of the teacher must lie in the capacity to adapt teaching to the circumstances of this or that group of learners – taking account of their experiences, respecting their 'voices', responding to their needs and aspirations. But such adaptation must take place within a nationally agreed, albeit broad and flexible framework. That framework, as set forth in Chapter 7, must include those forms of intellectual enquiry which enable the learners to make sense of the physical and social worlds they inhabit, the opportunities to excel and to have a sense of achievement, the development of practical and economically relevant capabilities, and the introduction to issues of profound social and personal concern. Development of the curriculum within such a framework is the professional job of the teacher, working cooperatively with other teachers across schools and colleges. Finally, the sheer complexity of the changing qualifications structure and of the needs of the local economies puts a major responsibility on the information, advice and guidance service to be constantly up to date and to be part of this curriculum framework.

Creating a unified qualifications framework

It is important, therefore, as argued in Chapter 8, that future qualifications in England and Wales support broader forms of attainment, involve all 14–19 year olds and encourage personal development and innovative learning. Qualifications should reflect rather than shape what is learnt; build on successful features of existing awards; move towards a more unified approach; and facilitate flexible routes into higher education, further training and employment.

The Review suggests that these aims will best be realised in England through a move towards a more unified approach that brings all qualifications within an over-arching framework for learning, such as an English Baccalaureate style of a unified qualifications framework, that guarantees an inclusive, broad and holistic educational experience for all 14–19 year olds. In Wales, the Review supports the continued development of the Welsh Bac so that it becomes the organising framework for all 14–19 curriculum and assessment in that country.

Ensuring progression from 14–19 into higher education and the 'labour market'

Smooth and clear progression routes right through from 14 into higher education, further training or employment have been high on the government's reform agenda. But getting that progression right is not easy, as is shown in Chapter 10. Higher education complains that young people are not well prepared for the more independent studies of university. Applicants are faced with an ever increasing number of selection hurdles which are not in the Qualifications Framework. Despite efforts on the part of higher education, entrance requirements and procedures for many courses need to be more transparent – particularly where vocational qualifications are concerned.

Chapter 9 points out that much the same goes for entry into further training and employment. There can be considerable regional and local variation in the opportunities available. Level 1 and 2 qualifications are not quite the passports into employment that they are made out to be. And the possibilities for work-based learning are fewer and fewer, despite the importance attached to that.

Apprenticeship and Advanced Apprenticeship can provide excellent pathways into employment, generating wage premiums as large as degrees in some cases. As a mode of formation training, apprenticeship is a tradition worth retaining. Whether or not the brand should be diluted by the widespread introduction of programme-led apprenticeship requires further discussion, but as avenues to employment these programmes might work well for some young people in some sectors. The key challenge is to encourage more employers, in particular in the public services, to offer apprenticeship opportunities. This is a key area where employers have to exercise responsibility. Perhaps simplification of the bureaucracy surrounding apprenticeship and better funding may encourage more employers to participate.

Creating strongly collaborative local learning systems

The current organisational arrangements for 14–19 education and training in England are complex and still fragile as a result of competition for learners. Collaboration is also expensive and the costs and benefits have to be weighed against simpler options, such as local reorganisation into a tertiary system. The Review, therefore, argued in Chapter 11 for a coherent institutional system of education and training, based on strongly collaborative learning partnerships between schools, colleges, higher education, training providers, the youth service and employers. The extent of each such partnership will depend on local economic and geographical conditions – no one pattern will fit all. Collaborative local learning systems can be facilitated by local authority leadership, by ensuring that policy levers, such as funding and performance measures, focus on collective action rather than competition and by a better balance between national, regional, local and institutional levels of decision-making, in which national government sets the broad framework for policy and allows regional and local government to play a stronger role in meeting the needs of all 14–19 year olds in a locality.

Seeking a more reflective and participative approach to policy

The success of policy for 14–19 education and training in England and Wales is not simply based on its content but also on how it is made. The development of an integrated and responsive 14–19 education and training system will require, as argued in Chapter 12, a different approach to policy and policy-making which will encourage the sustained commitment and involvement of key partners – learners, education professionals, parents, employers and higher education providers – who can make a difference to the learning experience of 14–19 year olds. Furthermore, decisions should be made as close to the learner as is practically possible, taking into account local conditions and local histories. This will mean a slower pace for policy development so that all social partners can be meaningfully involved in all stages of the policy process, from conception to implementation.

In sum, the Review makes five demands:

- The reassertion of a broader vision of education in which there is a profound respect for the whole person (not just the narrowly conceived 'intellectual excellence' or 'skills for economic prosperity'), irrespective of ability or ethnic and social background, and in which the learning contributes to a more just and cohesive society. That respect will be reflected in a language that expresses the essentially moral purpose of education – helping young people to develop their distinctively human qualities, and not impoverished by the prevailing language of 'performance management'.
- System performance indicators 'fit for purpose' in which measures of success reflect the range of educational aims.
- The redistribution of power and decision-making such that there can be greater room for the voice of the learner, for the expertise of the teacher and for the concerns of other stakeholders in the response to the learning needs of all young people in the different economic and social settings.
- The creation of strongly collaborative learning systems in which schools, colleges, higher education institutions, the youth service, independent training providers and voluntary bodies can work together for the common good – in curriculum development, in provision of opportunities and in ensuring appropriate progression into further education, training and employment.
- The development of a more unified system of qualifications to meet the diverse talents of young people and diverse needs of the wider community, but which avoids fragmentation, divisiveness and inequalities to which the present system is prone.

Appendix 1

Nuffield Review publications

Aims, Learning and Curriculum Working Group (Mar 2006) *Curriculum for the 21st Century*.

Bailey, Bill (Working Paper 3, Dec 2003) *14–19 Education and Training: Historical Roots and Lessons*.

Ball, Stephen (Working Paper 24, Oct 2004) *Participation and Progression in Education and Training 14–19: Working Draft of Ideas*.

Beresford, John (Briefing Paper 11, Jul 2006) *Wolverhampton 14–19 Learning Strategy*.

Besley, Steve (Briefing Paper 16, Jul 2006) *14–19 Policy in England: Developments 2005–06*.

Brockington, Dave (ALC series Discussion Paper 9, Mar 2005) *Nascent Futures: A Discussion Paper on the Ways in Which ASDAN Might Contribute to a Future Teaching and Learning Agenda from Aspects of its Current Practice*.

—— (Briefing Paper 3, Oct 2005) *An Update on the Status of Generic Employability Skills: Wider Key Skills in the National Qualifications Framework*.

—— (Briefing Paper 6, Oct 2005) *The National Qualifications Framework in England: A Summary Outline*.

Brockmann, Michaela, Clarke, Linda and Winch, Chris (Feb 2008) *Position Paper on the Relevance of Other European Vocational Education Systems to the English Situation*.

Buckley, Jane (Discussion Paper 27, Oct 2004) *How Can We Help Disaffected and Less Committed Young People Participate in Education and Training?*

Bynner, John (Working Paper 9, Feb 2004) *Participation and Progression: Use of Birth Cohort Study Data in Illuminating the Role of Basic Skills and Other Factors*.

Colley, Helen (Working Paper 36, Jun 2006) *Mentoring for Young People Not in Education, Employment or Training: A 'NEET' Solution, but to Whose Problems?*

Croxford, Linda and Raffe, David (Policy series Discussion Paper 4, Mar 2005) *Secondary School Organisation in England, Scotland and Wales Since the 1980s*.

David, Miriam (Research Report 4, Oct 2006) *The Education of 14–19 Year-Olds: Gender, Sexuality and Diversity in Socio-cultural Contexts*.

Davies, Peter and Fletcher, Mick (Working Paper 17, Apr 2004) *The Role of Strategic Area Reviews (StARs) and Potential Implications for 14–19 Education and Training*.

Ecclestone, Kathryn (Research Report 2, Aug 2006) *Assessment in Post-14 Education: The Implications of Principles, Practices and Politics for Learning and Achievement*.

Egan, David (Working Paper 19, May 2004) *14–19 Developments in Wales: Learning Pathways*.

—— (Briefing Paper 5, Nov 2005) *Progress with 14–19 Developments in Wales*.

—— (Briefing Paper 18, Jul 2006) *A Response to Chapter 2 (14–19 Institutional Developments in Wales in the Wider Policy Context: Observations from an English Reform Perspective) of the Nuffield Review Annual Report 2005–06*.

Ellis, Viv (ALC series Discussion Paper 5, Dec 2005) *Rethinking English in English Schools: Asking Questions of a 'Sack of Snakes'*.

Farlie, Victor (Working Paper 28, Oct 2004) *Are Apprenticeships any Longer a Credible Vocational Route for Young People, and Can the Supply Side Respond Effectively to Government Policy, and Address the Needs of Learners and Employers?*

Finlay, Ian and Egan, David (Working Paper 20, May 2004) *What Policy Trajectories are the National Governments in England, Wales, Northern Ireland and Scotland Following and are they Converging or Diverging?*

Fletcher, Mick (Working Paper 46, Jan 2009) *Funding the 14–19 phase in England.*

Foskett, Nick (Working Paper 25, Oct 2004) *IAG (Information, Advice and Guidance) and Young People's Participation Decisions 14–19.*

Fox, John (Working Paper 29, Oct 2004) *Ivor the Engine and Practical Curriculum Reform 14–16.*

—— (ALC series Discussion Paper 18, Sep 2005) *'... Restaurant Chefs, not Cookery Teachers' (White Paper, 14–19, Section 7.14): The Confusing Language of the 14–19 Debate and Three Case Studies of 'Other Providers'.*

—— (Briefing Paper 9, Jun 2006) *Starting Up: The East Oxfordshire Education Partnership (14–16 Phase).*

Fuller, Alison (Working Paper 10, Feb 2004) *Expecting Too Much? Modern Apprenticeship: Purposes, Participation and Attainment.*

Furlong, Andy (Working Paper 26, Oct 2004) *Cultural Dimensions of Decisions about Educational Participation among 14–19 Year-Olds.*

Gardner, Stuart (ID series Discussion Paper 6, May 2005) *An LSC Perspective on Key Policy Mechanisms, Their Effects and Opportunities for Reform.*

—— (Working Paper 42, Aug 2007) *GCE Advanced Level Providers in England.*

—— (Working Paper 43, Aug 2007) *Listening to the Voice of GCE A Level Students and Their Teachers.*

—— (Working Paper 44, Aug 2007) *The Experience of Learning by GCE A Level Students in England.*

—— (Working Paper 45, Aug 2007) *Value Added by GCE A Level Providers.*

Gay, John (ALC series Discussion Paper 11, Mar 2005) *Religious Education 14–19.*

Haines, Steve (Working Paper 37, Jun 2006) *14–19 Education and Training and Young Disabled People: Working Draft of Ideas.*

Hall, James (Briefing Paper 19, Oct 2006) *Rates of Return: What are Young People Doing?*

Harkin, Joe (ALC series Discussion Paper 16, May 2005) *14 to 16 Year Olds in Further Education.*

Hart, John and Tuck, Ron (Policy series Discussion Paper 7, Mar 2005) *Consultation, Consultation, Consultation: Policy Making in Action Plan, Higher Still and Beyond.*

Harwood, John (Discussion Paper 16, Apr 2004) *Reflections on the Role of the Learning and Skills Council.*

Hayward, Geoff (Discussion Paper 31, Apr 2005) *How Might the Tomlinson and White Paper Proposals Affect System Performance – Participation, Progression and Achievement?*

Hayward, Geoff, Hodgson, Ann, Johnson, Jill, Keep, Ewart, Oancea, Alis, Pring, Richard, Spours, Ken and Wright, Susannah (Oct 2004) *Nuffield Review of 14–19 Education and Training Annual Report 2003–04.*

—— (2004) *Nuffield Review of 14–19 Education and Training Annual Report 2003–04: Overview.*

Hayward, Geoff, Hodgson, Ann, Johnson, Jill, Oancea, Alis, Pring, Richard, Spours, Ken, Wilde, Stephanie and Wright, Susannah (Oct 2005) *Nuffield Review of 14–19 Education and Training Annual Report 2004–05.*

—— (2005) *Nuffield Review of 14–19 Education and Training Annual Report 2004–05: Executive Summary.*

—— (2006) *Nuffield Review of 14–19 Education and Training Annual Report 2005–06*.

—— (2006) *Nuffield Review of 14–19 Education and Training Annual Report 2005–06: Executive Summary*.

Hayward, Geoff, Wilde, Stephanie and Williams, Richard (Oct 2008) *Engaging Youth Enquiry Final Report for Consultation*.

Hewlett, Mark (Working Paper 47, Jan 2009) *Educating Young People for the 21st Century: Constructing an aims-led curriculum*.

Higham, Jeremy (Working Paper 4, Dec 2003) *Continuity and Discontinuity in the '14–19 Curriculum'*.

Higham, Jeremy and Yeomans, David (Policy series Discussion Paper 5, Mar 2005) *Policy Memory and Policy Amnesia in 14–19 Education: Learning from the Past?*

—— (ID series Discussion Paper 9, May 2005) *Collaborative Approaches to 14–19 Education and Training Provision*.

Hodgson, Ann and Spours, Ken (Working Paper 18, May 2004) *14–19 Education and Training: Politics, Policy and the Role of Research*.

—— (Policy series Discussion Paper 8, Mar 2005) *14–19 Education and Training in England: A Historical and System Approach to Policy Analysis*.

—— (Discussion Paper 35, Apr 2005) *Building a Strong 14–19 Phase in England? The Government's White Paper in its Wider System Context*.

—— (Briefing Paper 7, Apr 2006) *The Irish Upper Secondary Education and Training System: Report from a Research Visit in December 2005*.

—— (Discussion Paper 39, Jul 2006) *14–19 Institutional Arrangements in England in the Wider Governance and Policy Context*.

Hodgson, Ann, Spours, Ken and Wright, Susannah (ID series Discussion Paper 1, Feb 2005) *From Collaborative Initiatives to a Coherent 14–19 Phase?*

—— (ID series Discussion Paper 10, May 2005) *14–19 Collaborative Learning Systems*.

Hodkinson, Phil (Working Paper 12, Feb 2004) *Career Decision Making, Learning Careers and Career Progression*.

Holt, Maurice (Working Paper 41, Jan 2007) *The Case for the Slow School*.

Huddleston, Prue (Working Paper 11, Feb 2004) *Learning on the Edge: Second Chance Learning for 14–19 Year Olds*.

Huddleston, Prue, Keep, Ewart and Unwin, Lorna (Discussion Paper 33, Apr 2005) *What Might the Tomlinson and White Paper Proposals Mean for Vocational Education and Work-Based Learning?*

Johnson, Jill (Discussion Paper 34, Apr 2005) *What Would the Tomlinson and White Paper Proposals Mean for Higher Education Providers?*

Johnson, Martin (ID series Discussion Paper 7, May 2005) *The Effects of the Accountability Framework on 14–19 Education and Training and Institutional Arrangements*.

Jupp, Tom (ID series Discussion Paper 8, May 2005) *Key Policy Mechanisms and Their Impact on 14–19 Education and Training with Particular Reference to Colleges of Further Education*.

Keep, Ewart (Working Paper 22, May 2004) *Reflections on a Curious Absence – the Role of Employers, Labour Market Incentives and Labour Market Regulation*.

—— (Working Paper 23, Jul 2004) *The Multiple Dimensions of Performance – Performance as Defined by Whom, Measured in What Ways, to What Ends?*

Lambert, David (ALC series Discussion Paper 2, Feb 2005) *Why Subjects Really Matter*.

Lane, Graham (response to Issues Paper 1) *Nuffield Review of 14–19 Education: Document Download*.

Leney, Tom (Discussion Paper 6, Dec 2003) *Developing the 14 to 19 Curriculum and Qualifications in England – Aims and Purposes: International and Comparative Aspects*.

Lucas, Geoff (Working Paper, Feb 2008) *The 14–19 Curriculum and Qualifications: Options in Independent Schools.*

Lumby, Jacky and Foskett, Nick (Policy series Discussion Paper 6, Mar 2005) *Turbulence Masquerading as Change: Exploring 14–19 Policy.*

Maguire, Malcolm (Working Paper 15, Apr 2004) *Guidance Issues and the Role of Connexions.*

Maguire, Sue and Thompson, Jo (Research Report 3, Aug 2006) *Paying Young People to Stay on at School – Does it Work? Evidence from the Evaluation of the Piloting of the Education Maintenance Allowance (EMA).*

Mason, Peter (ALC series Discussion Paper 12, Mar 2005) *Curriculum 14–19: One Independent School Head's View.*

McPhee, Linda and Cumberland, Gill (ID series Discussion Paper 4, Feb 2005) *History of the Educational Provision for Secondary and Post-16 in the London Borough of Richmond Upon Thames.*

Nuffield Review (Jan 2007) *Written Evidence Submitted by the Nuffield Review of 14–19 Education and Training to the Education and Skills Select Committee.*

—— (Issues Paper 1, Nov 2007) *The New 14–19 Diplomas.*

—— (Issues Paper 2, Dec 2007) *14–19 Partnerships.*

—— (Issues Paper 3, Jan 2008) *Apprenticeship I: Prospects for Growth.*

—— (Issues Paper 4, Jan 2008) *Apprenticeship II: A High Quality Pathway for Young People?*

—— (Issues Paper 5, Feb 2008) *Guidance and Careers Education.*

—— (Issues Paper 6, Feb 2008) *Aims and Values.*

—— (Issues Paper 7, Apr 2008) *The Whole Curriculum 14–19.*

—— (Issues Paper 8, Apr 2008) *14–19 Curriculum: The Humanities.*

—— (Issues Paper 9, Jun 2008) *Applied Learning: The Case of Applied Science.*

—— (Issues Paper 10, Jun 2008) *General Education in the 14–19 Phase.*

—— (Issues Paper 11, Jul 2008) *Lessons from Detached Youth Work: Democratic Education.*

—— (Issues Paper 12, Aug 2008) *Learners and Learning.*

Nuffield Review/Rathbone (Engaging Youth Enquiry (EYE) Background Paper, May 2007) *New Approaches to Engaging Youth: Understanding the Problems and Implementing the Solutions.*

—— (EYE Briefing Paper, Sep 2007) *Engaging Youth Enquiry Briefing Paper.*

—— (EYE Briefing Paper 2, Feb 2008) *The Life Circumstances of Young People.*

—— (EYE Briefing Paper 3, Oct 2008) *Rates of Post-16 Non-Participation in England.*

—— (EYE Executive Summary, Oct 2008) *Final Report – Executive Summary.*

Oancea, Alis and Hayward, Geoff (Briefing Paper 1, Feb 2004) *Patterns of Participation and Attainment 14–19.*

Ozga, Jenny (Policy series Discussion Paper 1, Feb 2004) *Models of Policy Making and Policy Learning.*

Payne, Joan (Working Paper 7, Feb 2004) *Participation, Retention and Qualification Achievement in Education and Training from 16 to 19: Data from the England and Wales Youth Cohort Study.*

Plato, Penny (ID series Discussion Paper 3, Feb 2005) *14–19 Institutional Arrangements in Surrey – a Case Study.*

—— (Briefing Paper 17, Jul 2006) *The Experience of Current 14–19 Policy in Surrey: A Case Study.*

Pring, Richard (Working Paper 2, Dec 2003) *Aims and Purposes: Philosophical Issues.*

—— (ALC series Discussion Paper 1, Feb 2005) *The Strengths and Limitations of 'Subjects'.*

—— (Discussion Paper 30, Apr 2005) *What Would the White Paper Proposals Mean for the Aims and Purposes of the 14–19 Phase?*

—— (Oct 2005) *Nuffield Review of 14–19 Education and Training Annual Report 2004–05: Aims, Learning and Curriculum Summary.*

—— (Briefing Paper 8, May 2006) *Note of Meeting with Heads of Science Departments in Hillingdon Schools.*

—— (Briefing Paper 14, Aug 2006) *14–19 Partnerships: Stevenage.*

Pring, Richard and Roberts, Martin (Briefing Paper 12, Jul 2006) *Case Study: Kent.*

Raffe, David (Working Paper 5, Dec 2003) *The Aims of 14–19 Education: Learning from the Scottish Experience.*

—— (Policy series Discussion Paper 3, Mar 2005) *Learning from 'Home International' Comparisons: 14–19 Curriculum and Qualifications Reform in England, Scotland and Wales.*

Rawling, Eleanor (ALC series Discussion Paper 4, Feb 2005) *School Geography and the Process of Curriculum Change.*

—— (Working Paper 41, Oct 2006) *A Shift in the Zeitgeist? Are we Witnessing the Return of Curriculum Development?*

Roberts, Martin (Briefing Paper 13, Jul 2006) *Case Study: Oxfordshire.*

Roberts, Martin and Winch, Chris (ALC series Discussion Paper 3, Feb 2005) *Some Thoughts on the Role of the Humanities and History in the 14–19 Curriculum.*

Shaw, John (ALC series Discussion Paper 6, Feb 2005) *Organising a Relevant Curriculum.*

Somers, John (ALC series Discussion Paper 10, Mar 2005) *Drama as Alternative Pedagogy.*

Stanton, Geoff (Working Paper 13, Apr 2004) *The Organisation of Full Time 14–19 Provision in the State Sector.*

—— (ID series Discussion Paper 2, Feb 2005) *National Institutional Patterns and the Effects of These on Aspects of Participation, Attainment and Progression.*

—— (Working Paper 32, Apr 2005) *The Proposals for a New System of Specialist (Vocational) Diplomas.*

Stanton, Geoff and Fletcher, Mick (Working Paper 38, Sep 2006) *14–19 Institutional Arrangements in England: A Research Perspective on Collaboration, Competition and Patterns of Post-16 Provision.*

Stasz, Cathy and Wright, Susannah (Policy series Discussion Paper 2, Mar 2005) *A Framework for Understanding and Comparing 14–19 Policy in the UK.*

Truelove, Jez (ID series Discussion Paper 5, Feb 2005) *A Case Study of the Kingswood Partnership.*

Wake, Geoff (ALC series Discussion Paper 17, Aug 2005) *Functional Mathematics: More than 'Back to Basics'.*

Watson, Anne (ALC series Discussion Paper 13, May 2005) *Maths 14–19: Its Nature, Significance, Concepts and Modes of Engagement.*

Watson, Judith (Working Paper 8, Feb 2004) *Using Individual Learner Data to Investigate Progression.*

West, Ann (ALC series Discussion Paper 8, Mar 2005) *Successes that Challenge the System: The FE Perspective.*

—— (Briefing Paper 10, Jun 2006) *Case Study: Lewisham College.*

West, John (Working Paper 14, Apr 2004) *Work-Based Education and Training for Young People: Flexibility or Structure?*

Wilde, Stephanie, Wright, Susannah, Hayward, Geoff, Johnson, Jill and Skerrett, Richard (Research Report 1, Feb 2006) *Nuffield Review Higher Education Focus Groups Preliminary Report.*

Wilde, Stephanie, Hayward, Geoff and Oancea, Alis (Engaging Youth Enquiry Working Paper 1, Jan 2008) *New Approaches to Engaging Youth: Understanding the Problems and Implementing the Solutions.*

Winch, Chris (Working Paper 1, Dec 2003) *Some Philosophical and Policy Considerations Concerning Vocational and Pre-vocational Education.*

Winch, Chris, Roberts, Martin and Lambert, David (ALC series Discussion Paper 15, May 2005) *Civic Education for the 14–19 Age Group: How Subjects Might Contribute.*

Wood, David (ALC series Discussion Paper 14, May 2005) *The Arts 14–19.*

Wright, Susannah (Briefing Paper 4, Nov 2005) *Young People's Decision-Making in 14–19 Education and Training: A Review of the Literature.*

—— (Research Report 5, Oct 2006) *The Health of Subjects: Evidence from Examinations Entries.*
Wright, Susannah and Oancea, Alis (Briefing Paper 2, last updated Aug 2006) *Policies for 14–19 Education and Training in England, 1976 to the Present Day: A Chronology.*

- ALC = Aims, Learning and Curriculum working group (2004–5)
- ID = Institutional Dimension working group (2004–5)

Appendix 2

People who have contributed to the Nuffield Review

Core Group, many of whom have written papers for the Review or given presentations at events

Graham Able, Kate Anderson, Bill Bailey, Kathy Baker, Louise Bamfield, John Berkeley, Steve Besley, Tony Breslin, Dave Brockington, Michaela Brockmann, Jane Buckley, John Bynner, Nadine Cartner, Robert Cassen, Linda Clarke, Andy Cook, Jim Coyle, Norman Crowther, Miriam David, Mike Davies, Peter Davies, John Douglas, John Dunford, David Egan, Victor Farlie, Ian Ferguson, Ian Finlay, Mick Fletcher, Nick Foskett, John Fox, Alison Fuller, Leisha Fullick, Stuart Gardner, Denis Gleeson, Steve Godfrey, Paul Grainger, Maggie Greenwood, Steve Haines, Sonja Hall, John Harwood, Peter Hawthorne, Sue Hawthorne, Mark Hewlett, Jeremy Higham, Helen Hill, Prue Huddleston, Tina Isaacs, Martin Johnson, Tom Jupp, Sue Kirkham, Richard Larcombe, Simon Lebus, Jack Lewars, Geoff Lucas, Wendy Mappin, Alison Matthews, Ian McGimpsey, John Mitchell, Marian Morris, Sophie Moullin, Caroline Neville, Judith Norrington, Tim Oates, John Offord, Hugh Pitman, Penny Plato, Eleanor Rawling, Sonia Reynolds, Martin Roberts, Ann Rossiter, Paul Ryan, Hilary Sargeant, Maggie Scott, John Shaw, David Silk, Mandy Smart, Richard Steer, John Stevens, Gordon Stobart, Judy Stradling, Bridie Sullivan, Dan Taubman, Sylvia Thomson, Graeme Tiffany, Jim Tirrell, James Turner, David Turrell, Martyn Waring, Judith Watson, Ann West, John West, Richard Williams, John Wilson, Peter Wilson, Christopher Winch, Hannah Woodhouse, David Yeomans.

Others who have contributed to workshops and seminars or who have produced written or oral evidence

Marc Abbott, Fran Abrams, Keith Ajegbo, Nazir Ali C, Stephen Ball, Jacqui Bastock, Claire Bassett, John Beeby, Bahram Bekhradnia, Paul Bellamy, Natalie Bennett, John Beresford, Sir Michael Bichard, Mark Biffin, Angela Birch, Mark Blake, Maggie Blyth, Elspeth Boardley, Adrian Bostock, Ken Boston, Annie Bouder, Pauline Boundy, Richard Bowles, Karen Brierley, Derek Brogan, Deb Brown, Kim Brown, Jane Bryant, Peter Campbell, Roy Canning, Steve Capewell, Adrienne Carmichael, Alex Carrington, Sir John

Cassels, Robin Casson, John Chapman, Robert Cheesman, Stuart Chenery, Ann Childs, Suzanne Chisholm, Andrew Church, Rufus Clarke, Sarah Codrington, Helen Colley, Sheila Cooper, Nick Corrigan, Chris Cottam, John Craig, Michael Cresswell, Jeremy Cripps, Linda Croxford, Gill Cumberland, Mary Curnock Cook, Sonja Czabaniuk, Ella Davidoff, Arthur de Caux, Mike de Val, James de Winter, Jane Delfino, Simone Delorenzi, Sally Dicketts, Wendy DiMarco, Natalie Dodd, Julie Dodson, Jim Donnelly, Alaster Douglas, Harriet Dunbar-Goddet, Alison Eagles, Helen Eccles, Kathryn Ecclestone, Rebecca Edwards, Viv Ellis, Leighton Ernsberger, Caroline Erskine, Hubert Ertl, Jane Evans, Susan Fifer, John Fincham, Eric Fisk, Paul Fletcher, Judith Foster, Margaret Frostick, Andy Furlong, Ken Gadd, Jim Gallacher, Simon Gallacher, Lesley Gannon, Stephen Gardner, John Gay, Howard Gospel, Janet Graham, Sally Gran, Trevor Grant, Valerie Gray, Matt Haigh, Suzanna Hancock, Timothy Hands, Georg Hanf, Joe Harkin, John Hart, Abu Hasanath, Elaine Hendry, Kevin Hewison, Donna Higgins, Tony Hoare, Phil Hodksinson, Lorri Holding, Maurice Holt, Adrian Hooper, Deian Hopkin, Susan Hopkins, Aminul Hoque, Anan Hoque, Kate Hughes, Andrew Hunt, Dinar Hussain, Ruth Hutton, Suzanne Hyde, Jo Jamieson, Jean Jensen, Moira Jinks, Andrea Johnson, Claire Johnson, Mike Johnson, Stuart Johnson, Sarah Jones, Vinal Karania, Pauline Keeling, Steven Kenny, Reggie Kibel, Catherine Kirkup, David Knighton, Stuart Laing, David Lambert, Graham Lane, David Laverick, Peter Lauener, James Lawrence, Rob Lawy, Tom Leney, Jacky Lumby, Ginny Lunn, Stephen Machin, Malcom Maguire, Sue Maguire, Clare Makepeace, Peter Mason, Anne Matthews, Ken Mayhew, Jeff McCloud, Liz Mcdonnell, Ronnie McLeod, Austin McNamara, Jane McNicholl, Linda McPhee, Phillippe Mehaut, Dave Melia, David Miliband MP, Fiona Millar, Jeff Mills, Neil Mitchell, Robert Moehler, Jyoti Morar, Peet Morris, Stephanie Musialski, June Nelson, Richard Newton, Mike Nicholson, Paul Norris, Charmaine Odusina, Colin Osborne, Jenny Ozga, Rebecca Palmer, Asi Panditharatna, Joan Payne, Anna Pendry, Adrian Perry, Anne Pinney, Andrew Pollard, Tim Potter, Anne Quinlan, Jocey Quinn, Michael Reiss, Helen Reynolds, Debbie Ribchester, William Richardson, Graham Robb, Alison Robb-Webb, Jill Robson, Shirley Rogers, Neil Roscoe, John Rose, Sarah Ross, Carol Rowlands, Rebecca Rylatt, Tony Sacco, Syleta Samuel, Daniel Sandford Smith, Jayne Saul, Ellen Scott, Jenny Shackleton, Mark Shannon, David Shaw, Dan Shelley, Barry Sheerman MP, Paul Silvester, Richard Skerrett, Peter Sloane, John Somers, Thomas Spielhofer, Sandra Stalker, Jan Stapleton, Stef Stefanou, Brian Stevens, Rob Strettle, Heather Stretton, Phil Syrpis, Kate Taylor, Sam Tendeter, Marion Thomas, Jo Thompson, Joanna Tolley, Antony Tomei, Norman Tomlin, Sally Tomlinson, Samantha Tonner, Malcolm Trobe, Jez Truelove, Ron Tuck, Chris Tweedale, Anne Tyborczyk, Christine Usher, Geoff Wake, Susan Walker, Anna Wallis, Sue Wallis, Peter Walsh, Alan Wann, Mick Waters, Anne Watson, John Watts, Sally Weir, Anneke Westerhuis, Sally White, Kathy Wicksteed, Debbie Williams, Debbie Williamson, Lee Willows, Andrew Wilson, Louca Mai Wilson, Jonathan Winterton, Alison Wolf, David Wood, Sian Woods, Ruth Wright, Anya Zarod.

Bibliography

ALI Report (2006) *Greater Expectations: Provision for Learners with Disabilities*, London: Open Society Institute.

AoC (2006) *Post-16 Achievement and Attainment Tables 2006*, submitted to DfES.

Archer, L. and Yamashita, H. (2003) 'Knowing Their Limits: Identities, Inequalities and Inner City School Leavers', *Journal of Education Policy* 18(1).

Argyris, C. and Schön, D. (1978) *Organizational Learning: a Theory of Action Perspective*, New York: McGraw-Hill.

ASCL (2008) *Promoting Achievement, Valuing Success: a Strategy for 14–19 Qualifications*, Leicester: ASCL.

Ashton, D. and Sung, J. (2006) *How Competitive Strategy Matters: Understanding the Drivers of Training, Learning and Performance at Firm Level*, SKOPE Research Paper 66, University of Warwick.

Audit Commission (1996) *Trading Places: the Supply and Allocation of School Places*, London: Audit Commission.

Bailey, B. and Unwin, L. (2008) 'Fostering Habits of Reflection, Independent Study and Free Enquiry', *Journal of Vocational Education and Training* 60(1).

Ball, S.J. (2007) *Education Plc: Understanding Private Sector Participation in Public Sector Education*, London: Routledge.

—— (2008) *The Education Debate*, Bristol: Policy Press.

Barnardo's (2006) *Failed by the System*, London: Barnardo's.

Bates, P., Johnson, C. and Gifford, J. (2008) *Recruitment and Training among Large National Employers*, Coventry: LSC.

Bathmaker, A.M. *et al.* (2008) 'Dual-Sector Further and Higher Education: Policies, Organisations and Students in transition', *Research Papers in Education* 23(2).

Baxter, A., Tate, J. and Hatt, S. (2007) 'From Policy to Practice: Pupils' Responses to Widening Participation Initiatives', *Higher Education Quarterly* 61(3).

Baylis, V. (1999) *Opening Minds: Education for the 21st Century*, London: RSA.

Beard, C. and Wilson, J.P. (2002) *Experiential Learning*, London: Kogan Page.

Beaumont, G. (1995) *Review of 100 NVQs and SVQs*, London: DfEE.

Beecham Review (2006) *Beyond Boundaries: Citizen-centred Local Services for Wales*, Cardiff: WAG.

Beloe Report (1960) *Secondary School Examinations Other than GCE*, London: HMSO.

Bennett, R., Glennerster, H. and Nevison, D. (1992) *Learning Should Pay*, Poole: British Petroleum.

Bernstein, B. (1970) 'Education Cannot Compensate for Society', *New Society* 15(387).

Berthoud, R. (2007) *Work-rich and Work-poor: Three Decades of Change*, York: The Joseph Rowntree Foundation and Policy Press.

Black, P. and Wiliam, D. (1998) *Inside the Black Box: Raising Standards through Classroom Assessment*, NFER Nelson.

Bowles, S. and Gintis, H. (2002) 'Schooling in Capitalist America Revisited', *Sociology of Education* 75(1).

Boyd, S. (2002) *Partnership Working: European Social Partnership Models*, Glasgow: Scottish TUC.

British Crime Survey 2004–5 (SN 5347), London: Home Office.

—— 2007/8 *Drug Misuse Declared: Findings from the 2007/08, British Crime Survey*, London: Home Office.

Brockington, D. (2004) 'Nascent Futures: a Discussion Paper', www.nuffield14-19review.org. uk/documents.shtm

Brown, P. and Hesketh, A. (2004) *The Mismanagement of Talent*, Oxford: Oxford University Press.

Bruner, J. (1960) *The Process of Education*, Cambridge, Massachusetts: Harvard University Press.

—— (1966) *Towards a Theory of Instruction*, Cambridge, Massachusetts: Harvard University Press.

Bruntland Commission (1987) *Our Common Future*, Milton Keynes: Open University Press.

Bullock Report (1975) *Language for Life*, London: DES.

Bunt, K., McAndrew, F. and Kuechel, A. (2005) *Jobcentre plus Employer (Market View) Survey*, London: Department for Work and Pensions.

Bynner, J. (2004) *Participation and Progression: Use of Birth Cohort Study Data in Illuminating the Role of Basic Skills and Other Factors*, NR Working Paper 9.

Cabinet Office (2008) *Getting On, Getting Ahead. A Discussion Paper: Analysing the Trends and Drivers of Social Mobility*, The Strategy Unit, Cabinet Office.

Callender, C. and Jackson, J. (2005) 'Does the Fear of Debt Deter Students from Higher Education?' *Journal of Social Policy* 34(4).

Capey, J. (1995) *GNVQ Assestment Review Final Report*, London: NCVQ.

Cassells Report (2001) *Modern Apprenticeships: the Way to Work*, London: DfES.

Catan, L. (2003) *Youth, Citizenship and Social Change*, Swindon: ESRC Research Programme.

CBI (2007) *Shaping up for the Future: the Business Vision for Education and Skills*, London: CBI.

Chambers, D. and Lewis, J. (2008) *14–19 Qualification Reform: the A* and Extended Project*, London: DCSF.

CiLT (2007) *Language Trends: Languages in Secondary Schools*, National Centre for Languages.

Clarke, L. and Winch, C. (2007a) *Vocational Education in an International Context*, London: Routledge.

—— (eds) (2007b) *Vocational Education: International Approaches, Developments and Systems*, London: Routledge.

Cleaver, E. *et al.* (2006) 'Foundations and Baseline for Citizenship', in Breslin, T. and Dufour, B. (eds) *Developing Citizens*, London: Hodder.

Coffield, F. (2007) 'Running Ever Faster Down the Wrong Road: an Alternative Future for Education and Skills', Inaugural lecture, Institute of Education, University of London.

Coffield, F. and Edward, S. (2009) 'Good, Best, and Now Excellent Practice. What Next? Perfect Practice?' *British Educational Research Journal* In press.

Coffield, F. *et al.* (2007) *Public Sector Reform: Principles for Improving the Education System*, Paper 30, Institute of Education, University of London.

—— (2008) *Improving Learning, Skills and Inclusion: the Impact of Policy on Post-compulsory Education*, London: Routledge.

Coleman, J. and Hagell, A. (2007) *Adolescence, Risk and Resilience: Against the Odds*, Chichester: Wiley.

Coleman, J. and Schofield, J. (2007) *Key Data on Adolescence*, 6th edition, Brighton: Trust for the Study of Adolescence.

Coles, J. (2006) 'The Recent Announcement on the International Baccalaureate: Letter to Local Authorities, 5 Dec', London: DfES.

Connor, H. and Little, B. (2005) *Vocational Ladders or Crazy Paving: Making your Way to Higher Levels*, London: LSDA.

Conservative Party (2008) 'Building Skills, Transforming Lives: a Training and Apprenticeships Revolution', *Opportunity Agenda Policy Green Paper No. 7*, London.

Cooke, G. and Lawton, K. (2008) *Working out of Poverty*, London: IPPR.

CRG (Curriculum Review Group) (2004) *Curriculum for Excellence*, Edinburgh: Scottish Government.

Crick Report (1998) *Education for Citizenship and the Teaching of Democracy in Schools*, London: QCA.

Crowther Report (1959) *15–18*, London: HMSO.

Croxford, L. *et al.* (2006) 'Education and Youth Transitions across Britain 1984–2002', *Special CES Briefing 39*, Edinburgh: Centre for Educational Sociology.

Cummings, C. *et al.* (2006) 'Evaluation of the Full Service Extended School: Second Year', *Research Report 795*, London: DfES.

Curriculum Study Group (1963) *Working Papers on CSE Examinations*, London: Ministry of Education.

Dahrendorf Report (1995) *Wealth Creation and Social Cohesion in a Free Society*, London: Centre for European Reform.

Davies, C. (2007) 'Views of Young People', in *Theorising the Benefits of New Technology for Youth*, Report of ESRC Seminar, 12 March 2008, London: LSC.

Davies, S. and Thomas, C. (2008) 'The Welsh Baccalaureate Qualification', *14–19 Skills Bulletin 6*.

DCELLS (2008a) *Notice to Stakeholders*, Cardiff: WAG.

—— (2008b) *Delivering Skills that Work for Wales: Reducing the Proportion of Young People Not in Education, Employment or Training in Wales*, Cardiff: WAG.

—— (2008c) *Proposals for a Learning and Skills (Wales) Measure*, (046/2008), Cardiff: WAG.

—— (2008d) *Skills That Work for Wales: a Skills and Employment Strategy and Action Plan*, Cardiff: WAG.

DCLG (2006) *Strong and Prosperous Communities: the Local Government*, Cm 6939, London: Department for Communities and Local Government.

DCSF (2007a) *14–19 Partnerships and Plans*, London: DCSF.

—— (2007b) *Education and Training Statistics for the United Kingdom*, www.dcsf.gov.uk/rsgateway/DB/VOL/v000761/Vweb02–2007final.pdf

—— (2007c) *Changes to A Levels*, www.dfes.gov.uk/14–19/

—— (2007d) *Getting the Basics Right: Generic Definition of Functional Skills*. Online.

—— (2008a) 'Youth Cohort Study and Longitudinal Study of Young People in England: the Activities and Experiences of 16 Year-Olds: England 2007', *Statistical Bulletin*, London: DCSF/ONS.

—— (2008b) *Delivering 14–19 Reform: Next Steps*, London: DCSF.

—— (2008c) *14–19 Qualifications Strategy*, London: DCSF.

—— (2008d) *National Council for Educational Excellence: Recommendations*, London: DCSF.

—— (2008e) *Promoting Achievement, Valuing Success: a Strategy for 14–19 Qualifications*, London: DCSF.

—— (2008f) SFR 28/2008 *GCSE and Equivalent Results in England 2007/08* (provisional), www.dcsf.gov.uk

—— (2008g) SFR 13/2008 *Participation in Education, Training and Employment by 16–18 Year-Olds in England*, www.dcsf.gov.uk

DCSF/DIUS (2008a) *Raising Expectations: Enabling the System to Deliver*, London: DIUS.

—— (2008b) *World-class Apprenticeships: Unlocking Talent, Building Skills for All*, London: DIUS.

—— (2008c) *Youth Cohort Study and Longitudinal Study of Young People in England: The Activities and Experiences of 16 Year Olds: England 2007*, www.dcsf.gov.uk

Dearden, L. *et al.*. (2000) *The Returns to Academic, Vocational and Basic Skills in Britain*, DfEE Research Report 192, Nottingham: DfEE.

Dearden, L., McGranahan, L. and Sianesi, B. (2004) *An In-Depth Analysis of the Returns to National Vocational Qualifications Obtained at Level 2*, London: LSE, Centre for the Economics of Education.

Dearing Report (1994) *The National Curriculum and its Assessment*, London: SCAA.

—— (1996) *Review of Qualifications of 16–19 Year-Olds*, London: SCAA.

—— (2006) *Languages Review: Consultation Report*, London: DfES.

Desforges, C. and Abouchaar, A. (2003) *The Impact of Parental Involvement, Parental Support and Family Education on Pupil Achievement and Adjustment: A Review of Literature*, DfEE Research Report.

Devine, P. *et al.* (2007) *Feel-Bad Britain: A View from the Democratic Left*, www.hegemonics.co.uk

Dewey, J. (1902) 'The Child and the Curriculum', reprinted in Garforth, F.W. (1966) *John Dewey: Selected Writings*, London: Heinemann.

—— (1916) *Democracy and Education*, New York: The Free Press.

—— (1938) *Experience and Education*, New York: Touchstone.

DfEE (1998) *Teachers: Meeting the Challenge of Change, Green Paper*, London: DfEE.

DfES (2002) *14–19 Education: Extending Opportunities, Raising Standards*, London: Stationery Office.

—— (2003a) *Building Schools for the Future*, London: DCSF.

—— (2003b) *Every Child Matters*, London: Stationery Office.

—— (2003c) *The Skills Revolution: Realising Our Potential*, London: HMSO.

—— (2004) *Five Year Strategy for Children and Learners: Putting People at the Heart of Public Services*, Cm 6272, London: The Stationery Office.

—— (2005a) *14–19 Education and Skills*, London: DfES.

—— (2005b) *14–19 Implementation Plan*, London: DfES.

—— (2005c) *Youth Matters*, Cm 6629, London: DfES.

—— (2005d) *Skills: Getting on in Business, Getting on at Work, Part 2*, Cm 6483-II, London: DfES.

—— (2005e) *Higher Standards, Better Schools for All*, London: DfES.

—— (2006a) *Further Education: Raising Skills, Improving Life Chances*, London: DfES.

—— (2006b) *The Specialised Diploma Gateway*, London: DfES.

—— (2007) *Raising Expectations: Staying in Education and Training Post-16*, Cm 7065, London: The Stationery Office.

Dickerson, A. and Vignoles, A. (2007) *The Distribution and Returns to Qualifications in the Sector Skills Councils*, SSDA Research Report 21, Wath-upon-Dearne: SSDA.

Donnelly, J. (2005) 'Reforming Science in the School Curriculum: a Critical Analysis', *Oxford Review of Education* 31(2).

Dorling, D. *et al.* (2007) *Poverty, Wealth and Place in Britain 1968–2005*, York: Joseph Rowntree Foundation and Policy Press.

Drakeford, M. (2005) 'Wales and a Third Term of New Labour: Devolution and the Development of Difference', *Critical Social Policy* 25(4).

EDA (Education Development Agency) (1997) *Employability Phase 1: the Skills and Attributes Tyneside Employers Look for in School Leavers*, Newcastle: EDA.

EDS (Education Data Survey) (2006) 'Analysis of Applications to Teacher Training', *Monthly Commentary* 7(3).

Edward, S. *et al.* (2007) 'Endless Change in the Learning and Skills Sector: The Impact on Teaching Staff', *Journal of Vocational Education and Training* 59(2).

Eggins, H. (1992) *Arts Graduates, Their Skills and Their Employment*, London: Falmer Press.

Elliott, J. (1991) *Action Research for Educational Change*, Milton Keynes: Open University Press.

Ertl, H. *et al.*. (2007) *Reviewing Diploma Development: an Evaluation of the Design of the Diploma Qualifications*, Oxford: Oxford University Department of Education.

Estyn (2002) *Excellent Schools: A Vision for Schools in Wales in the 21st Century*, Cardiff: Estyn.

—— (2006a) *Collaboration between Schools with Sixth-Forms and Further Education Colleges*, Cardiff: Estyn.

—— (2006b) *Current Qualifications and the 14–19 Learning Pathways Initiative*, Cardiff: Estyn.

—— (2008a) *Choice and Flexibility for 14–19 Learners*, Cardiff: Estyn.

—— (2008b) *The Annual Report of Her Majesty's Chief Inspector of Education and Training in Wales 2006–2007*, Cardiff: Estyn.

—— (2008c) *The Welsh Baccalaureate in Key Stage 4*, Cardiff: Estyn.

Eurostat (2006) *Yearbook*, Luxembourg: Office for Official Publications of the European Communities.

Felstead, A. *et al.* (2007) *Skills at Work 1986–2006*, Cardiff and Oxford: SKOPE.

FEU (1979) *A Basis for Choice*, London: DES.

Fielding, M. *et al.* (2006) *Less is More: The Evaluation of Bishop Parks School, Essex*, Bath: Human Scale Education.

Fisher, L. (2007) 'Pedagogy and the Curriculum 2000 Reforms at Post-16: the "Learn it, Forget it" Culture?' *The Curriculum Journal* 18(1).

Fletcher, M. and Perry, A. (2008) *By Accident or Design: Is Our System of Post-16 Provision Fit for Purpose?* Reading: CfBT Education Trust.

Foskett, N., Dyke, M. and Maringe, F. (2008) 'The Influence of the School in the Decision to Participate in Learning Post-16', *British Educational Research Journal* 34(1).

Foster, A. (2005) *Realising the Potential: a Review of the Future Role of Further Education Colleges*, London: DfES.

Fox, J. (2004) *Ivor the Engine and Practical Curriculum Reform*, NR Working Paper 29.

Frankham, J. (2007) *School Exclusion: Making Relationships Outside Mainstream Education*, York: Joseph Rowntree Foundation.

Freedman, S. and Horner, S. (2008) *School Funding and Social Justice*, London: Policy Exchange.

Frost, D. (2007) 'New League Show "Shocking Truth" About Lack of Basic Skills', *British Chambers of Commerce News Release*, 10 January.

Fuller, A. and Heath, S. (2007) *Non-Participation in HE: Decision-Making as an Embedded Social Practice*, London: ESRC/TLRP.

Fuller, A. and Unwin, L. (2003) 'Creating a "Modern Apprenticeship": A Critique of the UK's Multi-Sector, Social Inclusion Approach', *Journal of Education and Work* 16(1).

—— (2004) 'Does Apprenticeship Still Have Meaning in the UK?', in Hayward, G. and James, S. (eds) *Balancing the Skills Equation*, Bristol: Policy Press.

—— (2008) *Towards Expansive Apprenticeships: TLRP Commentary*, London: ESRC/TLRP.

Gadd, K. and Campbell, P. (2007) *Characterising Applied Science*, briefing paper for NR Seminar, September 2007.

Gallie, D. (2000) 'The Labour Force', in Halsey, A.H. and Webb, J. (eds) *Twentieth-Century British Social Trends*, London: Macmillan.

Garner, R. (2008) *The Independent Education Average Student Debt Now £4,500 a Year*, www.independent.co.uk/news/education/education-news/average-student-debt-now-1634500-a-year-892852.html (accessed 13 August 2008).

General Household Survey (2004) *Living in Britain*, London: ONS.

Ghosh, S. (2006) 'Homelessness and Running Away: An Overview', in Horton, C. (ed.) *Working with Children*, London: Sage.

Gibbons, S., Machin, S. and Silva, O. (2006a) *Has Labour Delivered on the Policy Priorities of 'Education, Education, Education'? The Evidence on School Standards, Parental Choice and Staying on*. London: Centre for Economic Performance.

—— (2006b) *Choice, Competition and Pupil Achievement*, London: Centre for the Economics of Education Discussion Paper 56.

Giddens, A. (1998) *The Third Way: Renewal of Social Democracy*, London: Polity Press.

Gilbert Review (2007) *2020 Vision Report of the Teaching and Learning in 2020 Review Group*, London: DfES.

Gleeson, D. and Keep, E. (2004) 'Voice without Accountability: the Changing Relationship between Employers, the State and Education in England', *Oxford Review of Education* 30(1).

Goldthorpe, J.H. and Mills, C. (2004) 'Trends in Intergenerational Class Mobility in Britain in the Late Twentieth Century', in Breen, R. (ed.) *Social Mobility in Europe*, Oxford: Oxford University Press.

Gorard, S. (2000) 'Underachievement is Still an Ugly Word: Reconsidering the Relative Effectiveness of Schools in England and Wales', *Journal of Education Policy* 15(5).

Gorard, S. *et al.* (2006) *Review of Widening Participation Research: Addressing the Barriers to Participation in Higher Education*, Report to HEFCE, York: HE Academy and Institute for Access Studies.

Greatbach, D., Wilmut, J. and Bellin, W. (2006) *External Evaluation of the Welsh Baccalaureate Qualification Pilot*, Nottingham: Centre for Developing and Evaluating Lifelong Learning.

Green, A. (1998) 'Core Skills, Key Skills and General Culture: In Search of a Common Foundation for Vocational Education', *Evaluation and Research in Education* 12(1).

Green, A. and Owen, D. (2006) *The Geography of Poor Skills and Access to Work*, York: Joseph Rowntree Foundation.

Green, K. *et al.* (2005) *Mental Health of Children and Young People in Britain 2000*, London: ONS.

Grugulis, I. (2008) *Skills, Training and Human Resource Development: A Critical Text*, London: Palgrave Macmillan.

GTC (2008) *Annual Digest of Statistics 2007–08: Profiles of Registered Teachers in England*, London: GTC.

GTCW (2008) *Annual Statistics Digest, March 2008*, Cardiff: GTCW.

Gutierrez, R. (2002) 'Enabling the Practice of Mathematics Teachers in Context: Towards a New Equity Research Agenda', *Mathematical Thinking and Learning* 4.

Hadow Report (1926) *The Education of the Adolescent*, London: Board of Education.

Haines, K. *et al.* (2004) *Extending Entitlement: Making it Real*, a Pilot Evaluation of Extending Entitlement, Cardiff: WAG.

Haines, S. (2006) *14–19 Education and Training and Young Disabled People*, NR Working Paper 37.

Hall, C. (2006) 'A Picture of the UK Using the NS-SEC', *ONS Population Trends*, 125.

Halsey, K. *et al.* (2007) *The Voice of Young People: An Engine for Improvement? Scoping the Evidence*, Slough: NFER.

Hanley, P. *et al.* (2008) 'Teaching 21st Century Science', *School Science Review* 90(330).

Harlen, W. (2006) *The Role of Teachers in Assessment of Learning*, London: Assessment Reform Group, Nuffield Foundation.

Harold, G., Aitken, J. and Shelton, K. (2007) 'Inter-Parental Conflict and Children's Academic Attainment: A Longitudinal Analysis', *Journal of Child Psychology and Psychiatry* 48(12).

Hatcher, R. (2008) 'The Blair Legacy: Business Solutions for Schools and School Solutions for Business', *Oxford Review of Education* 34(6).

Hawton, K., Rodham, K. with Evans, E. (2007) *By Their Own Hand*, London: Jessica Kingsley Publishers.

Hay/McBer (2000) *Raising Achievement in Our Schools: Model of Effective Teaching*, Interim Report to DFEE, Hay Group, London: DFEE.

Hayden, M. and Thompson, J. (2007) 'Policy-Making in Practice: Issues Arising from Evaluation of the Welsh Baccalaureate', *Welsh Journal of Education* 14(1).

Hayward, G., Wilde, S. and Williams, R. (2008) *Engaging Youth Enquiry: Report for Consultation*, NR/Rathbone, www.nuffield14-19review.org.uk/cgi/documents

Heald, O. (2006) *Giving Responsibility to Local People and Local Communities*, Conservative Party, 12.10.06, www.conservatives.com

Heath, A. (2000) 'The Political Arithmetic Tradition in the Sociology of Education', *Oxford Review of Education* 26(3).

HEFCE (2005) *Young Participation in Higher Education*, Bristol: HEFCE.

—— (2008) *Compact Schemes in Higher Education Institutions*, www.hefce.ac.uk/pubs/hefce/2008/08_32/

Hesketh, A.J. (1998) 'Towards an Economic Sociology of the Student Financial Experience of Higher Education', *Journal of Education Policy* 14(4).

Higham, J. and Yeomans, D. (2006) *Emerging Provision and Practice in 14–19 Education and Training*, DfES Research Report 737, Nottingham: DfES.

—— (2007) 'Policy Memory and Policy Amnesia in 14–19 Education: Learning from the Past?' in Raffe, D. and Spours, K. (eds) *Policy-Making and Policy Learning in 14–19 Education*, Institute of Education, University of London.

Hill, R. (2008) *Achieving More Together: Adding Value through Partnership*, Leicester: ASCL.

Hirsch, D. (2006) *What Will it Take to End Child Poverty?* York: Joseph Rowntree Foundation.

HM Treasury, DTI, DfES (2004) *Science and Innovation Framework 2004–14*, London: The Stationery Office.

HoC (2006) Select Committee *Special Educational Needs* Third Report 2005–6, Education and Skills Committee, London: The Stationery Office.

—— (2007) Select Committee *14–19 Diplomas: Fifth Report of Session 2006–07*, HC249, London: The Stationery Office.

—— (2008) *Select Committee on Testing and Assessment: Government and Ofsted Responses to the Committee's Third Report of Session 2007–08*, HC4003, London: The Stationery Office.

Hodgson, A. and Spours, K. (2006) 'The Organisation of 14–19 Education and Training in England: Beyond Weakly Collaborative Arrangements', *Journal of Education and Work* 19(4).

—— (2007) 'Specialised Diplomas: Transforming the 14–19 Landscape in England?' *Journal of Education Policy* 22(6).

—— (2008a) '14–19 Education and Training: Transformation or Transformism?' *Journal of Education Policy* In press.

—— (2008b) *Education and Training 14–19: Curriculum, Qualifications and Organization*, London: Sage.

Hodgson, A., Spours, K. and Steer, R. (2007) 'All Change for the Learning and Skills Sector?' *Journal of Education and Work* 21(2).

Hodgson, A., Spours, K. and Waring, M. (2005) 'Higher Education, Curriculum 2000 and the Future Reform of 14–19 Qualifications in England', *Oxford Review of Education* 31(4).

Hoelscher, M., Hayward, G., Ertl, H. and Dunbar-Goddet, H. (2008) 'The Transition from Vocational Education and Training to Higher Education: A Successful Pathway?' *Research Papers in Education* 23(2).

HoL (2001) *Science in Schools*, Science and Technology Committee First Report 2000–2001, London: The Stationery Office.

—— (2007) *Apprenticeship: A Key Route to Skill*. Volume I: Report, Select Committee on Economic Affairs, London: The Stationery Office.

Hoyle, E. and Wallace, M. (2007) 'Educational Reform: An Ironic Perspective', *Educational Management Administration & Leadership* 35(1).

Hutchings, M. (2003) 'Financial Barriers to Participation', in Archer, L., Hutchings, M. and Ross, A. (eds) *Higher Education and Social Class: Issues of Exclusion and Inclusion*, London: Routledge Falmer.

IFF Research (2000) *Learning and Training at Work*, DfEE Research Report 202, Nottingham: DfEE.

Iles, P. and Salaman, G. (1995) 'Recruitment, Selection and Assessment', in Storey, J. (ed.) *Human Resource Management: A Critical Text*, London: Routledge.

IoD (2008) *Education Briefing Book*, in association with the University of Durham, London: Institute of Directors.

Jackson, M. (2001) 'Meritocracy, Education and Occupational Attainment: What Do Employers Really See As Merit?' Working Paper 2001–3, Oxford University, Department of Sociology.

Jackson, M., Goldthorpe, J. and Mills, C. (2002) *Education, Employers and Class Mobility*, paper presented at the meeting of the International Sociological Association, Research Committee 28, Oxford, April.

James, S. and Keep, E. (2008) *Recruitment and Selection: Towards a New Research Agenda*, SKOPE Research Paper, Cardiff University.

JCQ (2007a) 'Improvements in Results for English, Mathematics and Science at GCSE', News Release, 23 August.

—— (2007b) 'Improvement in A Level Results and Increased Entries in Maths, Science and Modern Foreign Languages', News Release, 16 October.

Jenkins, A., Greenwood, C. and Vignoles, A. (2007) *The Returns to Qualifications in England: Updating the Evidence Base on Level 2 and Level 3 Vocational Qualifications*, London: LSE, Centre for the Economics of Education.

Jessop, G. (1991) *Outcomes: NVQs and the Emerging Model of Education and Training*, London: Falmer Press.

Johnson, S. and Burden, T. (2003) *Young People, Employability and the Induction Process*, York: Joseph Rowntree Foundation.

Keep, E. (2005) 'Reflections on the Curious Absence of Employers, Labour Market Incentives and Labour Market Regulation in English 14–19 Policy: First Signs of a Change in Direction?' *Journal of Educational Policy* 20(5).

—— (2008) 'From Competence and Competition to the Leitch Review: The Utility of Comparative Analyses of Skills and Performance', IES WP17, Brighton: Institute of Employment Studies.

—— (2009) *Internal and External Incentives to Engage in Education and Training: A Framework for Analysing the Forces Acting on Individuals?* SKOPE Research Paper, Cardiff University.

Keep, E. and Mayhew, K. (1999) 'The Assessment: Knowledge, Skills and Competitiveness', *Oxford Review of Economic Policy* 15(1).

—— (2004) 'The Economic and Distributional Implications of Current Policies on Higher Education', *Oxford Review of Economic Policy* 20(2).

Keep, E. and Payne, J. (2002) 'Policy Interventions for a Vibrant Work-Based Route: Or When Policy Hits Reality's Fan (Again)', in Evans, K., Hodkinson, P. and Unwin, L. (eds) *Working to Learn: Transforming Learning in the Workplace*, London: Kogan Page.

—— (2004) 'I Can't Believe it's Not Skill: The Changing Meaning of Skill in the UK Context and Some Implications', in Hayward, G. and James, S. (eds) *Balance the Skills Equation: Key Issues and Challenges for Policy and Practice*, Bristol: Policy Press.

Keep, E., Mayhew, K. and Payne, J. (2006) 'From Skills Revolution to Productivity Miracle: Not As Easy As it Sounds?' *Oxford Review of Economic Policy* 22(4).

Kersley, B. *et al.* (2006) *Inside the Workplace: Findings from the 2004 Workplace Employment Relations Survey*, London: Routledge.

Kimberlee, R. (2002) 'Why Don't British Young People Vote at General Elections?', *Journal of Youth Studies* 5(1).

Kohlberg, L. (1975) 'The Just Community School: The Theory and the Cambridge Cluster School Experiment', in *Collected Papers from the Center for Moral Education*, Cambridge, Massachusset: Harvard University PRess.

Kooiman, J. (2003) *Governing as Governance*, London: Sage.

Lambert, D. (2008) 'Inconvenient Truths', *Geography* 93(1).

Langa-Rosada, D. and David, M. (2006) 'A Massive University or a University for the Masses? Continuity and Change in Higher Education in Spain and England', The Entity from Which ERIC Acquires the Content, Including Journal, Organization, and Conference Names, or by Means of Online Submission from the Author. *Journal of Education Policy* 21(3).

Larsen, T., Taylor-Gooby, P. and Kananen, J. (2006) 'New Labour's Policy Style: A Mix of Policy Approaches', *Journal of Social Policy* 35(4).

Larson, R.W. *et al.* (2006) 'Forms and Functions of Family Mealtimes: Multidisciplinary Perspectives', *New Directions for Child and Adolescent Development* 111.

Lawson, N. (2005) *Dare More Democracy: From Steam-Age Politics to Democratic Self-Government*, London: Compass.

Leadbeater, C. (2000) *Living on Thin Air*, London: Viking.

—— (2008) *What's Next? 21 Ideas for the 21st Century*, London: DCSF Innovations Unit.

Lebus, S. (2007) 'Intelligent Regulation: Trust and Risk', QCA seminar, November.

Leitch Review of Skills (2005) *Skills in the UK: The Long-Term Challenge (Interim Report)*, London: HM Treasury.

—— (2006) *Prosperity for All in the Global Economy: World Class Skills (Final Report)*, London: HM Treasury.

LGA (2004) *Local Government: Transforming Learning, Building Skills in Education, in Communities, at Work*, LGA Position Statement, London: LGA.

—— (2007) *Prosperous Communities II: vive la dévolution!* London: LGA.

Livingstone, S. (2007) *Introduction to Theorising the Benefits of New Technology for Youth*, Report of ESRC Seminar, 12 March 2008, London: LSC.

Livingstone, S. and Bober, M. (2005) 'UK Children Go Online', Report of ESRC Seminar, London: London School of Economics.

Lloyd, C., Mason, G. and Mayhew, K. (eds) (2008) *Low Waged Work in the UK*, New York: Russell Sage Foundation.

Local Futures (2006) *State of the Nation 2006*, London: Local Futures.

Lockyer, C. and Scholarios, D. (2007) 'The "Rain Dance" of Selection in Construction: Rationality as Ritual and the Logic of Informality', *Personnel Review* 36(4).

Lord, P. (2007) *What Young People Want from the Curriculum*, Slough: NFER.

LSC (2004) 'The Learning and Skills Council Announces a New Regional Management Structure', Press Release, 7 January, Coventry: LSC.

—— (2006) *National Employers Skills Survey 2005: Key Findings*, London: LSC.

—— (2008) *Further Education, Work-Based Learning and Train to Gain: LSC-Funded Learner Outcomes in England 2006/07*, www.lsc.gov.uk (accessed November 2008).

Lumby, J. and Foskett, N. (2005) *14–19 Education: Policy, Leadership and Learning*, London: Sage.

Lyons, T. (2006) 'Different Countries, Same Science Classes: Students' Experiences of School Science Classes in Their Own Words', *International Journal of Science Education* 28(6).

MacBeath, J. *et al.*. (2006) *The Costs of Inclusion: A Study of Inclusion Policy and Practice in English Primary, Secondary and Special Schools*, Cambridge: University of Cambridge Press.

MacDonald, B. (1973) 'The Evaluation of the Humanities Curriculum Project: A Holistic Approach', *CARE Theory into Practice*, University of East Anglia.

Mansell, W. (2007) *Education by Numbers: The Tyranny of Testing*, London: Methuen.

Marcenaro-Gutierrez, O., Galindo-Rueda, F. and Vignoles, A. (2007) 'Who Actually Goes to University?' *Empirical Economics* 32(2/3).

Margo, J. *et al.* (2008) *Those Who Can?* London: IPPR.

Marquand, D. (2004) *Decline of the Public*, Cambridge: Polity Press.

Marriott, P. (2007) 'An Analysis of First Experience Students' Financial Awareness and Attitude to Debt in a Post-1992 University', *Higher Education Quarterly* 61(4).

Marshall, T.F. (1999) *Restorative Justice: An Overview*, London: Home Office Research and Statistics Directorate.

McKinsey and Company (2007) *Consistently High Performance: Lessons from the World's Top Performing Schools Systems*, London: McKinsey.

Middleton, S. *et al.* (2005) *Evaluation of Education Maintenance Allowances: Young People 16–19*, DfES Research Report 678.

Millar, R. and Osborne, J. (1998) *Beyond 2000: Science Education for the Future*, London: KCL School of Education.

Miller, L., Acutt, B. and Kellie, D. (2001) 'Minimum and Preferred Entry Qualifications and Training Provision for British Workers', *International Journal of Training and Development* 6(3).

Miller, O., Keil, S. and Cobb, R. (2005) *A Review of Literature on Accessible Curricula, Qualifications and Assessment*, London: Disability Rights Commission.

Mills, S. and Frost, N. (2007) 'Growing up in Substitute Care', in Coleman, J. and Hagell, A. (eds) *Adolescence, Risk and Resilience: Against the Odds*, Chichester: Wiley.

Morgan, R. (2008) *Summary Justice: Fast but Fair?* London: Centre for Crime and Justice Studies.

Morrell, D. (1966) *Education and Change*, Lecture I, The Annual Joseph Payne Memorial Lectures, London: College of Preceptors.

Moser Report (1999) *A Fresh Start: Improving Literacy and Numeracy*, Sudbury: DfEE.

MSC (Manpower Training Commission) (1981) *A New Training Initiative: An Agenda for Action*, London: MSC.

NAHT (2008) *Promoting Achievement, Valuing Success*, Haywards Heath: NAHT.

NAO (2004) *Connexions Service: Advice and Guidance for All Young People*, London: NAO.

—— (2007) *Partnering for Success: Preparing to Deliver the 14–19 Education Reforms in England*, London: The Stationery Office.

National Learning Panel (2008).

NAWFC (2008) *Proposed Learning and Skills (Wales) Measure: Financial Information*, FIN(3) 12–08, Cardiff: NAW.

NAWPU (National Assembly for Wales Policy Unit) (2000) *Extending Entitlement: Supporting Young People in Wales*, Cardiff: NAW.

NCEE (2008) (National Council for Educational Excellence).

New Vision Group (2007) *A Letter to Gordon Brown*, The Guardian, 10 July 2007.

Newman, J. (2001) *Modernising Governance: New Labour, Policy and Society*, London: Sage.

Newman, J.H. (1852) *The Idea of a University*, New edition, 1907, New York: Longmans Green and Co.

Newsom Report (1963) *Half Our Future*, London: HMSO.

Newton, B. *et al.* (2005) *What Employers Look for When Recruiting the Unemployed and Inactive: Skills, Characteristics and Qualifications*, DWP Research Report 295, London: DWP.

NHS (2006) Drug Use, Smoking and Drinking amongst Young People in England in 2005, NHS Information Centre.

Nolan, P. and Wood, S. (2003) 'Mapping the Future of Work', *British Journal of Industrial Relations* 41(2).

Norwood Report (1943) *Curriculum and Examinations in Secondary Schools*, London: HMSO.

Nottingham University (2006) *External Evaluation of the Welsh Baccalaureate Qualification Pilot*, London: DCELL.

NR (Nuffield Review) (2004) *Annual Report 2003/4*, OUDES, University of Oxford.

NR (2005a) Discussion Paper 18 *The Confusing Language of the 14–19 Debate and Three Case Studies of Other Providers*, OUDES, University of Oxford.

—— (2005b) *Annual Report 2004/5*, OUDES, University of Oxford.

—— (2006) *Annual Report 2005/6*, OUDES, University of Oxford.

—— (2007) Issues Paper 2 *14–19 Partnerships: From Weakly Collaborative Arrangement to Strongly Collaborative Learning Systems*, Oxford: Nuffield Review.

—— (2008a) Issues Paper 3 *Apprenticeship I: Prospects for Growth*, Oxford: Nuffield Review.

—— (2008b) Issues Paper 4 *Apprenticeship II: A High Quality Pathway for Young People?*, Oxford: Nuffield Review.

—— (2008c) Issues Paper 5 *Guidance and Careers Education*, Oxford: Nuffield Review.

—— (2008d) Issues Paper 6 *Aims and Values*, Oxford: Nuffield Review.

—— (2008e) Issues Paper 7 *The Whole Curriculum 14–19*, Oxford: Nuffield Review.

—— (2008f) Issues Paper 8 *14–19 Curriculum: The Humanities*, Oxford: Nuffield Review.

—— (2008g) Issues Paper 9 *Applied Learning: The Case of Applied Science*, Oxford: Nuffield Review.

—— (2008h) Issues Paper 10 *General Education in the 14–19 Phase*, Oxford: Nuffield Review.

—— (2008i) Issues Paper 11 *Lessons from Detached Youth Work: Democratic Education*, Oxford: Nuffield Review.

Nuffield Foundation (2006) Twenty-First Century Science, Newsletter 2, www.nuffieldfoundation.gov

NUS (undated) *Broke and Broken: A Critique of the Higher Education Funding System*, www.nus.org.uk/PageFiles/3115/Brokeandbroken.pdf

NUT/UCU (2008) *14–19 Education: A Joint Statement by the National Union of Teachers and the University and College Union*, London: NUT/UCU.

Nutley, S. (2003) *Bridging the Policy/Research Divide: Reflections and Lessons from the UK*, University of St Andrews, Research Unit for Research Utilisation.

Oakeshott, M. (1972) 'Education: Its Engagements and Its Frustrations', in Fuller, T. (ed.) (1990) *Michael Oakeshott and Education*, London: Yale University Press.

—— (1975) 'A Place of Learning', in Fuller T. (ed.) (1990) *Michael Oakeshott and Education*, London: Yale University Press.

Oancea, A. (2007) 'From Procrustes to Proteus: Trends and Practices in the Assessment of Education Research', *International Journal of Research & Method in Education* 30(3).

Observer, 21 September 2008, 'Learn Languages or Lose Out On a Job'.

Odden, A. and Kelly, C. (1997) *Paying Teachers for What They Know and Do*, San Francisco, California: Corwin Press.

O'Donnell, L. *et al.*. (2006) *Evaluation of the Increased Flexibility for 14–16 Year-Olds Programme: Delivery for Cohorts 3 and 4 and the Future*, DfES Research Brief 790, London: DfES.

OECD (2007) *PISA 2006: Science Competencies for Tomorrow's World*, Volume 1: Analysis, Paris: OECD.

—— (2008) *Education at a Glance*, Paris: OECD.

Ofsted (2003) *The Initial Training of Further Education Teachers*, London: Stationery Office.

—— (2007a) *The Annual Report of Her Majesty's Chief Inspector of Education, Children's Services and Skills 2006–07*, London: The Stationery Office.

—— (2007b) *The Contribution Made by the Centres of Vocational Excellence to the Development of Vocational Work in Schools*, London: Ofsted.

—— (2008a) *A Comparison of the Effectiveness of Level 3 Provision in 25 Post-16 Providers*, London: Ofsted.

—— (2008b) *Implementation of 14–19 Reforms: An Evaluation of Progress*, London: Ofsted.

—— (2008c) *Mathematics: Understanding the Score*, London: Ofsted.

—— (2008d) *Curriculum Innovation in Schools*, London: Ofsted.

O'Hear, A. (1991) *Father of Child-centredness*, London: Centre for Policy Studies.

Ousley Report (2001) *Community Pride Not Prejudice*, Bradford LEA.

Ozga, J. and Sukhanandan, L. (1998) 'Undergraduate Non-Completion: Developing an Explanatory Model', *Higher Education Quarterly* 52(3).

Parsons, S. and Bynner, J. (2007) *Illuminating Disadvantage: Profiling the Experiences of Adults with Entry Level Literacy or Numeracy Over the Life Course*, Research Report, NRDC, London Institute of Education.

Paterson, L. and Iannelli, C. (2007a) 'Patterns of Absolute and Relative Social Mobility: A Comparative Study of England, Wales and Scotland', *Sociological Research Online* 12(6).

—— (2007b) 'Social Class and Educational Attainment: A Comparative Study of England, Wales and Scotland', *Sociology of Education* 80.

Paxton, W. and Dixon, M. (2004) *The State of the Nation*, London: IPPR.

Payne, J. (1999) *All Things to All People: Changing Perceptions of Skill among Britain's Policy Makers Since the 1950s and Their Implications*, SKOPE Research 2, University of Warwick.

Perry, A. and Simpson, M. (2006) *Delivering Quality and Choice: How Performance Indicators Help and How Performance Indicators Hinder*, London: LSDA.

Perry, P.J.C. (1976) *The Evolution of British Manpower Policy*, London: British Association of Commercial and Industrial Education.

Phillips, R. (2003) 'Education Policy, Comprehensive Schooling and Devolution in the Disunited Kingdom: An Historical "Home International" Analysis', *Journal of Education Policy* 18.

PMSU (2006) *The UK Government's Approach to Public Service Reform: A Discussion Paper*, London: Cabinet Office.

Pollard, A. *et al.* (2008) *University is Not Just for Young People: Working Adults' Perceptions of and Orientations to Higher Education*, DIUS Research Report 0608, London: DIUS.

Power, S. *et al.* (2008) *Out-Of-School Learning: Creation, Variation in Provision and Participation in Secondary Schools*, Cardiff: Research Papers in Education.

Pratchett, L. (2004) 'Local Autonomy, Local Democracy and the "New Localism"', *Political Studies* 52.

Pring, R. (2007) *John Dewey: The Philosopher of Education for the 21st Century*, London: Continuum.

—— (2008) 'Don't Forget the Past', in Hudson, C. (ed.) *The Sound and the Silence: Key Perspectives on Speaking and Listening and Skills for Life*, Coventry: Quality Improvement Agency.

QCA (2007) *Controlled Assessment*, London: QCA.

QCA/LSC (2007) *Foundation Learning Tier*, London: QCA.

Raffe, D. (1998) 'Does Learning Begin At Home? The Place of "Home International" Comparisons in UK Policy-Making', *Journal of Education Policy* 13.

Raffe, D., Brannen, K. and Croxford, L. (2001) 'The Transition from School to Work in the Early 1990s: A Comparison of England, Wales and Scotland', *Journal of Education and Work* 14(3).

Raffe, D., Howieson, C. and Tinklin, T. (2007) 'The Impact of a Unified Curriculum and Qualifications System: The Higher Still Reform of Post-16 Education in Scotland', *British Education Research Journal* 33(4).

Raffe, D. and Spours, K. (eds) (2007) *Policy-Making and Policy Learning in 14–19 Education*, London: Institute of Education Bedford Way Papers.

Raffo, C. *et al.* (2007) *Education and Poverty: A Critical Review of Theory, Policy and Practice*, York: Joseph Rowntree Foundation.

Ranson, S. (2006) 'Public Accountability in the Age of Neo-Liberal Governance', in Lingard, B. and Ozga, J. (eds) *Education Policy and Politics*, London: Routledge Falmer.

Rawlings, E. and Daugherty, R. (1996) *Geography into the 21st Century*, Chichester: Wiley.

Reay, D., David, M.E. and Ball, S. (2005) *Degrees of Choice: Social Class, Race and Gender in Higher Education*, Stoke on Trent: Trentham Books.

Rees, G. (2002) 'Devolution and the Restructuring of Post-16 Education and Training in the UK', in Adams, J. and Robinson, P. (eds) *Devolution in Practice: Public Policy Differences within the UK*, London: IPPR.

—— (2004) 'Democratic Devolution and Education Policy in Wales: The Emergence of a National System?', *Contemporary Wales* 17.

—— (2007) 'The Impacts of Parliamentary Devolution on Education Policy in Wales', *Welsh Journal of Education* 14(1).

Rees, G. and Taylor C. (2006) 'Devolution and the Restructuring of Participation in Higher Education in Wales', *Higher Education Quarterly* 60(4).

Rees, G., Williamson, H. and Winkler, V. (1989) 'The "New Vocationalism": Further Education and Local Labour Markets', *Journal of Education Policy* 4.

Reuter, P. and Stevens. A. (2007) *An Analysis of UK Drugs Policy*, London: UK Drug Policy Commission.

Reynolds, D. (1998) 'Teacher Effectiveness: Better Teachers, Better Schools', The Teacher Training Agency Annual Lecture, *Research Intelligence* 66.

—— (2008) 'New Labour, Education and Wales: The Devolution Decade', *Oxford Review of Education* 34(6).

Roberts Report (2002) *SET for Success: The Supply of People with Science, Technology, Engineering and Mathematics Skills*, London: HM Treasury.

Rowntree Foundation (2007) *Experience of Poverty and Educational Disadvantage*, www.jrf.org.uk/ knowledge/findings/socialpolicy/2123.asp

Royal Society (2006) *A Degree of Concern? UK First Degrees in Science, Technology and Mathematics*, London: Royal Society.

—— (2007) *The UK's Science and Mathematics Teaching Workforce: A 'State of the Nation' Report*, London: Royal Society.

—— (2008) *'State of the Nation' Report: Science and Mathematics Education, 14–19*, London: Royal Society.

RSA (1986) *Education for Capability*, London: RSA.

—— (2003) *Opening Minds: Taking Stock*, London: RSA.

—— (2005) *Open Minds: Giving Young People a Better Chance*, London: RSA.

—— (2006) *Increasing Uptake of Science Post-16*, Report of a RSA conference, 10 March 2006.

Rudduck, J., Brown, N. and Hendy, L. (2006) *Personalised Learning and Pupil Voice*, London: DCSF.

Rudduck, J. and McIntyre, D. (2007) *Improving Learning through Consulting Pupils*, London: Routledge.

Russell Group (2007) *Statement on University and School Partnerships*, www.russellgroup.ac.uk/ news/2007/statement-on-university-and-school-partnerships.html

Ryan, P. and Unwin, L. (2001) 'Apprenticeship in the British Training Market', *National Institute Economic Review* 178.

Schagen, I. *et al.*. (2006) *Do Post-16 Structures Matter? Evaluating the Impact of Local Patterns of Provision*, London: LSDA.

Schwartz Report (2004) *Admissions to HE Review: Fair Admissions to Higher Education: Recommendations for Good Practice*, Admissions to HE Steering Group, London: HMSO.

Seddon, J. (2008) 'Deliverology: The Science of Delivery, or Dogmatic Delusion?' in *Systems Thinking in the Public Sector*, Axminster: Triarchy Press.

Seddon, V. (2005) *An Analysis of the Progression of Advanced Apprentices to Higher Education in England*, Bolton: UVAC.

Simon, B. (1994) *The State and Educational Change*, London: Lawrence and Wishart.

Smith Report (2004) *Making Mathematics Count*, London: HMSO.

Smithers, A. and Robinson, P. (2005) *Teacher Turnover, Wastage and Movements between Schools*, DfES Research Brief 640, London: DfES.

—— (2008) *The Diploma: A Disaster Waiting to Happen?* Buckingham: University of Buckingham.

Social Trends (2004) No. 34, London: ONS.

—— (2006) No. 36, London: ONS.

Spencer, N. and Hirsch, D. (2008) *Health of Children in Poverty*, London: Campaign to End Child Poverty.

Spilsbury, M. and Lane, K. (2000) *Skill Needs and Recruitment Practices in Central London*, London: FOCUS Central London.

Spours, K., Coffield, F. and Gregson, M. (2007a) 'Mediation, Translation and Local Ecologies: Understanding the Impact of Policy Levers on FE Colleges', *Journal of Vocational Education and Training* 59(2).

Spours, K., Hodgson, A. and Yeomans, D. (2007) 'Learning from Local Experience: How Effective is the Government's 14–19 Learning Model?' in Raffe, D. and Spours, K. (eds) *Policy-Making and Policy Learning in 14–19 Education*, Institute of Education, University of London.

Stanton, G. (2008) *Learning Matters: Making the 14–19 Reforms Work for Learners*, London: CfBT Education Trust.

Stanton, G. and Fletcher, M. (2006) *14–19 Institutional Arrangements in England: A Research Perspective on Collaboration, Competition and Patterns of Post-16 Provision*, NR Working Paper 38, www.nuffield14-19review.org.uk

Stasz, C. and Wright, S. (2004) *Emerging Policy for Vocational Learning in England: Will it Lead to a Better System?* London: LSRC.

Steer, R. *et al.* (2007) '"Modernisation" and the Role of Policy Levers in the Learning and Skills Sector', *Journal of Vocational Education and Training* 59(2).

Stenhouse, L. (1975) *Introduction to Curriculum Research and Development*, London: Heinemann.

—— (1983) *Authority, Education and Emancipation*, London: Heinemann.

Sutton Trust (2008) *Increasing Higher Education Participation amongst Disadvantaged Young People and Schools in Poor Communities*, Report to NCEEHE, London: Sutton Trust.

Swann Report (1995) *Education for All*, London: HMSO.

Tait, T. (2003) *Credit Systems for Learning and Skills: Current Developments*, London: LSDA.

Tasker, M. (2003) *Smaller Structures in Secondary Education: A Research Digest*, Bristol: Human Scale Education.

Tawney, R.H. (1931) *Equality*, London: Geo. Allen and Unwin.

Taylor, C. (2008) *Personalisation through Participation: Twenty-One Ideas for 21st Century.*

Taylor, J. (2007) *The Impact of the Specialist Schools Programme on Exam Results*, Working Paper, Lancaster University Management School.

Thomas, B. and Dorling, D. (2007) *Identity in Britain*, Bristol: The Policy Press.

Thompson, P. (2004) *Skating on Thin Ice: the Knowledge Economy Myth*, Glasgow: University of Strathclyde.

TLRP (2008) *Degrees of Success; Learners' Transition from Vocational Education and Training to Higher Education*, Research Briefing 42, London: TLRP.

Tomlinson Report (2004) *Curriculum and Qualifications Reform*, London: DfES.

Tyler, R. (1949) *Basic Principles of Curriculum and Instruction*, Chicago: University of Chicago Press.

Tymms, P. *et al.* (2005) *Standards in English Schools: Changes Since 1997 and the Impact of Government Policies and Initiatives*, Durham University, CEM Centre.

UCAS (2008) www.ucas.com/about_us/stat_services/stats_online/data_tables

UCU (2006a) *Degrees of Decline? Core Science and Mathematics Degree Courses in the UK 1998–2007*, London: UCU.

—— (2006b) *Losing Our Tongues? Declining Numbers of Language Degree Courses 1998–2007*, London: UCU.

UNICEF Report (2007) *Child Poverty in Perspective: An Overview of Child Well-being in Rich Countries*, Florence: UNICEF Innocenti Research Centre.

Unwin, L. and Wellington, J. (2001) *Young People's Perspectives in Education, Training and Employment*, London: Kogan Page.

WAG (2001a) *Learning Country: Vision into Action*, Cardiff: WAG.

—— (2001b) *The Learning Country: A Comprehensive Education and Lifelong Learning Programme to 2010 in Wales*, Cardiff: WAG.

—— (2002a) *14–19 Learning Pathways and Beyond*, Cardiff: WAG.

—— (2002b) *Learning Pathways 14–19: Consultation Document*, Cardiff: WAG.

—— (2003) *Learning Country: Learning Pathways 14–19*, Cardiff: WAG.

—— (2004) *Learning Pathways 14–19 Guidance*, Cardiff: WAG.

—— (2006a) *14–19 Learning Pathways Action Plan*, Cardiff: WAG.

—— (2006b) *Learning Pathways 14–19 Guidance II*, Cardiff: WAG.

—— (2006c) *Professional Development, Recognition and Accreditation*, Cardiff: WAG.

—— (2008a) *Assessment and Examination Performance in Wales: Comparisons with England and its Regions 2007*, Cardiff: WAG.

—— (2008b) *Modernising Learning Provision*, Cardiff: WAG.

Wake, G. (2005) *Functional Mathematics: More than Back to Basics*, NR Discussion Paper 17, www.nuffield14-19review.org.uk

Wallace, G. (1996) 'Relating to Teachers', in Rudduck, J. *et al.. School Improvement: What Can Pupils Tell Us?* London: David Fulton.

Warhurst, C. and Nickson, D. (2001) *Looking Good, Sounding Right*, London: Industrial Society.

Warnock, M. (2005) 'Special Educational Needs: A New Look', *Impact No. 11*, Philosophy of Education Society of Great Britain.

Warnock Report (1978) *Special Educational Needs*, Cm 7212, London: HMSO.

Watson, J. (2008) *Achievement in the First Post-Compulsory Year*, briefing document to NR, Nuffield 14–19 Review, www.nuffield14-19review.org.uk

WBQ (2006) *How Did the Second Examination (2004–06) Cycle Go?* Cardiff: WBQ.

—— (2008) *Producing Better Undergraduates: Information for the Admissions Officers and Tutors*, www.welshbaccalaureate.org.uk

Webb Review (2007) *Promise and Performance: The Report of the Independent Review of the Mission and Purpose of Further Education in Wales in the Context of 'The Learning Country'*, Cardiff: WAG.

Wellcome Trust (2006) *Believers, Seekers and Sceptics: What Teachers Think about Professional Development*, London: Wellcome Trust.

West, J. (2005) *Improving Completion Rates in Apprenticeship: A Comparative and Numerical Approach*, Windsor: Apprenticeship Task Force.

Wiener, M. (1985) *English Culture and the Decline of the Industrial Spirit, 1850–1980*, Harmondsworth: Penguin.

Wilde, S. and Hoelscher, M. (2007) *Missed Opportunities? Non-Placed Applicants (NPAs) in the UCAS Data*, Cheltenham: UCAS.

Wilde, S. and Wright, S. (2007) 'On the Same Wavelength but Tuned to Different Frequencies?' *London Review of Education* 5(3).

Wilson, R. (1997) *Research into the Deployment and Impact of Support Staff Who Have Achieved HLTA Status*, Slough: NFER.

YJB (2006) Annual Statistics, www.yjb.gov.uk

Name index

Subject index